low-fat
low-cholesterol
Chinese Cookbook

low-fat
low-cholesterol
Chinese Cookbook

**200 DELICIOUS CHINESE &
FAR EAST ASIAN RECIPES
FOR HEALTH, GREAT TASTE,
LONG LIFE & FITNESS**

Consultant editors: Maggie Pannell
Jenni Fleetwood

HERMES
HOUSE

This edition is published by Hermes House, an imprint of Anness Publishing Ltd, Hermes House, 88–89 Blackfriars Road, London SE1 8HA; tel. 020 7401 2077; fax 020 7633 9499
www.hermeshouse.com; www.annesspublishing.com

If you like the images in this book and would like to investigate using them for publishing, promotions or advertising, please visit our website www.practicalpictures.com for more information.

Publisher: Joanna Lorenz
Editorial Director: Judith Simons
Project Editor: Lucy Doncaster
Consultant Editors: Maggie Pannell and Jenni Fleetwood
Designer: Bill Mason
Editorial Reader: Jay Thundercliffe

ETHICAL TRADING POLICY

Because of our ongoing ecological investment programme, you, as our customer, can have the pleasure and reassurance of knowing that a tree is being cultivated on your behalf to naturally replace the materials used to make the book you are holding. For further information about this scheme, go to www.annesspublishing.com/trees

Main front cover image shows Chilli-seared Scallops on Pak Choi – for recipe, see page 100

NOTES

Bracketed terms are intended for American readers.

For all recipes, quantities are given in both metric and imperial measures and, where appropriate, in standard cups and spoons. Follow one set, but not a mixture, because they are not interchangeable.

Standard spoon and cup measures are level. 1 tsp = 5ml, 1 tbsp = 15ml, 1 cup = 250ml/8fl oz.

Australian standard tablespoons are 20ml. Australian readers should use 3 tsp in place of 1 tbsp for measuring small quantities of gelatine, flour, salt etc.

The nutritional analysis given for each recipe is calculated per portion (i.e. serving or item), unless otherwise stated. If the recipe gives a range, such as Serves 4–6, then the nutritional analysis will be for the smaller portion size, i.e. 6 servings. Measurements for sodium do not include salt added to taste.
Medium (US large) eggs are used unless otherwise stated.

Each recipe title in this book is followed by a symbol that indicates the following:

★ = 5g of fat or fewer per serving
★★ = 10g of fat or fewer per serving
★★★ = 15g of fat or fewer per serving

CONTENTS

INTRODUCTION

The majority of people living in China and Far East Asia have a very healthy diet, which is low in fat, high in fibre, with plenty of vegetables and relatively small amounts of meat. Much of their protein comes from fish and tofu, both of which are low-fat foods. Noodles and rice form the bulk of most meals, and processed foods are seldom eaten. In part, this diet evolved through necessity. Subsistence workers could not afford to eat large quantities of meat on a daily basis, even though pork, duck and chickens were – and still remain – an important part of the diet. Unfortunately, as countries like China and Japan have become increasingly prosperous, more fat is being consumed. In major cities like Beijing, where individuals have adopted a more Western diet, the incidence of coronary heart disease is on the increase.

Some of the dishes exported to the West are none too healthy either. Pork that has been dipped in batter, deep-fried in fat and then coated in a syrupy sauce is never going to make it to the list of best choices for optimum nutrition. Nor is the practice of enriching a dish by stirring in pure lard to be recommended. There's been a lot of criticism of certain Chinese restaurants and takeaways in recent years, because of their devotion to the deep-fat fryer and their habit of slathering everything in thick, often very salty sauces, but such dishes – which are generally on the menu only because of Western demand – give a skewed picture of Asian cuisine.

China and the Far East can be a great source of healthy, low-fat recipes. Asian cooks are fussy about what they eat, and ingredients are chosen with considerable care. Visit any open-air market and you will see cooks sifting through piles of gourds to choose one that is at just the right state of ripeness for the meal they have planned. Meat

Right: Noodles add bulk and extra flavour to dishes without having a significant impact on fat levels. Fresh or dried egg noodles are available in various widths.

and fish must be very fresh, a fact that can be a bit daunting to the visitor invited to choose their meal while it is still swimming in a tank, but which proves beyond any doubt that the item in question will not have far to travel to their table. This passion for freshness is particularly apparent – and important – if the fish is to be eaten raw, as it is in sushi and sashimi.

A HEALTHY WAY OF COOKING

Steaming and stir-frying are two of the most popular cooking methods in China and Far East Asia. Both these methods are ideal for the low-fat cook, since they require little or no oil to be used. The wok is the principal utensil. This extraordinarily versatile pan, with its rounded bottom, was originally designed to fit snugly on a traditional Chinese brazier or stove. Modern versions have

flatter bases, to prevent wobble on electric stoves, but are still very efficient in the even way they conduct and retain heat. The sloping sides mean that the food always returns to the centre, where the heat is most intense.

Many of the woks on sale today are non-stick. Although traditional carbonized steel woks are the ones purists choose, because they are so efficient, non-stick woks are better for low-fat cooking, since they make it possible to stir-fry with the smallest amount of oil.

When stir-frying, the best technique is to place the wok over the heat without any oil. When the pan is hot, dribble drops of oil, necklace fashion, on to the inner surface just below the rim. As the drops slither down the pan, they coat the sides, then puddle on the base. You can get away with using just about a teaspoon of oil if you follow

Above: One of the reasons for cooking with fats is for flavour, but if you use aromatics like ginger (pictured) and garlic, there is no need to add oils or sauces for flavouring.

this method. Add the food to be cooked when the oil is very hot, and keep it moving. This is often done with a pair of chopsticks, but the easiest way is to use two spatulas or spoons, as when tossing a salad.

Add a metal trivet to a wok and it becomes a steamer. Better still, use a bamboo steamer. These attractive-looking utensils look rather like hat boxes, and come with tightly fitting domed lids. You can stack several tiers on top of each other over a wok partly filled with water. No fat will be needed and the food will taste delicious, with just a hint of fragrance from the bamboo.

A HEALTHY LIFESTYLE

Most of us eat fats in some form or another every day and we all need a small amount of fat in our diet to maintain a healthy, balanced eating plan. However, many of us eat far too much fat, and we should all be looking to reduce our overall fat intake, especially of saturated fats.

Regular exercise is also an important factor in a healthy lifestyle, and we should aim to exercise three times a week for a minimum of half an hour each session. Swimming, brisk walking, jogging, dancing, skipping and cycling are all good forms of aerobic exercise.

ABOUT THIS BOOK

This cookbook aims to bring you a wide selection of delicious and nutritious dishes from many regions of China and Far East Asia, all of which are low in fat, and are ideal to include as part of an everyday healthy and low-fat eating plan.

The book includes plenty of useful and informative advice. A short introduction gives a blueprint for healthy eating and has helpful hints and tips on low-fat and fat-free ingredients and cooking techniques. There are plenty of practical tips for reducing fat, especially saturated fat, in your diet, and the section on ingredients provides an insight into fruits, vegetables, flavourings and other essentials used in Chinese and Far East Asian cooking.

The tempting recipes – over 200 of them – will be enjoyed by all the family. They range from soups and appetizers to desserts and there are lots of delicious main course dishes for meat eaters and vegetarians. The emphasis throughout the book is on good food with maximum taste, and if you don't let on that the dishes are also low in fat, nobody is likely to guess.

Each recipe includes a nutritional breakdown, proving an at-a-glance guide to calorie and fat content (including saturated fat content) per serving, as well as other key components such as protein, carbohydrate, calcium, cholesterol, fibre and sodium. All the recipes in this collection are low in fat.

Above: Keep the food moving when cooking in a wok. Chopsticks like these can be used, or toss the food using two spatulas or wooden spoons.

Many contain less than five grams of total fat or less per serving, and a few are even lower in fat, with under one gram per serving. One or two classic recipes, such as Glazed Lamb and Duck and Ginger Chop Suey, contain slightly more fat, but even these contain less than in the traditional versions.

For ease of reference, throughout the recipe section, all recipes with a single * after the recipe title contain a maximum of five grams of total fat, those with ** contain a maximum of 10 grams of total fat and those with*** contain up to 15 grams of total fat per portion. Each recipe also has a complete breakdown of the energy, protein, carbohydrate, cholesterol, calcium, fibre and sodium values of the food.

Although the recipes are low in fat, they lose nothing in terms of flavour. This practical cookbook will enable you to enjoy healthy Chinese and Far East Asian food with a clear conscience. All the recipes are easy to cook and many are so quick that you'll have supper on the table in less time than it would have taken to collect a take-away.

Left: When food is cooked in a steamer, there is no need for any fat to be used. A bamboo steamer like this one is ideal. Several can be stacked on top of each other if needed.

THE LOW-FAT CHINESE AND FAR EAST ASIAN KITCHEN

Cooks in China and Far East Asia have much to teach us about low-fat cooking. Their traditional diet is largely composed of vegetables, with a healthy proportion of carbohydrate in the form of noodles or rice, protein in the form of tofu and only small amounts of meat or fish. Suggestions for using tofu and other ingredients specific to the region are given in this section, which also includes valuable advice about planning and maintaining a healthy low-fat diet.

HEALTHY EATING GUIDELINES

A healthy diet provides us with all the nutrients we need. By eating the right types, balance and proportions of foods, we are more likely to have more energy and a higher resistance to diseases and illnesses such as heart disease, cancers, bowel disorders and obesity.

By choosing a variety of foods every day, you are supplying your body with all the essential nutrients it needs. To get the balance right, it is important to know just how much of each type of food you should be eating.

Of the five main food groups, it is recommended that we eat at least five portions of fruit and vegetables a day, not including potatoes; carbohydrate foods such as noodles, cereals, rice and potatoes; moderate amounts of fish, poultry and dairy products; and small amounts of foods containing fat or sugar. A dish like Five-Flavour Noodles fits the prescription perfectly, with its balance of noodles, lean pork, cabbage, beansprouts and (bell) peppers.

THE ROLE OF FAT IN THE DIET

Fats shouldn't be cut out of our diets completely, as they are a valuable source of energy and make foods more palatable. However, lowering the fats, especially saturated fats, in your diet, may help you to lose weight, as well as reducing your risk of developing diseases.

Aim to limit your daily intake of fats to no more than 30–35 per cent of the total number of calories you consume. Each gram of fat provides nine calories, so a person eating 2,000 calories a day should not eat more than 70g/2¾oz of fat. Saturated fat should not comprise more than 10 per cent of the total calorie intake.

TYPES OF FAT

All fats in our foods are made up of building blocks of fatty acids and glycerol, and their properties vary according to each combination.

The two main types of fat are saturated and unsaturated. The unsaturated group is divided into

two further categories – polyunsaturated and monounsaturated fats. There is usually a combination of these types of unsaturated fat in foods that contain fat, but the amount of each type varies from one kind of food to another.

SATURATED FATS

These fats are usually hard at room temperature. They are not essential in the diet, and should be limited, as they are implicated in raising the level of cholesterol in the blood, which can increase the likelihood of heart disease.

The main sources of saturated fats are animal products, such as fatty cuts of meat and meat products; spreading fats that are solid at room temperature, such as butter, lard and margarine; and full-fat dairy products such as cream and cheese. Aside from meat, these ingredients are seldom found in Chinese and Far East Asian recipes, but it is also important to avoid coconut and palm oil, which are saturated fats of vegetable

Above: Tofu, which is also known as bean curd, is a highly nutritious vegetable protein. It is cholesterol-free and low in fat.

Above: Chinese greens like pak choi (bok choy) and Chinese leaves (Chinese cabbage) are delicious raw in salads or stir-fried with just a drop of oil.

Above: Oily fish like salmon are a good source of the Omega-3 fatty acids that are good for our hearts. Very fresh fish can be eaten raw in sushi or sashimi.

origin. More insidious are those fats which, when processed, change the nature of the fat from unsaturated fatty acids to saturated ones. These are called "hydrogenated" fats, and should be strictly limited, so look out for that term on food labels.

Saturated fats are also found in many processed foods, such as chips (French fries) and savoury snacks, as well as cookies, pastries and cakes.

POLYUNSATURATED FATS

Small amounts of polyunsaturated fats are essential for good health, as they provide energy, can help to reduce cholesterol levels and enable the absorption of the fat-soluble vitamins A and D. The body can't manufacture polyunsaturated fatty acids, so they must be obtained from food. There are two types: those of vegetable or plant origin, known as Omega-6, which are found in sunflower oil, soft margarine, nuts and seeds; and Omega-3 fatty acids, which come from oily fish such

Left: Far Eastern cuisine makes the most of a wide variety of fresh fruit and vegetables, carbohydrates such as rice and noodles, and a wealth of herbs, spices and other flavourings.

as tuna, salmon, herring, mackerel and sardines as well as walnuts, soya beans, wheatgerm and rapeseed (canola) oil.

MONOUNSATURATED FATS

The best known monounsaturated fat is olive oil. This is not used in Asian cooking, but another monounsaturated oil, groundnut (peanut) oil, is a popular choice. It is ideal for stir-frying and gives food a delicious flavour. Monounsaturated fatty acids are also found in nuts such as almonds, and oily fish. They are thought to have the beneficial effect of reducing blood cholesterol levels.

THE CHOLESTEROL QUESTION

Cholesterol is a fat-like substance that occurs naturally in the body, and which we also acquire from food. It has a vital role, since it is the material from which many essential hormones and vitamin D are made. Cholesterol is carried around the body, attached to proteins called high density lipoproteins (HDLs), low density lipoproteins (LDLs) and very low density lipoproteins (VLDLs or triglycerides).

Eating too much saturated fat encourages the body to make more cholesterol than it can use or can rid itself of. After food has been consumed, the LDLs carry the fat in the blood to

the cells where it is required. Any surplus should be excreted from the body, but if there are too many LDLs in the blood, some of the fat will be deposited on the walls of the arteries. This furring up gradually narrows the arteries and is one of the most common causes of heart attacks and strokes.

By way of contrast, HDLs appear to protect against heart disease. Whether high triglyceride levels are risk factors remains unknown.

CUTTING DOWN ON FATS AND SATURATED FATS IN THE DIET

It is relatively easy to cut down on obvious sources of fat in the diet, like butter, oils, margarine, cream, whole milk and full-fat cheese, but it is also important to know about and check consumption of "hidden" fats.

By educating yourself and being aware of which foods are high in fats, and by making simple changes, you can reduce the total fat content of your diet quite considerably. Choose low-fat alternatives when selecting items like milk, cheese and salad dressings. If you are hungry, fill up on very low-fat foods, such as fruits and vegetables, and foods that are high in carbohydrates, such as bread, potatoes, rice or noodles.

PLANNING A LOW-FAT DIET

Cutting down on fat on an everyday basis means that we need to keep a close eye on the fat content of everything that we eat. This section provides some general guidelines, which are applicable to all cuisines.

CUTTING DOWN ON FAT IN THE DIET

Most of us eat about 115g/4oz of fat every day. Yet just 10g/¼oz, about the amount in a single packet of crisps (US potato chips) or a thin slice of Cheddar cheese, is all that we actually need.

Current nutritional thinking is more lenient than this, however, and suggests an upper daily limit of about 70g/2¾oz total fat.

Using low-fat recipes helps to reduce the overall daily intake of fat, but there are also lots of other ways of reducing the fat in your diet. Just follow the "eat less, try instead" suggestions below to discover how easy it can be.

• Eat less butter, margarine, other spreading fats and cooking oils. Try instead reduced-fat spreads, low-fat spreads or fat-free spreads. Butter or hard margarine should first be softened at room temperature so that they can be spread thinly. Alternatively, use low-fat cream cheese or low-fat soft cheese for sandwiches and toast.

• Eat less full-fat dairy products such as whole milk, cream, butter, hard margarine, crème fraîche, whole-milk yogurts and hard cheese. Try instead semi-skimmed (low-fat) or skimmed milk, low-fat or reduced-fat milk products, such as low-fat yogurts and low-fat soft cheeses, reduced-fat hard cheeses such as Cheddar, and reduced-fat crème fraîche. Silken tofu can be used instead of cream in soups and sauces. It is a good source of calcium and an excellent protein food.

• Eat fewer fatty cuts of meat and high fat meat products, such as pâtés, burgers, pies and sausages. Try instead naturally low-fat meats such as skinless chicken and turkey, ostrich and venison. When cooking lamb, beef or pork, use only the leanest cuts. Always cut away any visible fat and skin from meat before cooking. Try substituting low-fat protein ingredients like dried beans, lentils or tofu for some or all of the meat in a recipe.

• Eat more fish. It is easy to cook, tastes great, and if you use a steamer, you won't need to add any extra fat at all.

• Eat fewer hard cooking fats, such as lard or hard margarine. Try instead polyunsaturated or monounsaturated oils, such as sunflower or corn oil, and don't use too much.

• Eat fewer rich salad dressings and less full-fat mayonnaise. Try instead reduced-fat or fat-free dressings, or just a squeeze of lemon juice. Use a reduced-fat mayonnaise and thin it with puréed silken tofu for an even greater fat saving.

• Eat less fried food, especially deep-fried. Try fat-free cooking methods like steaming, grilling (broiling), baking or microwaving. Use non-stick pans with spray oil. When roasting or grilling meat, place it on a rack and drain off excess fat frequently.

Below: Sardines are a good source of unsaturated fat.

• Eat fewer deep-fried or sautéed potatoes. Boil or bake them instead, or use other carbohydrates. Avoid chow-mein noodles, which are high in fat.

• Cut down on oil when cooking. Choose heavy, good-quality non-stick pans and use spray oil for the lightest coverage. Moisten food with fat-free or low-fat liquids such as fruit juice, defatted stock, wine or even beer.

• Eat fewer high-fat snacks, such as chocolate, cookies, chips (French fries) and crisps. Try instead a piece of fruit, some vegetable crudités or some home-baked low-fat fruit cake.

Below: Choose lean cuts of meat and naturally low-fat meats such as skinless chicken and turkey.

Above: Keep the fruit bowl stocked with fruit, including exotic varieties like lychees, and you'll always have a fat-free snack to hand.

FAT-FREE COOKING METHODS

Chinese and Far East Asian cooking uses a variety of low-fat and fat-free cooking methods, and by incorporating recipes from this region into your daily diet it is easy to bring down your total fat consumption. Where possible, steam, microwave or grill (broil) foods, without adding extra fat. Alternatively, braise in a defatted stock, wine or fruit juice, or stir-fry with just the merest amount of oil.

• By choosing a good quality, non-stick wok, such as the one above, you can keep the amount of fat needed for cooking foods to the absolute minimum. When cooking meat in a regular pan, dry-fry the meat to brown it, then tip it into a sieve and drain off the excess fat before returning it to the pan and adding the other ingredients. If you do need a little fat for cooking, choose an oil high in unsaturates, such as groundnut (peanut), sunflower or corn oil, or a spray oil.

• Eat less meat and more vegetables and noodles or other forms of pasta. A good method for making a small amount of meat such as beef steak go a long way is to place it in the freezer for 30 minutes and then slice it very thinly with a sharp knife. Meat prepared this way will cook very quickly with very little fat.

• When baking chicken or fish, wrap it in a loose package of foil or baking parchment, with a little wine or fruit juice. Add some fresh herbs or spices before sealing the parcel, if you like.

• It is often unnecessary to add fat when grilling (broiling) food. If the food shows signs of drying, lightly brush it with a small amount of unsaturated oil, such as sunflower, corn or olive oil. Microwaved foods seldom need the addition of fat, so add herbs or spices for extra flavour and colour.

• Steaming is the ideal way of cooking fish. If you like, arrange the fish on a bed of aromatic flavourings such as lemon or lime slices and sprigs of herbs. Alternatively, place finely shredded vegetables or seaweed in the base of the steamer to give the fish extra flavour.

• If you do not own a steamer, cook vegetables in a covered pan over low heat with just a little water, so that they cook in their own juices.
• Vegetables can be braised in the oven in low-fat or fat-free stock, wine or a little water with some chopped fresh or dried herbs.
• Try poaching foods such as chicken, fish or fruit in low-fat or fat-free stock or fruit juice.
• Plain rice or noodles make a very good low-fat accompaniment to most Chinese and Far East Asian dishes.

• The classic Asian technique of adding moisture and flavour to chicken by marinating it in a mixture of soy sauce and rice wine, with a little sesame oil, can be used with other meats too. You can also use a mixture of alcohol, herbs and spices, or vinegar or fruit juice. The marinade will also help to tenderize the meat and any remaining marinade can be used to baste the food while it is cooking.
• When serving vegetables, resist the temptation to add a knob or pat of butter. Instead, sprinkle with chopped fresh herbs.

LOW-FAT SPREADS IN COOKING

There is a huge variety of low-fat and reduced-fat spreads available at our supermarkets, along with some spreads that are very low in fat. Generally speaking, any very low-fat spreads with a fat content of around 20 per cent or less have a high water content. These are unsuitable for cooking and can only be used for spreading.

VEGETABLES

Naturally low in fat and bursting with vitamins and minerals, vegetables are one food group that should ideally make up the bulk of our daily diet. In China and Far East Asia cooks use vegetables freely in stir-fries and braised dishes, and have evolved a wide range of delicious vegetarian main courses to make the most of the abundant choice of vegetables on sale in markets.

Many of these vegetables are now commonplace in other parts of the world. Chinese leaves (Chinese cabbage), pak choi (bok choy) and beansprouts are usually available in supermarkets, and other greens, such as mizuna, Chinese mustard greens and Chinese broccoli, are often grown by small producers and can be found at farmers' markets.

CHINESE LEAVES

Also known as Chinese cabbage or Napa cabbage, this vegetable has pale green, crinkly leaves with long, wide, white ribs. It is pleasantly crunchy, has a sweet, nutty flavour and tastes wonderful raw or cooked. When buying Chinese leaves, look out for firm, slightly heavy heads with pale green leaves without blemishes or bruises. To prepare, peel off the outer leaves, cut off the root and slice the cabbage thinly or thickly. When stir-fried, Chinese leaves lose their subtle cabbage taste and take on the flavour of other ingredients in the dish.

Below: Chinese leaves have a mild, delicate flavour.

Right: Pak choi tastes similar to spinach.

PAK CHOI

Another member of the brassica family, pak choi (bok choy) has lots of noms-de-plume, including horse's ear, Chinese cabbage and Chinese white cabbage. There are several varieties, and one or other is usually on sale at the supermarket. Unlike Chinese leaves, pak choi doesn't keep well, so plan to use it within a day or two of purchase. The vegetable is generally cooked, although very young and tender pak choi can be eaten raw. The stems – regarded by many as the best part – need slightly longer cooking than the leaves.

CHOI SUM

Often sold in bunches, choi sum is a brassica with bright green leaves and thin, pale, slightly grooved stems. It has a pleasant aroma and mild taste, and remains crisp and tender if properly cooked. The leaves can be sliced, but are more often steamed whole. Choi sum will keep for a few days in the salad drawer, but is best used as soon as possible after purchase.

CHINESE BROCCOLI

With its somewhat straggly appearance, this brassica looks more like purple sprouting broccoli than prim Calabrese. Every part of Chinese broccoli is edible, and each has its own inimitable taste. To prepare, remove the tough outer leaves, then cut off the leaves. If the stems are tough, peel them. It is usual to blanch the vegetable briefly in salted boiling water or stock before stir-frying.

AUBERGINES

Popular throughout China and Far East Asia, aubergines (eggplants) come in a variety of shapes, sizes and colours. They have a smoky, slightly bitter taste and spongy flesh that readily absorbs other flavours and oils. To avoid the absorption of too much fat, cut the aubergine into slices, and dry-fry these in a wok over medium heat for 4–5 minutes. They can also be braised, stuffed or baked.

DAIKON

Also known as mooli, this Asian vegetable looks rather like a parsnip, but is actually related to the radish. The flavour is milder than that of most radishes, however, although the texture is similar: crisp and crunchy. Treat it like a carrot, scraping or peeling the outer skin and then slicing it in rounds or batons. It can be eaten raw or cooked.

BAMBOO SHOOTS

Fresh bamboo shoots are quite hard to buy outside Asia, but you may find them in big-city Asian markets. They must be parboiled before being cooked, as the raw vegetable contains a highly toxic oil. Remove the base and the hard outer leaves, then cut the core into chunks. Boil these in salted water for 30 minutes, then drain, rinse under cold water and drain again. Cut into slices, shreds or cubes for further cooking. Dried bamboo slices must be soaked in water for 2–3 hours before use. Canned bamboo shoots only need rinsing before being used.

Right: Choi sum is often used in stir-fries.

Above: There are numerous varieties of aubergines available.

WATER CHESTNUTS

Fresh, crisp water chestnuts are the corms of a plant that grows on the margins of rivers and lakes. They have snow-white flesh which stays crunchy even after long cooking. Fresh water chestnuts are often available from Asian markets. They keep well in a paper bag in the refrigerator. Once released from their dark brown jackets, however, they must be kept submerged in water in a covered container and used within one week. Canned water chestnuts should be rinsed before being used.

Below: Daikon has a crisp, crunchy texture and is delicious raw.

BEANSPROUTS

Mung beans and soy beans are the varieties of beansprout most often used, and they are an important ingredient in the Asian kitchen. It is important to use them as fresh as possible. Better still, sprout the beans yourself. Before use, rinse them to remove the husks and tiny roots. Use them in salads or stir-fries, but take care not to overcook them, or they will become limp and tasteless.

SPRING ONIONS

Slender and crisp, spring onions (scallions) are appreciated by Asian cooks not only for their aroma and flavour, but also for their perceived cooling qualities. Use spring onions raw in salads or lightly cooked in stir-fries. They need very little preparation. Just trim off the roots, strip off the wilted outer leaves and separate the white and green parts. Spring onion green is sometimes used in Asian dishes as ribbon, to tie tiny parcels of food, in which case it is first blanched so that it becomes more flexible.

MUSHROOMS

Several types of mushrooms are used in Asian cooking, and many of these are now available in Western supermarkets.

Shiitake mushrooms are prized in Far East Asia, both for their flavour and their medicinal qualities. They have a slightly acidic taste and a meaty, slippery texture. They contain twice as much protein as button mushrooms and their robust flavour makes them the ideal partner for noodles and rice. To prepare fresh shiitake mushrooms, remove the stems. The caps can be left whole, or sliced. If they are to be used in a salad, cook them briefly in low-fat stock first. Dried shiitake mushrooms must be reconstituted before being used. Soak them in cold water overnight, or in a bowl of warm water for at least 30 minutes before using, then strain the soaking liquid. Remove the stems before use.

Right: Spring onions

Oyster mushrooms have a mild flavour and are pastel-coloured in shades of pink, yellow or pearl grey. They need gentle handling. Tear, rather than cut, large specimens and don't overcook them, or they will become rubbery.

Enokitake mushrooms are tiny, with bud-like caps at the end of long, slender stems. To appreciate their crisp texture and sweet flavour, use them raw in salads.

SEAWEED

If you've never sampled seaweed before, it is a good idea to start with arame. Dried arame must be soaked in lukewarm water for 20 minutes before being used in salads or stir-fries, but it can be added straight from the packet to braised dishes or soups.

Konbu is a large seaweed, often called kelp. It is generally available dried, and must be reconstituted in cold water for 45 minutes before use. Don't wash off the powdery covering before soaking it; just wipe with a damp cloth. It is a rich source of vitamins and minerals, especially iodine.

Nori is wafer-thin dried seaweed, sold in sheets to be used as a wrapping for sushi. Grill (broil) the sheets briefly on one side for sushi, or on both sides for crumbling as a topping.

Wakame and Hijiki are similar forms of seaweed. Wakame is available fresh, and both are available dried, mostly pre-shredded. To prepare dried wakame or hijiki, soak in lukewarm water for 10–15 minutes until it softens and turns green, then drain it, blanch it in boiling water for 1 minute, drain again and refresh under cold water to set the colour. Use as directed in the recipe.

FRUIT AND NUTS

When embarking on a low-fat eating plan, it is all too easy to concentrate solely on the fat content of foods while ignoring the amount of sugar they contain. The occasional indulgence does no harm, but you should avoid following a sensible main course with a sugary dessert. Instead, end a meal with a piece of fresh fruit or a few nuts. The latter can be high in fat, but, with the exception of brazil nuts and coconuts, the fat in nuts is monounsaturated or polyunsaturated, and they are cholesterol-free. They are highly nutritious and are one of the best vegetable sources of vitamin E, which can help to protect against heart disease, stroke and certain cancers.

LYCHEES

These moist little fruits need no preparation once you have cracked the shells and peeled off the scaly red skin. The pearly white flesh inside can be nibbled off the stone (pit), or sliced and used in a fruit salad or savoury dish. Chinese cooks like to pair lychees with pork. They also go well with clementines. For a delectable sorbet, try puréed lychees with elderflower syrup. When buying fresh lychees, choose ones with pink or red shells; brown fruit are past their prime.

Below: Canned and fresh lychees

MANGOES

There are many types of mango. Most are oval in shape with blushed gold or pink skin, although there are also green, scarlet and orange varieties. All are highly scented, with meltingly soft flesh that is invariably sweet and juicy. When buying mangoes, choose fruit with smooth, unblemished skin. If mango chunks are required for a recipe, the easiest way to obtain these is to cut a thick lengthways slice off either side of the unpeeled fruit. Score the flesh on each slice with criss-cross lines, cutting down to the skin. Fold these slices inside out and then slice off the flesh, which will be neatly cubed. Cut the remaining flesh off the stone.

KUMQUATS

Although these look like tiny oranges, they are not in fact citrus fruits, but belong to a species of fruit classified as fortunella. The name comes from the Cantonese *kam kwat*, which translates as "golden orange". About the size of a large olive, the fruits have thin orange-coloured edible rind. This is sweet and provides an interesting contrast to the tangy, often quite bitter pulp it encloses. Kumquats can be eaten whole, halved or sliced into rings.

ASIAN PEARS

Unlike European pears, Asian pears – from Japan, China and Korea – do not soften when ripe, and are valued for their crunch. There are several varieties, most of which are round, rather than the conventional pear-shape, with golden or russet skin.

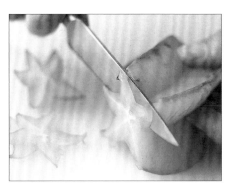

STAR FRUIT

The correct name for this fruit is carambola. Cylindrical in shape, the bright yellow waxy-looking fruit has five distinctive "wings" or protuberances which form the points of the star shapes revealed when the fruit is sliced. The flavour varies: fruits that have been picked straight from the tree in Asia are inevitably sweet and scented, but those that have travelled long distances in cold storage can be disappointing.

NUTS

Walnuts have been cultivated in Asia for centuries. They have a delicious sweet-sour flavour, but go rancid quite quickly, so are best used as soon as possible after purchase.

Cashew nuts have a sweet flavour and crumbly texture. They are never sold in the shell, since removing the seed from its outer casing requires an extensive heating process.

Almonds are valued for their aroma and crunchy texture.

Candlenuts look rather like macadamia nuts and are used as a thickener in Asian cooking. They are slightly toxic when raw, so must always be cooked.

Chinese chestnuts are sweeter and have a finer texture than the Japanese variety. They have a meaty texture and robust flavour, and taste particularly good with Chinese leaves (Chinese cabbage).

FLAVOURINGS

The principal flavourings favoured in Far East Asia have made a tremendous contribution to global cuisine. Ingredients like fresh ginger, lemon grass and lime now feature on menus the world over, not just in recipes that reflect their origin, but also in fusion food. Soy sauce is now a commonplace condiment and often finds its way into dishes that have no more than a nodding acquaintance with China or Japan.

GARLIC

Often used with spring onions (scallions) and ginger, garlic is an important ingredient in China and Korea, but is little used in Japan. The most common variety in the Far East has a purple skin, a fairly distinctive aroma and a hint of sweetness. In Taiwan, immature green garlic is popular. This is garlic that is harvested before the bulblets appear. It looks rather like a spring onion (scallion) and has a subtle garlic flavour. Garlic may dominate a dish, but is also used in more subtle ways, as when a garlic clove is heated in oil so that it imparts a mild flavour, but removed before other ingredients are added to the pan.

GINGER

Valued not just as an aromatic, but also for its medicinal qualities, ginger is used throughout Asia. Although commonly referred to as a root, ginger is actually a rhizome, or underground stem. When young, it is juicy and tender, with a sharp flavour suggestive of citrus. At this stage it can easily be sliced, chopped or pounded to a paste. Older roots are tougher and may need to be peeled and grated. Pickled ginger is delicious. The Chinese version, in rice vinegar, is quite pungent, while the Japanese type has a more delicate flavour.

CHILLIES

Although they did not originate in Far East Asia, chillies have been embraced so fervently by China that they are now irrevocably associated with the area. They are fundamental to Sichuan cooking and are also used in other regional cuisines, but it is for their flavour rather than their fire that they are most valued. Be careful when you are handling chillies. They contain a substance called capsaicin, which is a powerful irritant. If this comes into contact with delicate skin or the eyes, it can cause considerable pain. Either wear gloves when handling chillies or wash your hands thoroughly in hot soapy water afterwards.

LEMON GRASS

A perennial tufted plant with a bulbous base, lemon grass looks like a plump spring onion (scallion) and doesn't seem very promising as an ingredient until the stalk is cut or bruised. It is only then that the lively, but not acidic, citrus aroma becomes evident. There are two main ways of using lemon grass. The stalk can be kept whole, bruised, then cooked slowly in liquid until it releases its flavour and is removed, or the tender lower portion of the stalk can be sliced or finely chopped and then stir-fried.

Left: Red and green chillies

RICE VINEGAR

Vinegar fermented from rice, or distilled from rice grains, is used extensively in Chinese and Far East Asian cooking. The former is dark amber in colour and is referred to in China as red or black vinegar; the latter is clear, so it is called white vinegar. Unless labelled *yonezu* (pure rice vinegar), most Japanese vinegars, called *su* or *kokumotso-su* (grain vinegar), contain other grains besides rice.

MIRIN

This amber-coloured, heavily sweetened sake is made from distilled sake. It is only used in cooking, and adds a mild sweetness, a slight alcoholic flavour and a shiny glaze to food. It is used for simmered dishes and in glazing sauces.

SOY SAUCE

Made from fermented soya beans, this popular condiment is used all over Far East Asia. Chinese soy sauce can be light, dark or a blend of the two. Japan has similar products. Shoyu is a full-flavoured sauce made from fermented soya beans, wheat and salt. *Koikuchi* is dark shoyu, and *usukuchi* is light shoyu. *Usukuchi* is an all-purpose shoyu and is slightly less salty than its Chinese equivalent. Miso is one of the oldest traditional Japanese ingredients, and it has a strong fermented bean flavour. There are three types: *shiro-miso*, which is the lightest in saltiness and flavour; *aka-miso*, which has a medium flavour; and *kuro-miso*, which has the strongest flavour.

Above: Lemon grass

DASHI STOCK

Dashi is a fish stock made from water, konbu and dried skipjack tuna. It can be made at home, or you can buy freeze-dried granules called *dashi-no-moto* for an instant stock, if you prefer.

RICE <u>AND</u> NOODLES

These low-fat, high-carbohydrate foods are immensely important in China and Far East Asia, forming the bulk of most meals. People in the north of China favour noodles, while those in the south prefer rice. Japanese and Korean cooks make excellent use of both.

Below: Black and white glutinous rice

RICE

Many Asians eat rice three times a day and it is no coincidence that the Chinese character for cooked rice, *fan*, also stands for nourishment and good health. Rice is the essential element of the meal and anything served with it is merely relish.

Rice is a non-allergenic food, rich in complex carbohydrates and low in salts and fats. It contains small amounts of easily digestible protein, together with phosphorous, magnesium, potassium and zinc. Brown rice, which retains the bran, yields vitamin E and some B-group vitamins, and is also a source of fibre. Although it is healthier than white rice, it is the latter that is preferred in Far East Asia.

There are thousands of varieties of rice, many of which are known only in the areas where they are cultivated. The simplest method of classification is by the length of the grain, which can be long, medium or short. Long grain rice is three or four times as long as it is wide. When cooked, the individual grains remain separate. If the rice is medium grain, cooking will cause the grains to soften and start to cling together. This is even more marked in short grain rice, which absorbs liquid during cooking and becomes sticky and creamy. Glutinous rice has grains that stick together exceptionally well. In China, the everyday rice is a long grain variety, *xian*, but *geng*, a glutinous rice, is used for puddings and dim sum. In Japan, two basic types of rice are eaten. The first is a plump, short grained variety called *uruchimai*. This is the rice used for sushi. The grains cling together when cooked, although not as cohesively as when the second type, Japanese glutinous rice, is cooked. Steaming is the recommended method for cooking glutinous rice, since this encourages the rice to cook through without collapsing into mush.

NOODLES

Second only to rice as a staple food, noodles are enjoyed all over Asia. Usually mixed with other ingredients such as vegetables or seafood, rather than being served solo as an accompaniment, noodles are eaten at all times of day and are a popular breakfast food. Asian noodles are made from flours from a wide range of sources, including wheat, rice, mung bean, buckwheat, seaweed and devil's tongue, which is a plant related to the arum lily. Some noodles are plain, others are enriched with egg. They are sold fresh and dried.

Wheat noodles are made from water, wheat flour and salt. Japanese wheat noodles, udon, come in several thicknesses, and are usually sold in bundles, held in place by a paper band. The thin white ones are called somen.

PREPARING AND COOKING NOODLES

All noodles are easy to prepare but techniques vary for each type, so do check the package instructions. Before being used in a stir-fry or similar dish, some varieties only need to be warmed through in hot water, while others must be boiled briefly.

Egg noodles, which are enriched wheat noodles, are extremely popular. They are made in various thicknesses and may be fresh or dried, in coils or blocks. Japanese egg noodles are sold as ramen.

Cellophane noodles consist of very fine, clear strands. They are also known as mung bean noodles, transparent noodles, bean thread noodles or glass noodles. In Japan they are known as *harusame*. When cooked, they remain firm, and it is their texture, rather than their bland taste, that appeals.

Rice noodles come in various forms, from very thin strands called rice vermicelli to flattened sheets.

Buckwheat noodles are darker in colour than wheat varieties. They are popular in Korea and also in Japan, where they are called soba.

Right: Fresh egg noodles

MEAT AND POULTRY

It is traditional in China and Far East Asia for the meat element in a dish to be a relatively small percentage of the whole, with vegetables and noodles or rice making up the major portion. This is good news for anyone on a low-fat diet. When meat is included, it is usually used in stir-fries, soups and braised or grilled (broiled) dishes, none of which require much additional fat. Chicken is immensely popular and is the leanest meat. Pork, which comes a close second, is not quite such a healthy choice, although the breeding of new and leaner animals has reduced the fat content of pork in recent years. Lamb is not widely eaten, but there's a burgeoning interest in beef, partly because of the proliferation of fast-food restaurants in major cities.

Below: A whole raw chicken

CHICKEN

A whole chicken is a popular purchase almost everywhere in Far East Asia. The breast portion will be sliced or diced for a stir-fry; the rest of the meat will be carefully cut off the carcass and used in a red-cooked dish or a curry and the bones will be simmered in water to make a stock or soup. The giblets are also valued, as are the feet.

DUCK

Much higher in saturated fat than chicken, especially if you eat the skin, duck is best kept for occasional treats, or used in small quantities to flavour a dish like chop suey. When buying duck, look for a bird with a long body and a plump breast. The skin should be unmarked and should look creamy and slightly waxy. The healthiest way of cooking duck breast fillets is to steam them for about an hour, having first removed the skin. The meat can then be sliced and moistened with a little of the water from the steamer. Duck cooked this way is delicious in a salad.

PORK

The leanest cut of pork is fillet (tenderloin). There's very little waste with this cut, and it is perfect for stir-frying. Choose fillets that are pale pink all over. The flesh should be fairly firm, and should be slightly moist to the touch. Avoid any meat with discoloured areas. To prepare pork fillet, pull away the membrane that surrounds the meat, removing any fat at the same time. The sinew, which looks like a tougher strip of membrane, must be sliced away.

BEEF

In much of China and Far East Asia, the cow was for many centuries regarded solely as a beast of burden, thus too precious to be slaughtered for food. Today, however, thanks to the fast-food industry, beef consumption is on the increase all over China, and even in Japan, which was for centuries a Buddhist (and therefore vegetarian) culture. When buying beef, look for deep red meat. For slow-cooked dishes, a generous marbling of fat is required, but if the meat is to be stir-fried, a leaner cut such as fillet (tenderloin) or rump (round) steak should be used.

LAMB

Although not as popular as pork or beef, lamb is nevertheless an important ingredient in some classic Asian dishes, particularly those that originated in Mongolia or Tibet. Remove any visible fat before cooking, and use sparingly, padding out the meal with vegetables or carbohydrates.

Above: Lean pork fillet and ribs

TOFU: AN ALTERNATIVE PROTEIN

Packed with vitamins, tofu, or beancurd as it is known in China, is a gift to the health-conscious cook. An excellent source of vegetable protein, it contains the eight essential amino acids that cannot be synthesized in the body, plus vitamins A and B. It is also low in fat, cholesterol-free and easy to digest. Substituting tofu for meat in just a couple of meals a week is an easy way of reducing overall fat consumption.

Made from soya beans that have been boiled, mashed, sieved (strained) and curdled, tofu comes in various forms. The firm type is sold in blocks and can be cubed or sliced for use in a stir-fry, as kebabs or in salads. Silken tofu, which has a smooth texture, is ideal for sauces and dips, and is a useful non-dairy alternative to cream, soft cheese or yogurt. Smoked, marinated and deep-fried tofu, called *atsu-age* in Japan, are also available.

Of itself, tofu has little flavour, but its sponge-like texture means that it absorbs other flavours easily. Seasonings such as garlic, ginger, chillies, soy sauce, oyster sauce and fermented black beans go particularly well with tofu.

FISH AND SHELLFISH

Fish is an extremely important food source in China and Far East Asia, where coastal waters, rivers and lakes provide an abundant harvest. From a healthy eating perspective, bass and sea bass, cod, sea bream, sole and plaice are excellent low-fat protein foods, but the darker-fleshed oily fish like tuna, salmon, carp, trout, mackerel, sardines and herring excite even more interest. The Omega-3 fatty acids they contain benefit the heart, helping to lower cholesterol and triglyceride levels and reduce blood pressure. Scallops and squid are also a good source of Omega-3 fatty acids, and these, along with prawns (shrimp), crab and clams are used to great effect by Asian cooks, whether steamed, poached, baked or fried. In Japan, a country with one of the highest rates of fish consumption in the world, exceedingly fresh fish is frequently served raw as sashimi or sushi.

CARP

This freshwater fish is widely farmed in Asia. It has meaty, moist flesh that can taste a little muddy to those unfamiliar with the distinctive taste. When buying carp, ask the fishmonger to remove the scales and strong dorsal fins. A favourite Chinese way of cooking carp is to stuff it with ginger and spring onions (scallions) and serve it with a sweet pickle sauce.

Below: Blue swimming crabs

Right from top: Freshwater carp, mackerel and grey mullet.

CRAB

Several varieties of crab are found in Asian waters, including the giant spider crabs of Japan, and the blue crabs that are so popular in Korea that there have been serious skirmishes between fishermen intent on catching them. Crab meat has a distinctive taste that goes well with Oriental flavours. Dim sum often include steamed crab. The phrase "dim sum" translates as "heart's delight", which seems very apt in this instance. A crab meat sauce tastes good with asparagus.

MACKEREL

Easily recognized by the wavy dark blue markings on its silvery green body, mackerel is ideal for grilling (broiling) or poaching with miso. Like herring, the fish tastes best with a sharp sauce to counteract the richness of the flesh. When buying mackerel, insist on absolute freshness and use it on the day of purchase. Mackerel can be used for sashimi. It has a succulent flavour but can smell rather pungent, so salted mackerel is sometimes substituted in its place.

SALMON

The finest wild salmon has a superb flavour and makes excellent sashimi. It is costly, however, and so may not be affordable on a regular basis. Responsibly farmed salmon is more economical to buy, and although the flavour is not quite as good as that of wild salmon, it is still delicious. The rosy flesh is beautifully moist and responds very well to being poached or baked, either on its own or with herbs and spices or aromatics. Salmon can take quite robust flavours. Try it with sweet soy sauce and noodles, or in that classic dish, Salmon Teriyaki. If buying salmon for sashimi, have a good fishmonger cut you a chunk from a large salmon; do not use ready-cut steaks. Smoked salmon can be used for sushi.

GREY MULLET

This fish has dark stripes along the back, lots of thick scales and a heavy head. The flesh is soft and rather coarse, but responds well when it is cooked with distinctive flavours, such as ginger, garlic, spring onion (scallion) and chilli.

Above: Raw, unshelled prawns

SCALLOPS

The tender, sweet flesh of this seafood needs very little cooking. Whenever possible, buy scallops fresh. If they are to be used for sashimi, the coral (roe), black stomach and frill must be removed first. In cooked dishes, the coral can be retained and is regarded as a delicacy.

SEA BASS

Characterized by the delicate flavour of its flesh, sea bass is enjoyed throughout Asia. It holds its shape when cooked, and can be grilled (broiled), steamed, baked or barbecued whole. Sea bass fillets taste delicious when they have been marinated, then cooked on a ridged griddle pan. Chunks or strips make a sensational stir-fry.

SHRIMPS AND PRAWNS

If you ask for shrimp in Britain, you will be given tiny crustaceans, while in America, the term is used for the larger shellfish which the British call prawns. Asian cooks use both words fairly indiscriminately, so check exactly what a recipe requires. Buy raw shellfish if possible, and then cook it yourself. This applies equally to fresh and frozen mixed seafood. If frozen, thaw slowly and pat them dry before cooking.

SQUID

The cardinal rule with squid is to either cook it very quickly, or simmer it for a long time. Anything in between will result in seafood that is tough and rubbery. It is an ideal candidate for stir-frying with flavours like ginger, garlic, spring onion (scallion) and chilli, and also makes an interesting salad. For a slow-cooked dish, try squid cooked in a clay pot with chillies and noodles.

TUNA

This very large fish is usually sold as steaks, which can be pink or red, depending on the variety. Avoid steaks with heavy discoloration around the bone, or which are brownish and dull-looking. The flesh should be solid and compact. Tuna loses its colour and can become dry when overcooked, so cook it only briefly over high heat, or stew it gently with moist ingredients like tomatoes and peppers.

Below: Tuna steaks and salmon cutlets

SASHIMI AND SUSHI

Glowing colours, exquisite presentation and pure, clean flavours are just some of the reasons why sashimi and sushi have become popular the world over. Both these Japanese specialities are generally, but not inevitably, based upon raw fish, which must be absolutely fresh and of the finest quality.

For sashimi, fish is shaved into paper-thin slices or cut into chunks or finger-width slices. It is traditionally served with wasabi, an extremely hot condiment made from a plant that grows near mountain streams.

Sushi is a general term relating to a variety of snacks or light dishes based on rice that has been prepared in a particular way. It frequently includes fish. The most familiar version, *hoso-maki*, involves laying the rice on a sheet of nori seaweed and rolling it around one or more ingredients before slicing it into rolls. The rice can also be compressed into blocks and topped with fresh or smoked fish (as pictured above), or shaped by hand and coated in sesame seeds to make *onigiri*.

FAT AND CALORIE CONTENTS OF FOOD

The figures show the weight of fat (g) and the energy content per 100g (3½oz) of each of the following foods used in Chinese and Far East Asian cooking. Use the table to help work out the fat content of favourite dishes.

	fat (g)	Energy kcals/kJ		fat (g)	Energy kcals/kJ
MEATS			**VEGETABLES**		
Beef minced (ground), raw	16.2	225kcal/934kJ	Asparagus	0.0	12.5kcal/52.5kJ
Beef, rump (round) steak, lean only	4.1	125kcal/526kJ	Aubergine (eggplant)	0.4	15kcal/63kJ
Beef, fillet (tenderloin) steak	8.5	191kcal/799kJ	Bamboo shoots	0.0	29kcal/120kJ
Chicken, minced (ground), raw	8.5	106kcal/449kJ	Beansprouts	1.6	10kcal/42kJ
Chicken fillet, raw	1.1	106kcal/449kJ	(Bell) peppers	0.4	32kcals/128kJ
Chicken thighs, without skin, raw	6.0	126kcal/530kJ	Beans, fine green	0.0	7kcal/29kJ
Duck, without skin, cooked	9.5	182kcal/765kJ	Beetroot (beets)	0.1	36kcal/151kJ
Lamb leg, lean, cooked	6.3	198kcal/831kJ	Broccoli	0.9	33kcal/138kJ
Liver, lamb's, raw	6.2	137kcal/575kJ	Carrot	0.3	35kcal/156kJ
Pork, average, lean, raw	4.0	123kcal/519kJ	Celery	0.2	7kcal/142kJ
Pork, lean roast	4.0	163kcal/685kJ	Chilli, fresh	0.0	30kcal/120kJ
Pork, minced (ground), raw	4.0	123kcal/519kJ	Chinese leaves (Chinese cabbage)	0.0	8kcal/35kJ
Pork, ribs, raw	10.0	114kcal/480kJ	Courgettes (zucchini)	0.4	18kcal74kJ
Turkey, meat only, raw	1.6	105kcal/443kJ	Cucumber	0.1	10kcal/40kJ
Turkey, minced (ground), raw	6.5	170kcal/715kJ	Daikon (mooli)	0.1	18kcal74kJ
			Fennel	0.0	12kcal/50kJ
FISH AND SHELLFISH			Leek	0.3	20kcal/87kJ
Cod, raw	0.7	80kcal/337kJ	Mangetouts (snow peas)	0.4	81kcal/339kJ
Crab meat, raw	0.5	54kcal/230kJ	Mushrooms, button (white)	0.5	24kcal/100kJ
Mackerel, raw	16.0	221kcal/930kJ	Mushrooms, shiitake	0.2	55kcal/230kJ
Monkfish, raw	1.5	76kcal/320kJ	Mushrooms, dried Chinese	0.0	56kcal/240kJ
Mussels, raw, weight without shells	1.8	74kcal/312kJ	Onion	0.2	36kcal/151kJ
Mussels, raw, weight with shells	0.6	24kcal/98kJ	Pak choi (bok choy)	0.0	13kcal/53kJ
Oysters, raw	4.2	120kcal/508kJ	Spinach (fresh, cooked)	0.0	20kcal/87kJ
Prawns (shrimp)	1.0	76kcal/320kJ	Spring onion (scallion)	0.0	17kcal/83kJ
Salmon, steamed	13.0	200kcal/837kJ	Sweet potato (peeled, boiled)	0.0	84kcal/358kJ
Scallops, raw	1.6	105kcal/440kJ	Water chestnuts	0.0	98kcal/410kJ
Sardine fillets, grilled	10.4	195kcal/815kJ			
Sardines, grilled, weight with bones	6.3	19kcal/497kJ	**NUTS AND SEEDS**		
Sea bass, raw	2.0	97kcal/406kJ	Almonds	55.8	612kcal/2534kJ
Squid, boiled	1.0	79kcal/330kJ	Cashew nuts	48.0	573kcal/2406kJ
Swordfish, grilled	5.1	155kcal/649kJ	Chestnuts	2.7	169kcal/714kJ
Tuna, grilled	6.3	184kcal/770kJ	Sesame seeds	47.0	507kcal/2113kJ

Below: Red meat such as beef, lamb and pork have a higher quantity of fat per 100g than white meat.

Below: Seafood is a good source of vitamins, minerals and protein. Oily fish contains high levels of Omega-3 fatty acids.

FRUIT	fat (g)	Energy kcals/kJ
Apples, eating	0.1	47kcal/199kJ
Bananas	0.3	95kcal/403kJ
Grapefruit	0.1	30kcal/126kJ
Grapes (green)	0.0	56kcal/235kJ
Lychees	0.1	58kcal/248kJ
Mangoes	0.0	60Kcal/251kJ
Nectarine	0.0	40kcal/169kJ
Oranges	0.1	37kcal/158kJ
Peaches	0.0	31kcal/132kJ
Pears	0.1	40kcal/169kJ
Pineapple, fresh	0.0	50Kcal/209kJ
Pineapple, canned chunks	0.2	63Kcal/264kJ
Raspberries	0.0	28Kcal/117kJ
Star fruit (carambola)	0.0	25Kcal/105kJ
Strawberries	0.0	27kcal/113kJ
Watermelon	0.0	23kcal/95kJ

BEANS, CEREALS AND TOFU	fat (g)	Energy kcals/kJ
Aduki beans, cooked	0.2	123kcal/525kJ
Noodles, cellophane	trace	351kcal/1468kJ
Noodles, egg	0.5	62kcal/264kJ
Noodles, plain wheat	2.5	354kcal/1190kJ
Noodles, rice	0.1	360kcal/1506kJ
Noodles, soba	0.1	99kcal/414kJ
Rice, brown, uncooked	2.8	357kcal/1518kJ
Rice, white, uncooked	3.6	383kcal/1630kJ
Tofu, firm	4.2	73kcal/304kJ
Tofu, silken	2.5	55kcal/230kJ

BAKING AND PANTRY	fat (g)	Energy kcals/kJ
Cornflour (cornstarch)	0.7	354kcal/1508kJ
Flour, plain (all-purpose) white	1.3	341kcal/1450kJ
Flour, self-raising (self-rising)	1.2	330kcal/1407kJ
Flour, wholemeal (whole-wheat)	2.2	310kcal/1318kJ
Tapioca	0.0	28kcal/119kJ
Honey	0.0	288kcal/1229kJ
Soy sauce, per 5ml/1 tsp	0.0	9kcal/40kJ
Sugar, white	0.3	94kcal/1680kJ

FATS, OILS AND EGGS	fat (g)	Energy kcals/kJ
Butter	81.7	737kcal/3031kJ
Low-fat spread	40.5	390kcal/1605kJ
Very low-fat spread	25.0	273kcal/1128kJ
Oil, corn, per 1 tbsp/15ml	13.8	124kcal/511kJ
Oil, groundnut (peanut), per 1 tbsp/15ml	14.9	134kcal/552kJ
Oil, rapeseed (canola), per 1 tbsp/15ml	13.7	124kcal/511kJ
Oil, sesame seed, per 1 tbsp/15ml	14.9	134kcal/552kJ
Oil, sunflower, per 1 tbsp/15ml	13.8	124kcal/511kJ
Eggs	10.8	147kcal/612kJ
Egg yolk	30.5	339kcal/1402kJ
Egg white	Trace	36kcal/153kJ

DAIRY PRODUCTS	fat (g)	Energy kcals/kJ
Cheese, Cheddar	34.4	412kcal/1708kJ
Cheese, Cheddar-type, reduced fat	15.0	261kcal/1091kJ
Cheese, cottage	3.9	98kcal/413kJ
Cheese, cream	47.4	439kcal/1807kJ
Cream, double (heavy)	48.0	449kcal/1849kJ
Cream, reduced-fat double (heavy)	24.0	243kcal/1002kJ
Cream, single (light)	19.1	198kcal/817kJ
Cream, whipping	39.3	373kcal/1539kJ
Crème fraîche	40.0	379kcal/156kJ
Crème fraîche, reduced fat	15.0	165kcal/683kJ
Fromage frais, plain	7.1	113kcal/469kJ
Fromage frais, very low fat	0.2	58kcal/247kJ
Milk, full cream (whole)	3.9	66kcal/275kJ
Milk, semi-skimmed (low-fat)	1.5	35kcal/146kJ
Milk, skimmed	0.1	33kcal/130kJ
Yogurt, low-fat natural (plain)	0.8	56kcal/236kJ
Yogurt, Greek (US strained plain)	9.1	115kcal/477kJ

Below: Vegetables are very low in fat. Eat them raw for a filling snack, or steam them to retain maximum nutritional value.

Below: Soya products, such as tofu, soya milk and soya beans, contain isoflavones that are thought to lower cholesterol levels.

SOUPS AND APPETIZERS

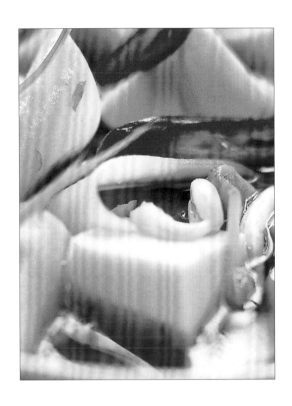

These superb dishes are uniformly low in fat but hit the heights when it comes to flavour and presentation. Unusual soups such as Cheat's Shark's Fin Soup or Miso Broth with Tofu make a marvellous opening to a special meal, and Prawn Toasts with Sesame Seeds or Stuffed Chillies are great with drinks. For something slightly more substantial, opt for Chinese-style Cabbage and Noodle Parcels. These leafy packages are tied with spring onion strips and have a pork and mushroom filling.

HOT AND SOUR SOUP ★

THIS SPICY, WARMING SOUP REALLY WHETS THE APPETITE AND IS THE PERFECT INTRODUCTION TO A SIMPLE CHINESE MEAL. USE HOME-MADE VEGETABLE STOCK FOR THE BEST POSSIBLE FLAVOUR.

SERVES 4

INGREDIENTS

10g/¼oz dried cloud ear
 (wood ear) mushrooms
8 fresh shiitake mushrooms
75g/3oz firm tofu
50g/2oz/½ cup sliced, drained,
 canned bamboo shoots
900ml/1½ pints/3¾ cups
 vegetable stock
15ml/1 tbsp caster (superfine) sugar
45ml/3 tbsp rice vinegar
15ml/1 tbsp light soy sauce
1.5ml/¼ tsp chilli oil
2.5ml/½ tsp salt
large pinch of ground white pepper
15ml/1 tbsp cornflour (cornstarch)
15ml/1 tbsp cold water
1 egg white
5ml/1 tsp sesame oil
2 spring onions (scallions),
 cut into fine rings

1 Soak the dried cloud ears in hot water for 20 minutes or until soft. Drain, trim off and discard the hard base from each cloud ear and then chop the fungus roughly.

2 Remove and discard the stems from the shiitake mushrooms. Cut the caps into thin strips.

3 Cut the tofu into 1cm/½in cubes and shred the bamboo shoots finely.

4 Place the stock, mushrooms, tofu, bamboo shoots and cloud ear mushrooms in a large pan. Bring the stock to the boil, lower the heat and simmer for about 5 minutes.

5 Stir in the sugar, vinegar, soy sauce, chilli oil, salt and pepper. Mix the cornflour to a paste with the water. Add the mixture to the soup, stirring constantly with a spoon or whisk until it thickens slightly.

6 Lightly beat the egg white, then pour it slowly into the soup in a steady stream, stirring constantly. Cook, stirring, until the egg white changes colour and becomes thready.

7 Add the sesame oil just before serving. Ladle into heated bowls and top each portion with spring onion rings.

COOK'S TIP
To transform this tasty soup into a nutritious light meal, simply add extra mushrooms, tofu, bamboo shoots and noodles.

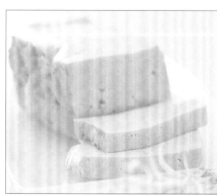

Energy 60Kcal/254kJ; Protein 3.2g; Carbohydrate 8.4g, of which sugars 4.6g; Fat 1.8g, of which saturates 0.3g; Cholesterol 0mg; Calcium 103mg; Fibre 0.5g; Sodium 287mg.

TOMATO AND BEEF SOUP ★

*MAKE THIS BEEF BROTH IN LATE SUMMER, WHEN FARMERS' MARKETS AND ROADSIDE STALLS SELL
FRESHLY PICKED RIPE TOMATOES. IT TAKES VERY LITTLE TIME TO COOK AND TASTES SUPERB.*

SERVES 4

INGREDIENTS

    75g/3oz rump (round) steak,
      trimmed of fat
    900ml/1½ pints/3¾ cups beef stock
    30ml/2 tbsp tomato
      purée (paste)
    6 tomatoes, halved, seeded
      and chopped
    10ml/2 tsp caster (superfine) sugar
    15ml/1 tbsp cornflour (cornstarch)
    15ml/1 tbsp cold water
    1 egg white
    2.5ml/½ tsp sesame oil
    2 spring onions (scallions),
      finely shredded
    salt and ground black pepper

1 Cut the beef into thin strips and place it in a pan. Pour over boiling water to cover. Cook for 2 minutes, then drain thoroughly and set aside.

2 Bring the stock to the boil in a clean pan. Stir in the tomato purée, then the tomatoes and sugar. Add the beef strips, allow the stock to boil again, then lower the heat and simmer for 2 minutes.

3 Mix the cornflour to a paste with the water. Add the mixture to the soup, stirring constantly until it thickens slightly. Lightly beat the egg white in a cup.

4 Pour the egg white into the soup in a steady stream, stirring all the time. As soon as the egg white changes colour and become thready, add salt and pepper, stir the soup and pour it into heated bowls.

5 Drizzle each portion of soup with a few drops of sesame oil, sprinkle the shredded spring onions over the top and serve immediately.

VARIATION

Instead of using spring onions, top the soup with finely chopped red (bell) peppers.

Energy 68Kcal/287kJ; Protein 6.2g; Carbohydrate 7.7g, of which sugars 7.7g; Fat 1.6g, of which saturates 0.5g; Cholesterol 11mg; Calcium 16mg; Fibre 1.5g; Sodium 56mg.

CHEAT'S SHARK'S FIN SOUP ★

SHARK'S FIN SOUP IS A RENOWNED DELICACY. IN THIS VEGETARIAN VERSION TRANSPARENT CELLOPHANE NOODLES MASQUERADE AS SHARK'S FIN NEEDLES, WITH REMARKABLE EFFECTS.

6 Add the stock to the pan. Bring to the boil, then simmer for 15–20 minutes.

7 Season with salt, pepper and soy sauce. Blend the arrowroot or potato flour with about 30ml/2 tbsp water. Pour into the soup, stirring all the time to prevent lumps from forming as the soup continues to simmer.

SERVES 4–6

INGREDIENTS

    4 dried Chinese mushrooms
    25ml/1½ tbsp dried cloud ear
      (wood ear) mushrooms
    115g/4oz cellophane noodles
    30ml/2 tbsp vegetable oil
    2 carrots, cut into fine strips
    115g/4oz canned bamboo shoots,
      rinsed, drained and cut into strips
    1 litre/1¾ pints/4 cups
      vegetable stock
    15ml/1 tbsp light soy sauce
    15ml/1 tbsp arrowroot or
      potato flour
    1 egg white, beaten (optional)
    5ml/1 tsp sesame oil
    salt and ground black pepper
    2 spring onions (scallions), finely
      chopped, to garnish
    Chinese red vinegar, to
      serve (optional)

1 Soak the mushrooms and cloud ears in separate bowls of warm water for 20 minutes. Drain.

2 Remove the mushroom stems from the water and slice the caps thinly. Cut the cloud ears into fine strips, discarding any hard bits.

3 Soak the noodles in hot water until soft. Drain and cut into short lengths.

4 Heat the oil in a large pan. Add the mushrooms and stir-fry for 2 minutes.

5 Add the cloud ears, stir-fry for 2 minutes, then stir in the carrots, bamboo shoots and noodles.

COOK'S TIP
Also known as mung bean or transparent noodles, cellophane noodles retain their firm texture when cooked.

8 Remove the pan from the heat. Stir in the egg white, if using, so that it sets to form small threads in the hot soup. Stir in the sesame oil, then pour the soup into individual heated bowls.

9 Sprinkle with chopped spring onions and offer the Chinese red vinegar separately, if you are using it.

Energy 124Kcal/518kJ; Protein 2.4g; Carbohydrate 18.9g, of which sugars 1.2g; Fat 4.4g, of which saturates 0.5g; Cholesterol 0mg; Calcium 11mg; Fibre 0.5g; Sodium 184mg.

CORN AND CHICKEN SOUP ★

USING A COMBINATION OF CHICKEN, CREAMED CORN AND WHOLE KERNELS GIVES THIS CLASSIC CHINESE SOUP A LOVELY TEXTURE. IT TASTES DELICIOUS AND IS VERY EASY TO MAKE.

SERVES 4–6

INGREDIENTS

1 skinless chicken breast fillet, about 115g/4oz, cubed
10ml/2 tsp light soy sauce
15ml/1 tbsp Chinese rice wine
5ml/1 tsp cornflour (cornstarch)
60ml/4 tbsp cold water
5ml/1 tsp sesame oil
15ml/1 tbsp vegetable oil
5ml/1 tsp grated fresh root ginger
1 litre/1¾ pints/4 cups chicken stock
425g/15oz can creamed corn
225g/8oz can whole kernel corn
2 eggs, beaten
2–3 spring onions (scallions), green parts only, cut into tiny rounds
salt and ground black pepper

3 Spoon about 90ml/6 tbsp of the hot liquid into the chicken mixture until it forms a smooth paste and stir. Return to the wok. Slowly bring to the boil, stirring constantly, then simmer for 2–3 minutes or until the chicken is cooked.

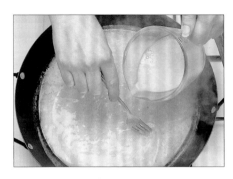

4 Pour the beaten eggs into the soup in a slow steady stream, using a fork or chopsticks to stir the top of the soup in a figure-of-eight pattern. The egg should set in lacy shreds. Serve immediately with the spring onions sprinkled over.

1 Mince (grind) the chicken in a food processor, taking care not to over-process. Transfer the chicken to a bowl and stir in the soy sauce, rice wine, cornflour, water, sesame oil and seasoning. Cover with clear film (plastic wrap) and leave for about 15 minutes to absorb the flavours.

2 Heat a wok over medium heat. Add the vegetable oil and swirl it around. Add the ginger and stir-fry for a few seconds. Pour in the stock with the creamed corn and corn kernels. Bring to just below boiling point.

VARIATION
For a seafood twist, add 175g/6oz/1 cup drained canned crab meat in place of the chicken.

Energy 196Kcal/831kJ; Protein 10g; Carbohydrate 29.9g, of which sugars 10.7g; Fat 4.7g, of which saturates 1g; Cholesterol 77mg; Calcium 17mg; Fibre 1.6g; Sodium 447mg.

TOFU AND BEANSPROUT SOUP ★

THIS LIGHT AND REFRESHING SOUP IS AN EXCELLENT PICK-ME-UP. THE AROMATIC, SPICY BROTH IS SIMMERED FIRST, AND THEN THE TOFU, BEANSPROUTS AND NOODLES ARE ADDED.

SERVES 4

INGREDIENTS
    150g/5oz dried thick rice noodles
    1 litre/1¾ pints/4 cups
      vegetable stock
    1 red chilli, seeded and
      finely sliced
    15ml/1 tbsp light soy sauce
    juice of ½ lemon
    10ml/2 tsp sugar
    5ml/1 tsp finely sliced garlic
    5ml/1 tsp finely chopped fresh
      root ginger
    200g/7oz firm tofu, cubed
    90g/3½oz beansprouts
    50g/2oz peanuts
    15ml/1 tbsp chopped fresh
      coriander (cilantro)
    spring onion (scallion) slivers and
      red chilli slivers, to garnish

1 Spread out the noodles in a shallow dish and and cook according to the packet instructions until they are just tender. Drain, rinse and set aside.

2 Meanwhile, place the stock, red chilli, soy sauce, lemon juice, sugar, garlic and ginger in a wok over high heat. Bring to the boil, cover, reduce to low heat and simmer gently for 10–12 minutes.

3 Cut the tofu into cubes. Add it to the wok with the drained noodles and beansprouts. Cook the mixture gently for 2–3 minutes.

4 Roast the peanuts in a dry non-stick wok, then chop them. Stir the coriander into the soup. Serve in warm bowls with peanuts, spring onions and chilli on top.

Energy 190Kcal/795kJ; Protein 6.7g; Carbohydrate 34.7g, of which sugars 3.5g; Fat 2.3g, of which saturates 0.3g; Cholesterol 0mg; Calcium 266mg; Fibre 0.4g; Sodium 275mg.

JAPANESE-STYLE NOODLE SOUP ★

THIS DELICATE, FRAGRANT SOUP IS FLAVOURED WITH JUST A HINT OF CHILLI. IT IS BEST SERVED AS A LIGHT LUNCH OR AS A FIRST COURSE. IT LOOKS VERY PRETTY WITH THE NOODLES AND VEGETABLES.

SERVES 4

INGREDIENTS

    45ml/3 tbsp *aka-miso*
    200g/7oz/scant 2 cups udon noodles,
      soba noodles or egg noodles
    30ml/2 tbsp sake or dry sherry
    15ml/1 tbsp rice or wine vinegar
    45ml/3 tbsp shoyu
    115g/4oz asparagus tips or
      mangetouts (snow peas), thinly
      sliced diagonally
    50g/2oz/scant 1 cup shiitake
      mushrooms, stalks removed and
      caps thinly sliced
    1 carrot, sliced into julienne strips
    3 spring onions (scallions), thinly
      sliced diagonally
    salt and ground black pepper
    5ml/1 tsp dried chilli flakes, to serve

1 Bring 1 litre/1¾ pints/4 cups water to the boil in a pan. Pour 150ml/¼ pint/⅔ cup of the boiling water over the miso and stir until it has dissolved.

2 Meanwhile, bring another large pan of lightly salted water to the boil, add the noodles and cook according to the packet instructions until they are just tender.

3 Drain the noodles in a colander. Rinse under cold water, then drain again.

COOK'S TIP
Miso is a thick fermented paste based on cooked soya beans with rice or a similar cereal. It adds a savoury flavour to dishes. There are various types, *aka-miso* being medium strength.

4 Thoroughly combine the sake or sherry, vinegar and soy sauce in a small bowl, then add to the pan of boiling water.

5 Boil the mixture gently for 3 minutes, then reduce the heat and stir in the miso mixture.

6 Add the asparagus or mangetouts, mushrooms, carrot and spring onions, and simmer for 2 minutes until the vegetables are just tender. Season.

7 Divide the noodles among four warm bowls and pour the soup over the top. Serve sprinkled with the chilli flakes.

Energy 223Kcal/942kJ; Protein 7.5g; Carbohydrate 40.9g, of which sugars 3.8g; Fat 3.4g, of which saturates 0.1g; Cholesterol 0mg; Calcium 29mg; Fibre 2.5g; Sodium 807mg.

MISO BROTH WITH TOFU ★

THE JAPANESE EAT MISO BROTH, A SIMPLE BUT HIGHLY NUTRITIOUS SOUP, ALMOST EVERY DAY — IT IS STANDARD BREAKFAST FARE AND IT IS ALSO EATEN WITH RICE OR NOODLES LATER IN THE DAY.

SERVES 4

INGREDIENTS

1 bunch of spring onions (scallions)
  or 5 baby leeks
15g/½ oz fresh coriander (cilantro),
  including the stalks
3 thin slices fresh root ginger
2 star anise
1 small dried red chilli
1.2 litres/2 pints/5 cups dashi stock
  or vegetable stock
225g/8oz pak choi (bok choy) or
  other Asian greens, thickly sliced
200g/7oz firm tofu, cut into
  2.5cm/1in cubes
60ml/4 tbsp red miso
30–45ml/2–3 tbsp shoyu
1 fresh red chilli, seeded and
  shredded (optional)

1 Cut the coarse green tops off the spring onions or baby leeks and slice the rest finely on the diagonal. Place the tops in a large pan.

2 Remove the coriander leaves from the stalks, and set the leaves aside. Add the coriander stalks, fresh root ginger, star anise and dried chilli to the pan. Pour in the dashi or vegetable stock.

3 Heat the mixture gently until it is boiling, then lower the heat and simmer for 10 minutes. Strain, return to the pan and reheat until simmering.

4 Add the green portion of the sliced spring onions or leeks to the soup with the pak choi or greens and tofu. Cook for 2 minutes.

5 Mix 45ml/3 tbsp of the miso with a little of the hot soup in a bowl, then stir it into the soup. Taste the soup and add more miso with soy sauce to taste.

6 Chop the reserved coriander leaves roughly and stir most of them into the soup with the white part of the spring onions or leeks.

7 Cook for 1 minute, then ladle the soup into warmed serving bowls. Sprinkle with the remaining coriander and the fresh red chilli, if using, and serve at once.

COOK'S TIP
• Dashi powder is available in most Asian and Chinese stores. Alternatively, make your own by gently simmering 10–15cm/4–6in konbu seaweed in 1.2 litres/2 pints/5 cups water for 10 minutes. Do not boil the stock vigorously as this makes the dashi bitter. Remove the konbu, then add 15g/½oz dried bonito flakes and bring to the boil. Strain immediately through a fine sieve.
• If you prefer not to use dashi stock, you can substitute instant or home-made vegetable stock in its place.

Energy 71Kcal/297kJ; Protein 7.2g; Carbohydrate 4.2g, of which sugars 3.5g; Fat 2.9g, of which saturates 0.4g; Cholesterol 0mg; Calcium 372mg; Fibre 2.6g; Sodium 884mg.

MISO SOUP WITH PORK AND VEGETABLES ★★

THIS IS QUITE A RICH AND FILLING SOUP. ITS JAPANESE NAME, TANUKI JIRU, MEANS RACCOON SOUP FOR HUNTERS, BUT AS RACCOONS ARE NOT EATEN NOWADAYS, IT IS BASED ON PORK.

SERVES 4

INGREDIENTS

- 200g/7oz lean boneless pork
- 15cm/6in piece *gobo* or 1 parsnip
- 50g/2oz daikon (mooli)
- 4 fresh shiitake mushrooms
- ½ *konnyaku* or 115g/4oz firm tofu
- 15ml/1 tbsp sesame oil, for stir-frying
- 600ml/1 pint/2½ cups instant dashi stock
- 70ml/4½ tbsp miso
- 2 spring onions (scallions), chopped
- 5ml/1 tsp sesame seeds

1 Slice the meat horizontally into very thin long strips, then cut the strips crossways into stamp-size pieces. Set the pork aside.

2 Peel the *gobo*, then cut it diagonally into 1cm/½in thick slices. Quickly plunge the slices into a bowl of cold water. If you are using parsnip, peel, cut it in half lengthways, then cut it into 1cm/½in thick half-moon-shaped slices.

3 Peel and slice the daikon into 1.5cm/⅔in thick discs. Shave the edge of the discs, then cut into 1.5cm/⅔in cubes.

4 Remove the shiitake stalks and cut the caps into quarters.

5 Cook the *konnyaku* in a pan of boiling water for 1 minute. Drain and cool. Cut in quarters lengthways, then crossways into 3mm/⅛in thick pieces.

6 Heat the sesame oil in a heavy pan. Stir-fry the pork, then add tofu, if using, *konnyaku* and all the vegetables except the spring onions. As soon as the colour of the meat changes, add the stock.

7 Bring to the boil over a medium heat. Keep skimming off the foam until the soup looks clear. Reduce the heat, cover, and simmer for 15 minutes.

8 Mix the miso with 60ml/4 tbsp hot stock to make a smooth paste. Stir one-third into the soup. Taste and add more if required. Add the spring onions and remove the pan from the heat. Serve hot in soup bowls and sprinkle with sesame seeds.

Energy 134Kcal/558kJ; Protein 14.4g; Carbohydrate 3.4g, of which sugars 1.9g; Fat 7.1g, of which saturates 1.4g; Cholesterol 32mg; Calcium 173mg; Fibre 1.4g; Sodium 308mg.

BEEF AND VEGETABLES IN TABLE-TOP BROTH ★★★

THE PERFECT INTRODUCTION TO JAPANESE COOKING, THIS DISH IS GREAT FUN FOR A SPECIAL DINNER PARTY AS GUESTS CHOOSE THEIR OWN INGREDIENTS AND COOK THEM AT THE TABLE.

SERVES 4–6

INGREDIENTS

    450g/1lb lean sirloin beef,
      fat trimmed off
    1.75 litres/3 pints/7 ½ cups water
      with ½ sachet instant dashi
      powder, or ½ vegetable (bouillon)
      stock cube
    150g/5oz carrots
    6 spring onions (scallions),
      trimmed and sliced
    150g/5oz Chinese leaves (Chinese
      cabbage), roughly shredded
    225g/8oz daikon (mooli),
      peeled and shredded
    275g/10oz udon or fine wheat
      noodles, cooked
    115g/4oz canned bamboo
      shoots, sliced
    175g/6oz firm tofu, cubed
    10 shiitake mushrooms, sliced
For the sesame dipping sauce
    30ml/2 tbsp tahini paste
    120ml/4fl oz/½ cup instant
      dashi stock or vegetable stock
    60ml/4 tbsp dark soy sauce
    10ml/2 tsp sugar
    30ml/2 tbsp sake (optional)
    10ml/2 tsp wasabi powder (optional)
For the ponzu dipping sauce
    75ml/5 tbsp lemon juice
    15ml/1 tbsp rice wine or
      white wine vinegar
    75ml/5 tbsp dark soy sauce
    15ml/1 tbsp tamari sauce
    15ml/1 tbsp mirin or 1 tsp sugar
    1.5ml/¼ tsp instant dashi powder
      or ¼ vegetable stock (bouillon) cube

1 Slice the meat thinly with a large knife or cleaver. Arrange neatly on a plate, cover and set aside.

2 In a covered, flameproof casserole that is unglazed on the outside, bring the dashi powder or stock cube and water to the boil. Cover and simmer for 8–10 minutes over a medium heat.

3 Place the casserole on a hot tray or a similar heat source, on the table.

4 Shred the daikon finely. Peel the carrots and cut grooves along their length with a canelle knife, then slice thinly into rounds. Bring a pan of lightly salted water to the boil. Blanch the sliced carrots, spring onions, Chinese leaves and daikon separately in the boiling water.

5 Drain the vegetables and arrange on a platter with the noodles, bamboo shoots, tofu and mushrooms.

6 Make the sesame dipping sauce by mixing all of the ingredients well and pouring them into a shallow dish.

7 To make the ponzu dipping sauce, put the ingredients into a screw-top jar and shake well. Provide your guests with chopsticks and bowls, so they can cook their choice of meat and vegetables in the stock and flavour with either the sesame or ponzu dipping sauces.

8 Near the end of the meal, each guest takes a portion of noodles and ladles the stock over them.

Energy 376Kcal/1583kJ; Protein 27.2g; Carbohydrate 41.8g, of which sugars 7.5g; Fat 12.3g, of which saturates 2.2g; Cholesterol 44mg; Calcium 244mg; Fibre 3.4g; Sodium 1250mg.

SEAFOOD SOUP <u>WITH</u> NOODLES ★★

AUDIBLE SOUNDS OF ENJOYMENT ARE A COMPLIMENT TO THE CHINESE COOK, SO SLURPING THIS SUPERB SEAFOOD SOUP IS NOT ONLY PERMISSIBLE, BUT POSITIVELY DESIRABLE.

SERVES 6

INGREDIENTS
175g/6oz tiger prawns (jumbo shrimp), peeled and deveined
225g/8oz monkfish fillet, cut into chunks
225g/8oz salmon fillet, cut into chunks
5ml/1 tsp vegetable oil
15ml/1 tbsp dry white wine
225g/8oz/2 cups dried egg vermicelli
1.2 litres/2 pints/5 cups fish stock
1 carrot, thinly sliced
225g/8oz asparagus, cut into 5cm/2in lengths
30ml/2 tbsp dark soy sauce
5ml/1 tsp sesame oil
salt and ground black pepper
2 spring onions (scallions), cut into thin rings, to garnish

4 Bring the fish stock to the boil over high heat in a separate pan. Add the prawns and monkfish, cook for 1 minute, then add the salmon and cook for 2 minutes more.

5 Using a slotted spoon, lift the fish and prawns out of the stock, add to the noodles in the bowls and keep hot.

6 Strain the stock through a sieve (strainer) lined with muslin or cheesecloth into a clean pan. Bring to the boil and cook the carrot and asparagus for 2 minutes, then add the soy sauce and sesame oil, with salt to taste. Stir well.

7 Pour the stock and the vegetables over the hot noodles and seafood, garnish with the spring onions and serve immediately.

1 Mix the prawns and fish together in a bowl. Add the vegetable oil and wine with 1.5ml/¼ tsp salt and a little ground pepper. Mix lightly, cover with clear film (plastic wrap) and marinate in a cool place for 15 minutes.

2 Bring a large pan of lightly salted water to the boil and cook the noodles for 4 minutes until just tender, or according to the instructions on the noodle packet.

3 Drain the noodles thoroughly and divide them among four deep serving bowls. Set to one side and keep the bowls of noodles hot.

Energy 274Kcal/1147kJ; Protein 23.2g; Carbohydrate 31.5g, of which sugars 2g; Fat 5.9g, of which saturates 1g; Cholesterol 81mg; Calcium 57mg; Fibre 0.9g; Sodium 442mg.

SEAFOOD WONTON SOUP ★

THIS IS A VARIATION ON THE POPULAR WONTON SOUP THAT IS TRADITIONALLY PREPARED USING PORK. IN THIS VERSION THE FAT CONTENT IS REDUCED BY SUBSTITUTING PRAWNS, SCALLOPS AND COD.

SERVES 4

INGREDIENTS

  50g/2oz raw tiger prawns
    (jumbo shrimp)
  50g/2oz queen scallops
  75g/3oz skinless cod fillet,
    roughly chopped
  15ml/1 tbsp finely chopped chives
  5ml/1 tsp dry sherry
  1 small egg white, lightly beaten
  2.5ml/½ tsp sesame oil
  1.5ml/¼ tsp salt
  large pinch of ground white pepper
  20 wonton wrappers
  900ml/1½ pints/3¾ cups fish stock
  2 cos lettuce leaves, shredded
  fresh coriander (cilantro) leaves and
    garlic chives, to garnish

3 Place the cod in a food processor and process until a smooth paste is formed. Scrape the paste into a bowl and stir in the prawns, scallops, chives, sherry, egg white, sesame oil, salt and pepper.

4 Mix all of the ingredients thoroughly, cover with clear film (plastic wrap) and leave in a cool place to marinate for at least 20 minutes.

8 Bring a large pan of water to the boil. Add the wontons to the pan using a spoon. When the water returns to the boil, lower the heat and simmer the wontons gently for 5 minutes or until they float to the surface. Drain the wontons and divide them among four heated soup bowls.

1 Peel the prawns, then devein them using the point of a sharp knife. Rinse them well, pat them dry on kitchen paper and cut them into small pieces.

5 Make the wontons. Place a teaspoonful of the seafood filling in the centre of a wonton wrapper, then bring the corners together to meet at the top.

6 Twist the edges of the wonton together to completely enclose the filling. Fill the remaining wonton wrappers in the same way.

9 Add a portion of shredded lettuce to each bowl. Ladle the hot fish stock into each bowl, garnish each portion with coriander leaves and garlic chives and serve immediately.

2 Rinse the scallops in a sieve (strainer) under cold water. Pat them dry, using kitchen paper. Chop them into small pieces so that they are the same size as the prawns.

7 Pour the fish stock into a pan and heat it gently over low heat. Do not let it boil, but ensure that it is piping hot.

COOK'S TIP
The filled wonton wrappers can be made ahead, then frozen for several weeks and cooked in boiling water for 8 minutes straight from the freezer.

Energy 113Kcal/478kJ; Protein 11.3g; Carbohydrate 15.7g, of which sugars 0.9g; Fat 0.8g, of which saturates 0.2g; Cholesterol 39mg; Calcium 53mg; Fibre 0.9g; Sodium 75mg.

BEEF NOODLE SOUP ★★★

THIS RICH, SATISFYING SOUP IS PACKED WITH ALL SORTS OF FLAVOURS AND TEXTURES, BROUGHT TOGETHER WITH DELICIOUS EGG NOODLES. THE GINGER GIVES IT A DELIGHTFUL TANG.

SERVES 4

INGREDIENTS

10g/¼oz dried porcini mushrooms
6 spring onions (scallions)
115g/4oz carrots
350g/12oz lean rump (round) steak
about 30ml/2 tbsp oil
1 garlic clove, crushed
2.5cm/1in fresh root ginger,
  finely chopped
1.2 litres/2 pints/5 cups beef stock
45ml/3 tbsp light soy sauce
60ml/4 tbsp sake or dry sherry
75g/3oz dried thin egg noodles
75g/3oz spinach, shredded
salt and ground black pepper

1 Break the dried porcini into small pieces, place them in a small heatproof bowl and pour over 150ml/¼ pint/⅔ cup boiling water. Cover the bowl and leave the mushrooms to soak for 15 minutes.

2 Cut the spring onions and carrots into fine 5cm/2in-long strips. Trim any fat off the meat and slice into thin strips.

3 Heat the oil in a large pan and cook the beef in batches until browned, adding a little more oil if necessary. Remove the beef with a slotted spoon and drain on kitchen paper.

4 Add the garlic, ginger, spring onions and carrots to the pan and stir-fry for 3 minutes.

5 Add the beef stock, the mushrooms and their soaking liquid, the soy sauce, sherry and plenty of seasoning. Bring to the boil, reduce the heat and simmer, covered, for 10 minutes.

6 Break up the noodles slightly and add to the pan, with the spinach. Simmer gently for 5 minutes, or until the beef is tender. Adjust the seasoning before serving in warmed bowls.

COOK'S TIP
Chilling the beef briefly in the freezer will make it much easier to slice into thin strips.

Energy 273Kcal/1143kJ; Protein 22.9g; Carbohydrate 17.6g, of which sugars 4.2g; Fat 10.9g, of which saturates 2.6g; Cholesterol 57mg; Calcium 57mg; Fibre 1.9g; Sodium 923mg.

BEEF SOUP WITH NOODLES AND MEATBALLS ★★★

EGG NOODLES AND SPICY MEATBALLS MAKE THIS A REALLY SUSTAINING MAIN MEAL SOUP. IN THE EAST IT IS OFTEN SERVED FROM STREET STALLS, TO MAKE A CONVENIENT LUNCH FOR OFFICE WORKERS.

SERVES 6

INGREDIENTS
    450g/1lb dried medium egg noodles
    30ml/2 tbsp vegetable oil
    1 large onion, finely sliced
    2 garlic cloves, crushed
    2.5cm/1in fresh root ginger,
      cut into thin matchsticks
    1.2 litres/2 pints/5 cups beef stock
    30ml/2 tbsp dark soy sauce
    2 celery sticks, sliced, leaves reserved
    6 Chinese leaves (Chinese cabbage),
      cut into small pieces
    1 handful mangetouts (snow peas),
      cut into strips
    salt and ground black pepper
For the meatballs
    1 large onion, roughly chopped
    1–2 fresh red chillies, seeded
      and chopped
    2 garlic cloves, crushed
    1cm/½in cube shrimp paste
    450g/1lb/2 cups lean minced
      (ground) beef
    15ml/1 tbsp ground coriander
    5ml/1 tsp ground cumin
    10ml/2 tsp dark soy sauce
    5ml/1 tsp dark brown sugar
    juice of ½ lemon
    a little beaten egg

1 To make the meatballs, put the onion, chillies, garlic and shrimp paste in a food processor. Process in short bursts, taking care not to over-chop the onion.

2 Put the meat in a large bowl. Stir in the onion mixture. Add the ground coriander and cumin, soy sauce, sugar, lemon juice and seasoning.

3 Bind the mixture with a little beaten egg and shape into small balls.

4 Cook the noodles in a large pan of boiling, salted water for 3–4 minutes, or until just tender.

5 Drain in a colander and rinse with plenty of cold water. Set aside.

6 Heat the oil in a wide pan and fry the onion, garlic and ginger until soft but not browned. Add the stock and soy sauce and bring to the boil.

COOK'S TIP
Shrimp paste, or terasi, has a strong, salty, distinctive flavour and smell. Use sparingly if unsure of its flavour.

7 Add the meatballs, half-cover and simmer until they are cooked, about 5–8 minutes. Just before serving, add the sliced celery. Cook for 2 minutes more, then add the Chinese leaves and mangetouts. Adjust the seasoning. Divide among soup bowls. Garnish with the reserved celery leaves.

Energy 464Kcal/1955kJ; Protein 27.2g; Carbohydrate 58.6g, of which sugars 5.6g; Fat 15.0g, of which saturates 4.8g; Cholesterol 66mg; Calcium 44mg; Fibre 2.9g; Sodium 905mg.

PRAWN TOASTS <u>WITH</u> SESAME SEEDS ★

THIS HEALTHY VERSION OF THE EVER-POPULAR APPETIZER HAS LOST NONE OF ITS CLASSIC CRUNCH AND TASTE. SERVE IT AS A SNACK, TOO. IT IS GREAT FOR GETTING A PARTY OFF TO A GOOD START.

2 Meanwhile, put the prawns in a food processor with the water chestnuts, egg white, sesame oil and salt. Process the mixture, using the pulse facility if you have it, until a coarse purée is formed.

3 Scrape the mixture into a bowl, stir in the chopped spring onions and sherry and set aside for 10 minutes at room temperature to allow the flavours to blend.

SERVES 4–6

INGREDIENTS
  6 slices medium-cut white bread,
    crusts removed
  225g/8oz raw tiger prawns (jumbo
    shrimp), peeled and deveined
  50g/2oz/⅓ cup drained,
    canned water chestnuts
  1 egg white
  5ml/1 tsp sesame oil
  2.5ml/½ tsp salt
  2 spring onions (scallions),
    finely chopped
  10ml/2 tsp dry sherry
  15ml/1 tbsp sesame seeds, toasted
    (see Cook's Tip)
  shredded spring onion (scallion),
    to garnish

1 Preheat the oven to 120°C/250°F/ Gas ½. Cut each slice of bread into four triangles. Spread out on a baking sheet and bake for 25 minutes or until crisp.

COOK'S TIP
To toast sesame seeds, put them in a dry frying pan and place over a medium heat until the seeds change colour. Shake the pan constantly so the seeds brown evenly and do not burn.

4 Remove the toast from the oven and raise the temperature to 200°C/400°F/ Gas 6. Spread the prawn mixture on the toast, sprinkle with the sesame seeds and bake for 12 minutes. Garnish the prawn toasts with spring onion and serve hot or warm.

Energy 120Kcal/506kJ; Protein 10.1g; Carbohydrate 13.8g, of which sugars 1g; Fat 2.8g, of which saturates 0.3g; Cholesterol 73mg; Calcium 80mg; Fibre 0.8g; Sodium 223mg.

MUSSELS IN BLACK BEAN SAUCE ★

LARGE GREEN-SHELLED MUSSELS ARE PERFECT FOR THIS DELICIOUS DISH. BUY THE COOKED MUSSELS ON THE HALF SHELL, AND TAKE CARE NOT TO OVERCOOK THEM, OR THEY WILL BE TOUGH.

SERVES 4

INGREDIENTS

15ml/1 tbsp vegetable oil
2.5cm/1in piece fresh root ginger, finely chopped
2 garlic cloves, finely chopped
1 fresh red chilli, seeded and chopped
15ml/1 tbsp black bean sauce
15ml/1 tbsp sake or dry sherry
5ml/1 tsp caster (superfine) sugar
5ml/1 tsp sesame oil
10ml/2 tsp dark soy sauce
20 cooked (New Zealand) green-shelled mussels
2 spring onions (scallions), 1 shredded and 1 cut into fine rings

1 Heat the vegetable oil in a small frying pan until very hot. Fry the ginger, garlic and chilli with the black bean sauce for a few seconds, then add the sake or sherry and caster sugar and cook for 30 seconds more.

2 Remove the sauce from the heat and stir in the sesame oil and soy sauce. Mix thoroughly, using a pair of chopsticks or a wooden spoon.

3 Place a trivet in the base of a heavy pan, then pour in boiling water to a depth of 5cm/2in. Place the mussels on a heatproof plate that will fit over the trivet. Spoon over the sauce.

4 Sprinkle the spring onions over the mussels, cover the plate tightly with foil and place it on the trivet in the pan.

5 Steam the mussels over a high heat for about 10 minutes or until the mussels have heated through.

6 Lift the plate carefully out of the pan and serve immediately.

COOK'S TIP

Large scallops in their shells taste delicious when they are cooked in the same way. Do not overcook the shellfish or it will become rubbery.

Energy 83Kcal/348kJ; Protein 6.6g; Carbohydrate 3.5g, of which sugars 1.5g; Fat 4.4g, of which saturates 0.7g; Cholesterol 21mg; Calcium 22mg; Fibre 0.2g; Sodium 413mg.

WAKAME WITH PRAWNS AND CUCUMBER ★

THIS SALAD-STYLE DISH, CALLED SUNO-MONO IN JAPAN, USES WAKAME SEAWEED, WHICH IS NOT ONLY RICH IN MINERALS, B COMPLEX VITAMINS AND VITAMIN C, BUT ALSO MAKES YOUR HAIR SHINY.

SERVES 4

INGREDIENTS
   10g/¼oz dried wakame seaweed
   12 medium raw tiger prawns
      (jumbo shrimp), heads removed
      but tails intact
   ½ cucumber
   salt
For the dressing
   60ml/4 tbsp rice vinegar
   15ml/1 tbsp shoyu
   7.5ml/1½ tsp caster
      (superfine) sugar
   2.5cm/1in fresh root ginger, peeled
      and cut into thin strips, to garnish

1 Soak the wakame in a pan or bowl of cold water for 15 minutes until fully open. The wakame expands to three to five times its original size. Drain.

VARIATION
For a vegetarian version, replace the shellfish with some toasted pine nuts.

2 Peel the prawns, including the tails. Insert a cocktail stick (toothpick) into the back of each prawn and gently scoop up the thin black vein running down its length. Pull it out, then throw it away.

3 Add the prawns to a pan of lightly salted boiling water and cook until they curl up completely to make full circles. Drain and cool.

4 Halve the cucumber lengthways. Peel away half of the green skin with a zester or vegetable peeler to create green and white stripes. Scoop out the centre with a tablespoon. Slice the cucumber very thinly with a sharp knife or a mandolin. Sprinkle with 5ml/1 tsp salt, and leave for 15 minutes in a sieve (strainer), to draw out excess liquid.

5 Bring a large pan of water to the boil and blanch the wakame briefly. Drain and cool under cold running water. Add to the cucumber in the sieve.

6 Press the cucumber and wakame to remove the excess liquid. Repeat the rinsing, draining and pressing process two to three times.

7 Mix the dressing ingredients in a mixing bowl. Stir well until the sugar has dissolved. Add the wakame and cucumber to the dressing and mix.

8 Pile up the wakame mixture in four small bowls or on four plates. Prop the prawns against the heap. Garnish with ginger and serve immediately.

Energy 37Kcal/154kJ; Protein 6.9g; Carbohydrate 1.7g, of which sugars 1.7g; Fat 0.3g, of which saturates 0g; Cholesterol 73mg; Calcium 35mg; Fibre 0.2g; Sodium 339mg.

CRAB CAKES WITH GINGER AND WASABI ★★★

THERE'S MORE THAN A HINT OF HEAT IN THESE CRAB CAKES, THANKS TO WASABI, A POWERFUL JAPANESE CONDIMENT, AND ROOT GINGER. THE DIPPING SAUCE DOUBLES THE DRAMATIC IMPACT.

SERVES 6

INGREDIENTS
  4 spring onions (scallions)
  450g/1lb fresh dressed crab meat
    (brown and white meat)
  2.5cm/1in piece fresh root
    ginger, grated
  30ml/2 tbsp chopped fresh
    coriander (cilantro)
  30ml/2 tbsp low-fat mayonnaise
  2.5–5ml/½–1 tsp wasabi paste
  15ml/1 tbsp sesame oil
  50–115g/2–4oz/1–2 cups fresh
    white breadcrumbs
  30ml/2 tbsp vegetable oil, for frying
  salt and ground black pepper
For the dipping sauce
  5ml/1 tsp wasabi paste
  90ml/6 tbsp soy sauce

1 Make the dipping sauce. Mix the wasabi and soy sauce in a small bowl. Set aside.

2 Chop the spring onions. Mix the crab meat, spring onions, ginger, coriander, mayonnaise, wasabi paste and sesame oil in a bowl. Season and stir in enough breadcrumbs to make a mixture that is firm enough to form patties. Chill the mixture for 30 minutes.

COOK'S TIPS
• Fresh crab meat will have the best flavour, but if it is not available, use frozen or canned crab meat.
• Wasabi is often described as horseradish mustard, although this Japanese paste is unrelated to either condiment. It is very hot.

3 Form the crab mixture into 12 cakes. Heat the oil in a non-stick frying pan and fry the crab cakes for about 3–4 minutes on each side, until browned.

4 Serve with the dipping sauce. Chilli and spring onion slices can be used as a garnish, and the crab cakes served with lettuce and lime slices.

Energy 190Kcal/795kJ; Protein 16.2g; Carbohydrate 7.1g, of which sugars 0.6g; Fat 11g, of which saturates 1.4g; Cholesterol 55mg; Calcium 35mg; Fibre 0.3g; Sodium 388mg.

ORIENTAL SCALLOPS <u>WITH</u> GINGER RELISH ★★

BUY SCALLOPS IN THEIR SHELLS TO BE SURE OF THEIR FRESHNESS; YOUR FISHMONGER WILL OPEN THEM FOR YOU IF YOU FIND THIS DIFFICULT. THE SHELLS MAKE EXCELLENT SERVING DISHES.

SERVES 4

INGREDIENTS
    8 king or queen scallops
    4 whole star anise
    30ml/2 tbsp vegetable oil
    salt and ground white pepper
    fresh coriander (cilantro) sprigs and
        whole star anise, to garnish
For the relish
    ½ cucumber, peeled
    salt, for sprinkling
    5cm/2in piece fresh root
        ginger, peeled
    10ml/2 tsp caster (superfine) sugar
    45ml/3 tbsp rice wine vinegar
    10ml/2 tsp syrup from a jar of
        preserved stem ginger
    5ml/1 tsp sesame seeds,
        for sprinkling

1 To make the relish, halve the cucumber lengthways, scoop out all of the seeds with a teaspoon and discard.

2 Cut the cucumber into 2.5cm/1in pieces, place in a colander and sprinkle liberally with salt. Set the cucumber aside, placing it in the sink to drain for 30 minutes.

3 To prepare the scallops, cut each into 2–3 slices. Coarsely grind the star anise using a mortar and pestle.

4 Place the scallop slices with the corals in a bowl and add the star anise and seasoning. Cover the bowl and marinate the scallops in the refrigerator for about 1 hour.

5 Rinse the cucumber under cold water, then drain and pat dry with kitchen paper. Place the cucumber in a bowl.

6 Cut the ginger into thin julienne strips and add to the cucumber with the sugar, rice wine and syrup. Mix well, then cover with clear film (plastic wrap) and chill until the relish is needed.

7 Heat the wok and add the oil. When the oil is very hot, add the scallop slices and stir-fry them for 2–3 minutes. Place the cooked scallops on kitchen paper to drain off any excess oil.

8 Garnish with sprigs of coriander and whole star anise, and serve with the cucumber relish, sprinkled with sesame seeds.

Energy 130Kcal/542kJ; Protein 12.1g; Carbohydrate 4.9g, of which sugars 3.2g; Fat 7g, of which saturates 1g; Cholesterol 24mg; Calcium 31mg; Fibre 0.3g; Sodium 92mg.

STUFFED CHILLIES ★

*WITH LESS THAN 3 GRAMS OF TOTAL FAT, THIS IS A GOOD CHOICE FOR A FIRST COURSE OR FOR
SERVING WITH DRINKS. IT ISN'T TOO HOT — UNLESS YOU'VE CHOSEN ESPECIALLY FIERY CHILLIES.*

SERVES 4

INGREDIENTS

    10 fat fresh green chillies
    115g/4oz lean pork, chopped
    75g/3oz raw tiger prawns (jumbo
      shrimp), peeled and deveined
    15g/½oz/½ cup fresh coriander
      (cilantro) leaves
    5ml/1 tsp cornflour (cornstarch)
    10ml/2 tsp sake or dry sherry
    10ml/2 tsp soy sauce
    5ml/1 tsp sesame oil
    2.5ml/½ tsp salt
    15ml/1 tbsp cold water
    1 fresh red and 1 fresh green chilli,
      seeded and sliced into rings, and
      cooked peas, to garnish

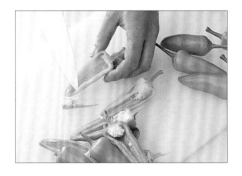

1 Cut all the chillies in half lengthways,
keeping the stalk. Scrape out and discard
the seeds and set the chillies aside.

2 Mix the chopped pork, prawns and
coriander leaves in a food processor.
Process until smooth. Scrape into a
bowl and mix in the cornflour, sherry,
soy sauce, sesame oil, salt and water.
Cover the bowl and leave to marinate
for 10 minutes.

3 Fill each half chilli with some of the
meat mixture. Have ready a steamer or
a heatproof plate and a pan with about
5cm/2in boiling water in the bottom.

COOK'S TIP
If you prefer a slightly hotter taste, leave
seeds in some of the chillies.

4 Place the stuffed chillies in the
steamer or on a plate, meat side
up, and cover them with a lid or foil.

5 Steam steadily for 15 minutes or
until the meat filling is cooked. Serve
immediately, garnished with the
chilli rings and peas.

Energy 74Kcal/309kJ; Protein 9.9g; Carbohydrate 3.1g, of which sugars 1.8g; Fat 2.2g, of which saturates 0.6g; Cholesterol 55mg; Calcium 27mg; Fibre 0.6g; Sodium 237mg.

DRUNKEN CHICKEN ★

AS THE CHICKEN IS MARINATED FOR SEVERAL DAYS, IT IS IMPORTANT TO USE A VERY FRESH BIRD FROM A REPUTABLE SUPPLIER. "DRUNKEN" FOODS ARE USUALLY SERVED COLD AS PART OF AN APPETIZER.

3 Pour 300ml/½ pint/1¼ cups stock into a jug (pitcher). Freeze the remainder.

4 Remove the skin from the chicken, joint it neatly. Divide each leg into a drumstick and thigh. Make two portions from the wings and some of the breast, then cut away the remainder of the breast pieces (still on the bone) and divide each into two even-size portions.

5 Arrange the chicken portions in a single layer in a shallow dish. Rub salt into the chicken and cover closely with clear film (plastic wrap). Leave in a cool place for several hours or overnight in the refrigerator.

SERVES 4–6

INGREDIENTS
1 chicken, about 1.3kg/3lb
1cm/½in piece fresh root ginger, peeled and thinly sliced
2 spring onions (scallions), trimmed
1.75 litres/3 pints/7½ cups water or to cover
15ml/1 tbsp salt
300ml/½ pint/1¼ cups sake or dry sherry
spring onions (scalllions), shredded, and fresh herbs, to garnish

1 Rinse and dry the chicken inside and out. Place the ginger and spring onions in the body cavity. Put the chicken in a large pan or flameproof casserole and just cover with water. Bring to the boil, skim and cook for 15 minutes.

2 Turn off the heat, cover the pan or casserole tightly and leave the chicken in the cooking liquid for 3–4 hours, by which time it will be cooked. Drain well.

6 When the stock has cooled completely, lift off any fat that has congealed on the surface. Mix the sherry and reserved stock in a jug (pitcher) and pour over the chicken. Cover again and leave in the refrigerator to marinate for a further 2 or 3 days.

7 When ready to serve, cut the chicken through the bone into chunky pieces and arrange on a serving platter garnished with spring onion shreds and herbs.

VARIATION
To serve as a cocktail snack, take the meat off the bones, cut it into bite-size pieces, then spear each piece on a cocktail stick (toothpick).

Energy 200Kcal/843kJ; Protein 32.2g; Carbohydrate 0.8g, of which sugars 0.8g; Fat 1.5g, of which saturates 0.4g; Cholesterol 93mg; Calcium 12mg; Fibre 0.1g; Sodium 1068mg.

LETTUCE PARCELS ★★

KNOWN AS SANG CHOY IN HONG KONG, THIS IS A POPULAR "ASSEMBLE-IT-YOURSELF" TREAT. THE FILLING IS SERVED WITH CRISP LETTUCE LEAVES, WHICH ARE USED AS WRAPPERS.

SERVES 6

INGREDIENTS

2 chicken breast fillets, total weight about 350g/12oz
4 dried Chinese mushrooms, soaked for 20 minutes in warm water to cover
30ml/2 tbsp vegetable oil
2 garlic cloves, crushed
6 drained canned water chestnuts, thinly sliced
30ml/2 tbsp light soy sauce
5ml/1 tsp Sichuan peppercorns, dry fried and crushed
4 spring onions (scallions), finely chopped
5ml/1 tsp sesame oil
vegetable oil, for deep frying
50g/2oz cellophane noodles
salt and ground black pepper (optional)
1 crisp lettuce and 60ml/4 tbsp hoisin sauce, to serve

4 Add the sliced mushrooms, water chestnuts, soy sauce and peppercorns. Toss for 2–3 minutes, then season, if needed. Stir in half the spring onions, then the sesame oil. Remove from the heat and set aside.

5 Cook the noodles in a large pan of lightly salted boiling water for 3–4 minutes or according to the packet instructions. Drain thoroughly.

6 Add the cooked noodles to the wok and toss over a high heat to warm through. Transfer to a serving dish and add the remaining spring onions. Wash the lettuce leaves, pat dry and arrange on a large platter.

7 Toss the chicken and noodles together using chopsticks or wooden spoons.

8 Invite guests to take one or two lettuce leaves, spread the inside with hoisin sauce and add a spoonful of filling, before rolling them into a parcel.

1 Remove the skin from the chicken breast fillets, if they have any, then pat the fillets dry with kitchen towel. Chop the chicken into thin strips.

2 Drain the soaked mushrooms. Cut off and discard the mushroom stems. Slice the caps finely and set them aside.

3 Heat the vegetable oil in a wok or large frying pan over high heat. When the oil is very hot, add the garlic, then add the chicken strips and stir-fry for 2–3 minutes until the pieces of chicken are cooked through and no longer pink.

Energy 168Kcal/705kJ; Protein 15.6g; Carbohydrate 7.5g, of which sugars 1.2g; Fat 8.6g, of which saturates 1.1g; Cholesterol 41mg; Calcium 14mg; Fibre 0.6g; Sodium 393mg.

CRISPY TURKEY BALLS ★

TURKEY IS LOW IN SATURATED FAT, SO ALTHOUGH IT IS NOT TRADITIONALLY USED IN CHINESE COOKING, IT IS AN EXCELLENT CHOICE FOR HEALTHY EATING AND WORKS WELL IN THIS RECIPE.

SERVES 4–6

INGREDIENTS

  4 thin slices white bread,
    crusts removed
  5ml/1 tsp vegetable oil
  225g/8oz skinless, boneless turkey
    meat, roughly chopped
  50g/2oz/⅓ cup drained, canned
    water chestnuts
  2 fresh red chillies, seeded and
    roughly chopped
  1 egg white
  10g/¼oz/¼ cup fresh coriander
    (cilantro) leaves
  5ml/1 tsp cornflour (cornstarch)
  2.5ml/½ tsp salt
  1.5ml/¼ tsp ground white pepper
  30ml/2 tbsp light soy sauce
  5ml/1 tsp sugar
  30ml/2 tbsp rice vinegar
  2.5ml/½ tsp chilli oil
  shredded fresh red chillies and fresh
    coriander (cilantro) sprigs, to garnish

4 Remove the toasted bread cubes from the oven and set them aside. Raise the oven temperature to 200°C/400°F/ Gas 6. With dampened hands, divide the turkey mixture into 12 portions and form into balls.

5 Roughly crush the toasted bread cubes, then transfer to a plate. Roll each ball in turn over the toasted crumbs until coated. Place on a baking sheet and bake for about 20 minutes or until the coating is brown and the turkey filling has cooked through.

6 In a small bowl, mix the remaining soy sauce with the sugar, rice vinegar and chilli oil. Serve the sauce with the turkey balls, garnished with shredded chillies and coriander sprigs.

VARIATION
Chicken can be used instead of turkey, with equally delicious results.

1 Preheat the oven to 120°C/250°F/ Gas ½. Brush the bread slices lightly with vegetable oil and cut them into 5mm/¼in cubes. Spread on a baking sheet and bake for 15 minutes they are until dry and crisp.

2 Meanwhile, mix the turkey meat, water chestnuts and chillies in a food processor. Process to a coarse paste.

3 Add the egg white, coriander leaves, cornflour, salt and pepper. Pour in half the soy sauce and process for about 30 seconds. Scrape into a bowl, cover and leave in a cool place for 20 minutes.

Energy 93Kcal/393kJ; Protein 11.4g; Carbohydrate 9.7g, of which sugars 1g; Fat 1.2g, of which saturates 0.2g; Cholesterol 21mg; Calcium 23mg; Fibre 0.4g; Sodium 472mg.

CABBAGE AND NOODLE PARCELS ★★

THE NOODLES AND CHINESE MUSHROOMS GIVE A DELIGHTFUL ORIENTAL FLAVOUR TO THE FILLING FOR THESE TRADITIONAL CABBAGE ROLLS, WHICH ARE SIMMERED IN A TASTY TOMATO SAUCE.

SERVES 6

INGREDIENTS

  4 dried Chinese mushrooms, soaked
    in hot water until soft
  50g/2oz cellophane noodles, soaked
    in hot water until soft
  450g/1lb/2 cups minced (ground) pork
  2 garlic cloves, finely chopped
  8 spring onions (scallions)
  30ml/2 tbsp Thai fish sauce
  12 large outer green cabbage leaves
For the sauce
  15ml/1 tbsp vegetable oil
  1 small onion, finely chopped
  2 garlic cloves, crushed
  400g/14oz can chopped
    plum tomatoes
  pinch of sugar
  salt and ground black pepper

1 Drain the mushrooms, discard the stems and chop the caps. Put them in a bowl. Next, drain the noodles and cut them into short lengths. Add to the bowl with the pork and garlic.

2 Chop two of the spring onions and add to the bowl. Season with the fish sauce and pepper.

3 Blanch the cabbage leaves a few at a time in a pan of boiling, lightly salted water for about 1 minute. Remove the leaves from the pan with a spoon and refresh under cold water.

4 Drain the leaves and dry them well on kitchen paper. Blanch the remaining six spring onions in the same fashion. Drain well.

5 Fill one of the cabbage leaves with a generous spoonful of the pork and noodle filling.

6 Taking hold of the corner closest to yourself, roll up the leaf sufficiently to enclose the filling, then tuck in the sides and continue rolling the leaf to make a tight parcel. Make more parcels in the same way.

7 Split each spring onion lengthways by cutting through the bulb and then tearing upwards.

8 Tie each of the cabbage parcels with a length of spring onion.

9 To make the sauce, heat the oil in a large frying pan and add the onion and garlic. Fry for 2 minutes until soft. Tip the tomatoes into a bowl. Mash with a fork, then add to the onion mixture.

10 Season with salt, pepper and a pinch of sugar, then bring to simmering point. Add the cabbage parcels. Cover and cook gently for 20–25 minutes. Check the seasoning and serve immediately.

Energy 159Kcal/670kJ; Protein 18g; Carbohydrate 9.8g, of which sugars 3.4g; Fat 5.6g, of which saturates 1.4g; Cholesterol 47mg; Calcium 20mg; Fibre 1.3g; Sodium 238mg.

MINI PHOENIX ROLLS ★★

THESE FILLED OMELETTE PARCELS ARE SO TASTY THAT THEIR FAME IS ALMOST AS LEGENDARY AS THAT OF THE MYTHICAL BIRD AFTER WHICH THEY ARE NAMED. THE SLICES LOOK GOOD AND TASTE BETTER.

4 Scrape the pork paste into a bowl. Stir in the egg white, sherry, remaining water, salt and pepper. Mix thoroughly, cover the bowl and leave in cool place for about 15 minutes.

5 Half-fill a steamer with boiling water and fit the insert, making sure it is clear of the water.

SERVES 4

INGREDIENTS

2 large eggs, plus 1 egg white
75ml/5 tbsp cold water
5ml/1 tsp vegetable oil
175g/6oz lean pork, diced
75g/3oz/½ cup drained, canned
    water chestnuts
5cm/2in piece fresh root
    ginger, grated
4 dried Chinese mushrooms, soaked
    in hot water until soft
15ml/1 tbsp dry sherry
1.5ml/¼ tsp salt
large pinch of ground white pepper
30ml/2 tbsp rice vinegar
2.5ml/½ tsp caster (superfine) sugar
fresh coriander (cilantro) or flat leaf
    parsley, to garnish

1 Lightly beat the 2 whole eggs with 45ml/3 tbsp of the water. Heat a 20cm/8in non-stick omelette pan and brush with a little of the oil.

2 Pour in a quarter of the egg mixture, swirling the pan to coat the base lightly. Cook the omelette until the top is set. Slide it on to a plate. Make three more omelettes in the same way.

3 Mix the pork and water chestnuts in a food processor. Add 5ml/1 tsp of the root ginger. Drain the mushrooms, chop the caps roughly and add these to the mixture. Process until smooth.

COOK'S TIP
These rolls can be prepared a day in advance and steamed just before serving.

6 Divide the pork mixture among the omelettes and spread into a large square shape in the centre of each of the omelettes.

7 Bring the sides of each omelette over the filling and roll up from the bottom to the top. Arrange the rolls in the steamer. Cover tightly and steam over a high heat for 15 minutes.

8 Make a dipping sauce by mixing the remaining ginger with the rice vinegar and sugar in a small dish.

9 Lift the rolls out of the steamer, then cut them diagonally in 1cm/½in slices, arrange them on a plate, garnish with the coriander or flat leaf parsley leaves and serve with the sauce.

Energy 110Kcal/460kJ; Protein 13.8g; Carbohydrate 0.8g, of which sugars 0.5g; Fat 5.4g, of which saturates 1.5g; Cholesterol 123mg; Calcium 22mg; Fibre 0.3g; Sodium 82mg.

SAVOURY CHIFFON CUSTARDS ★★

IT IS THE CONTRAST IN TEXTURES THAT MAKES THESE SO APPEALING. THE PORK AND MUSHROOM MIXTURE IS TOPPED WITH EGG, WHICH BECOMES A VELVETY CUSTARD WHEN STEAMED.

SERVES 4

INGREDIENTS
15g/½oz dried shrimps
4 dried Chinese mushrooms
175g/6oz lean pork, roughly chopped
3 large eggs
475ml/16fl oz/2 cups chicken stock
salt and ground white pepper
30ml/2 tbsp chopped chives
plaited whole chives, to garnish

1 Soak the dried shrimps in water to cover for about 1 hour or until softened.

2 Soak the mushrooms in a bowl of hot water for 30 minutes until soft. Drain, remove the hard stems, then cut the mushroom caps into small pieces.

3 Place the pork and mushrooms in a food processor. Drain the shrimps, then add them with 1.5ml/¼ tsp salt and a pinch of pepper. Process until finely ground. Scrape into a bowl and set aside.

4 Break the eggs into a bowl, then whisk in the stock. Add 2.5ml/½ tsp salt and a large pinch of pepper. Beat well, then strain into a jug (pitcher).

5 Stir a little of the egg mixture into the pork mixture to loosen it. Divide among four 300ml/½ pint/1¼ cup soufflé dishes and divide the remaining egg mixture equally among the soufflé dishes.

6 Sprinkle over the chives. Cover tightly with clear film (plastic wrap) and then foil and place in a steamer.

7 Bring a pan containing about 5cm/2in water to the boil.

8 Cover the steamer and position above the pan of boiling water.

9 Steam the custards for about 10 minutes, then lower the heat and continue steaming for a further 20 minutes until the custards are just set.

10 Serve the custards immediately, garnished with plaited whole chives.

VARIATION
For a delicious alternative, replace the pork mixture with fresh or frozen white crabmeat; this gives a more subtle taste. The crabmeat custards would make a great appetizer.

Energy 118Kcal/493kJ; Protein 16.2g; Carbohydrate 0g, of which sugars 0g; Fat 6g, of which saturates 1.8g; Cholesterol 189mg; Calcium 70mg; Fibre 0g; Sodium 246mg.

LIGHT
BITES

These bites are light in every sense of the word. Not only are

they served in relatively small, easy-to-digest portions, but they

are also low in fat. In visual terms, they are immensely

satisfying, thanks to the Chinese and Far East Asian passion

for perfect presentation. This is clearly evident in recipes such

as Chicken and Vegetable Bundles, Steamed Flower Rolls,

Nori-rolled Sushi and Seaweed-wrapped Prawn and

Water Chestnut Rolls, to name but a few.

CHICKEN AND VEGETABLE BUNDLES ★

LEEKS FORM THE WRAPPERS FOR THESE ENCHANTING LITTLE VEGETABLE BUNDLES. THEY TASTE GOOD ON THEIR OWN, BUT EVEN BETTER WITH THE SOY AND SESAME OIL DIP.

SERVES 4

INGREDIENTS
  4 skinless, boneless
    chicken thighs
  5ml/1 tsp cornflour (cornstarch)
  10ml/2 tsp sake or dry sherry
  30ml/2 tbsp light soy sauce
  2.5ml/½ tsp salt
  large pinch of ground
    white pepper
  4 fresh shiitake mushrooms
  50g/2oz/½ cup sliced, drained,
    canned bamboo shoots
  1 small carrot
  1 small courgette (zucchini)
  1 leek, trimmed
  1.5ml/¼ tsp sesame oil

3 Remove and discard the mushroom stems, then cut each mushroom cap in half (or in slices if very large). Cut the carrot and courgette into eight batons, each about 5cm/2in long, then mix the mushroom halves and bamboo shoots together in a bowl.

5 Divide the marinated chicken into eight portions. Do the same with the vegetables. Wrap each strip of leek around a portion of chicken and vegetables to make eight neat bundles. Half-fill the steamer with boiling water and fit the insert, making sure that it is clear of the water.

1 Remove any fat from the chicken thighs before cutting each thigh lengthways into eight strips. Place the strips in a bowl.

4 Bring a small pan of water to the boil. Add the leek and blanch until soft. Drain thoroughly, then slit the leek down its length. Separate each layer to give eight long strips.

6 Place the chicken and vegetable bundles in the steamer with a lid. Cover and steam over a high heat for 12–15 minutes or until the filling is cooked.

7 Meanwhile, mix the remaining soy sauce with the sesame oil and use as a sauce for the bundles.

VARIATION
You could use skinless, boneless turkey thighs, if preferred.

COOK'S TIP
Chicken is a good low-fat source of protein and B vitamins, especially if you poach, grill or steam it. Those on a low-fat diet should remove the skin where possible before cooking, as it makes up about 50 per cent of the total fat content of chicken.

2 Add the cornflour, sherry and half the soy sauce to the chicken in the bowl. Stir in the salt and pepper and mix well. Cover with clear film (plastic wrap) and leave in a cool place to marinate for 10 minutes.

Energy 136Kcal/576kJ; Protein 25.7g; Carbohydrate 4.5g, of which sugars 2.8g; Fat 1.5g, of which saturates 0.4g; Cholesterol 70mg; Calcium 25mg; Fibre 1.4g; Sodium 600mg.

STEAMED PORK BALLS <u>WITH</u> DIPPING SAUCE ★★★

*BITESIZE BALLS OF STEAMED PORK AND MUSHROOMS ROLLED IN JASMINE RICE MAKE A FABULOUS SNACK
TO SERVE WITH PRE-DINNER DRINKS, OR AS PART OF A SELECTION OF DIM SUM.*

SERVES 4

INGREDIENTS
    30ml/2 tbsp vegetable oil
    200g/7oz/scant 3 cups finely
      chopped shiitake mushrooms
    400g/14oz lean minced (ground) pork
    4 spring onions (scallions), chopped
    2 garlic cloves, crushed
    15ml/1 tbsp fish sauce
    15ml/1 tbsp soy sauce
    15ml/1 tsp grated fresh root ginger
    60ml/4 tbsp finely chopped
      coriander (cilantro)
    1 egg, lightly beaten
    salt and ground black pepper
    200g/7oz/1 cup cooked jasmine rice
For the dipping sauce
    120ml/4fl oz/½ cup sweet
      chilli sauce
    105ml/7 tbsp soy sauce
    15ml/1 tbsp Chinese rice wine
    5–10ml/1–2 tsp chilli oil

1 Heat the oil in a large wok, then add
the mushrooms and stir-fry over a high
heat for 2–3 minutes. Transfer to a food
processor with the pork, spring onions,
garlic, fish sauce, soy sauce, ginger,
coriander and beaten egg. Process
for 30–40 seconds.

2 Scrape the pork mixture into a bowl
and make sure all the ingredients are
well combined. Cover and chill in the
refrigerator for 3–4 hours or overnight.

3 Place the jasmine rice in a bowl.
With wet hands, divide the mushroom
mixture into 20 portions and roll each
one into a firm ball. Roll each ball in
the rice then arrange the balls, spaced
apart, in two baking parchment-lined
tiers of a bamboo steamer.

4 Cover the steamer and place over
a wok of simmering water. Steam for
1 hour 15 minutes.

5 Meanwhile, combine all the dipping
sauce ingredients in a small bowl.

6 When the pork balls are fully cooked,
remove them from the steamer and
serve them warm with the spicy
dipping sauce.

COOK'S TIP
Check the water level in the wok
regularly and top up as required.

Energy 322Kcal/1353kJ; Protein 25.8g; Carbohydrate 29.9g, of which sugars 14.3g; Fat 11.8g, of which saturates 2.7g; Cholesterol 111mg; Calcium 39mg; Fibre 0.8g; Sodium 893mg.

STEAMED CRAB DIM SUM <u>WITH</u> CHINESE CHIVES ★

THESE DELECTABLE CHINESE-STYLE DUMPLINGS HAVE A WONDERFULLY STICKY TEXTURE AND MAKE A PERFECT APPETIZER. YOU CAN MAKE THEM IN ADVANCE, AND STEAM THEM JUST BEFORE SERVING.

SERVES 4

INGREDIENTS

- 150g/5oz fresh white crab meat
- 115g/4oz/½ cup lean minced (ground) pork
- 30ml/2 tbsp chopped Chinese chives
- 15ml/1 tbsp finely chopped red (bell) pepper
- 30ml/2 tbsp sweet chilli sauce
- 30ml/2 tbsp hoisin sauce
- 24 fresh dumpling wrappers (available from Asian stores)
- Chinese chives, to garnish
- chilli oil and soy sauce, to serve

1 Place the crab meat, pork and chopped chives in a bowl. Add the red pepper, sweet chilli and hoisin sauces and mix well to combine.

2 Working with 2–3 wrappers at a time, put a small spoonful of the crab meat and pork mixture into the centre of each wrapper.

3 Brush the edges of each wrapper with water and fold over to form a half-moon shape. Press and pleat the edges to seal, and tap the base of each dumpling to flatten.

4 Cover with a clean, damp cloth and make the remaining dumplings in the same way.

VARIATION

To make a delicious variation on these crab dim sum, try using chopped raw tiger prawns (jumbo shrimp) in place of the crab meat.

5 Arrange the dumplings on one or more lightly oiled plates and fit inside one or more tiers of a bamboo steamer.

6 Cover the steamer and place over a wok of simmering water (making sure the water does not touch the steamer). Steam for 8–10 minutes, or until the dumplings are cooked through and become slightly translucent.

7 Make a dipping sauce by mixing equal amounts of chilli oil and soy sauce in a bowl.

8 Divide the dumplings among four plates. Garnish with Chinese chives and serve immediately with the sauce.

Energy 146Kcal/617kJ; Protein 15.3g; Carbohydrate 14.8g, of which sugars 5.2g; Fat 3.3g, of which saturates 0.7g; Cholesterol 45mg; Calcium 35mg; Fibre 0.5g; Sodium 961mg.

STEAMED PORK BUNS ★★★

THESE DELICIOUSLY LIGHT STUFFED BUNS PUSH THE BOUNDARIES WHEN IT COMES TO THE FAT CONTENT,
SO SAVE THEM FOR SERVING AS OCCASIONAL TREATS. THE MEAT FILLING IS SWEET AND SPICY.

SERVES 4

INGREDIENTS

For the basic dough
   250ml/8fl oz/1 cup hand-hot water
   30ml/2 tbsp golden caster
     (superfine) sugar
   10ml/2 tsp dried yeast
   300g/11oz/2¾ cups plain
     (all-purpose) flour
   30ml/2 tbsp sunflower oil
   10ml/2 tsp baking powder
For the filling
   250g/9oz good quality lean
     pork sausages
   15ml/1 tbsp barbecue sauce
   30ml/2 tbsp oyster sauce
   15ml/1 tbsp sweet chilli sauce
   15ml/1 tbsp Chinese rice wine
   15ml/1 tbsp hoisin sauce
   5ml/1 tsp chilli oil

1 To make the dough, pour the water into a bowl. Add the sugar and stir to dissolve. Stir in the yeast, cover and leave in a warm place for 15 minutes.

2 Sift the flour into a large mixing bowl and make a well in the centre with the back of a spoon. Pour the sugar and yeast mixture into the well, together with the sunflower oil. Fold the mixture together, using your fingers, until it forms a ball. Turn out on to a lightly floured surface.

3 Knead the dough for 8–10 minutes until it becomes smooth and elastic. Place the dough in a lightly oiled bowl, cover with a perfectly clean dish towel and leave the dough to rise in a warm place for 3–4 hours.

4 When the dough has risen, place it on a lightly floured surface, knock back (punch down) and shape it into a large circle with your hands.

5 Sprinkle the baking powder in the centre of the dough circle, bring all the edges towards the centre and knead for 6–8 minutes.

6 Divide the dough into 12 balls of equal size, cover with a clean, damp dishtowel and set aside.

7 Squeeze the sausage meat from the casings into a large bowl and stir in the barbecue sauce, oyster sauce, sweet chilli sauce, rice wine, hoisin sauce and chilli oil. Mix thoroughly, using clean fingers, to combine.

8 Press each dough ball with the palm of your hand to form a round, 12cm/4½in in diameter.

9 Place a large spoonful of the pork mixture in the centre of each round of dough and bring the edges up to the centre, then press together firmly to seal and form a bun shape.

10 Arrange the pork buns on several tiers of a large bamboo steamer. Bring a large pan or wok of water to the boil.

11 Cover the steamer, position over the pan or wok of simmering water and steam the pork buns for 20–25 minutes, or until the buns have puffed up and the pork is cooked through. Serve the buns immediately.

Energy 498Kcal/2100kJ; Protein 17.6g; Carbohydrate 77.7g, of which sugars 14.3g; Fat 15.0g, of which saturates 3.9g; Cholesterol 34mg; Calcium 194mg; Fibre 3.3g; Sodium 1542mg.

STEAMED FLOWER ROLLS ★

THESE ELEGANT STEAMED ROLLS ARE DELICIOUS AND ARE SO PRETTY THAT THEY LOOK ALMOST TOO GOOD TO EAT. THE TECHNIQUE FOR MAKING THEM IS A BIT TRICKY, BUT WELL WORTH THE EFFORT.

MAKES 16

INGREDIENTS
   1 quantity basic dough (see Steamed
   Pork Buns) made using only
   5ml/1 tsp sugar
   15ml/1 tbsp sesame seed oil
   chives, to garnish

1 Divide the risen and flattened dough into two equal portions. Roll each into a rectangle measuring 30 x 20cm/ 12 x 8in. Brush the surface of one with sesame oil and lay the other on top. Roll up like a Swiss roll (jelly roll). Cut into 16 pieces.

2 Take each dough roll in turn and press down firmly on the rolled side with a chopstick. Place the rolls on the work surface, coiled side uppermost.

3 Pinch the opposite ends of each roll with the fingers of both hands, then pull the ends underneath and seal. The dough should separate into petals.

4 Place the buns on baking parchment in a steamer and leave to double in bulk. Steam over rapidly boiling water for 30–35 minutes. Serve hot, garnished with chives.

COOK'S TIP
When lining the steamer, fold the paper several times, then cut small holes like a doily. This lets the steam circulate, yet prevents the steamed flower rolls from sticking to the steamer.

Energy 84Kcal/353kJ; Protein 1.8g; Carbohydrate 14.9g, of which sugars 0.6g; Fat 2.3g, of which saturates 0.3g; Cholesterol 0mg; Calcium 27mg; Fibre 0.6g; Sodium 1mg.

ROLLED OMELETTE ★★★

THIS IS A FIRMLY SET, ROLLED OMELETTE, CUT INTO NEAT PIECES AND SERVED COLD. THE TEXTURE SHOULD BE SMOOTH AND SOFT, NOT LEATHERY, AND THE FLAVOUR IS SWEET-SAVOURY.

SERVES 4

INGREDIENTS

4 eggs
30ml/2 tbsp sugar
10ml/2 tsp shoyu, plus extra
 to serve
45ml/3 tbsp sake or dry white wine
30ml/2 tbsp vegetable oil, for cooking
wasabi and pickled ginger, to garnish

COOK'S TIP
Use the wasabi sparingly as it is
extremely hot.

1 Crack the eggs into a large bowl
and lightly mix them, using a pair
of chopsticks and a cutting action.

2 Mix the sugar with the soy sauce and
sake or wine in a small bowl. Lightly stir
this mixture into the eggs.

3 Heat a little of the oil in a non-stick
frying pan, then wipe off the excess.
Pour a quarter of the egg mixture
into the pan, tilting the pan to coat
it thinly. When the edge has set, but
the middle is still moist, roll up the
omelette towards you.

4 Moisten a paper towel with a little
of the oil and grease the empty side of
the pan. Pour a third of the remaining
egg into the pan. Carefully lift up the
rolled egg with your chopsticks and let
the raw egg run underneath it. When
the edge has set, roll the omelette up
in the opposite direction, tilting the
pan away from you.

5 Slide the roll towards you, grease
the pan and pour in half the remaining
mixture, letting the egg run under.

6 When the egg is set, insert chopsticks
in the side of the rolled omelette, then
flip over towards the opposite side. Cook
the remainder in the same way. Slide the
roll so that its join is underneath. Cook
for 10 seconds.

7 Slide the roll out on to a bamboo
mat and roll up tightly, then press
neatly into a rectangular shape. Leave to
cool. Slice the cold omelette into
2.5cm/1in pieces, arrange on a platter
and garnish with a little wasabi and
some *gari* (pickled ginger). Serve
with soy sauce.

Energy 161Kcal/671kJ; Protein 6.4g; Carbohydrate 8.1g, of which sugars 8.1g; Fat 11.1g, of which saturates 2.2g; Cholesterol 190mg; Calcium 34mg; Fibre 0g; Sodium 249mg.

EGG FOO YUNG – CANTONESE STYLE ★★★

HEARTY AND FULL OF FLAVOUR, THIS CAN BE COOKED EITHER AS ONE LARGE OMELETTE OR AS INDIVIDUAL OMELETTES. EITHER WAY, IT IS A CLEVER WAY OF USING UP LEFTOVER ROAST PORK.

SERVES 4

INGREDIENTS

- 6 dried Chinese mushrooms soaked for 20 minutes in warm water
- 50g/2oz/1 cup beansprouts
- 6 drained canned water chestnuts, finely chopped
- 50g/2oz baby spinach leaves, washed
- 45ml/3 tbsp vegetable oil
- 50g/2oz lean roast pork, cut into strips
- 3 eggs
- 2.5ml/½ tsp sugar
- 5ml/1 tsp rice wine or dry sherry
- salt and ground black pepper
- fresh coriander (cilantro) sprigs, to garnish

1 Drain the mushrooms. Cut off and discard the stems; slice the caps finely and mix with the beansprouts, water chestnuts and spinach leaves. Heat 15ml/1 tbsp oil in a large heavy frying pan. Add the pork and vegetables and toss over the heat for 1 minute.

2 Beat the eggs in a bowl. Add the meat and vegetables and mix well.

3 Wipe the frying pan and heat the remaining oil. Pour in the egg mixture and tilt the pan so that it covers the base. When the omelette has set on the underside, sprinkle the top with salt, pepper and sugar.

4 Invert a plate over the pan, turn both the pan and the plate over, and slide the omelette back into the pan to cook on the other side. Drizzle with rice wine or sherry and serve immediately, garnished with sprigs of coriander.

Energy 153Kcal/634kJ; Protein 8.1g; Carbohydrate 0.7g, of which sugars 0.5g; Fat 13.1g, of which saturates 2.3g; Cholesterol 151mg; Calcium 46mg; Fibre 0.5g; Sodium 80mg.

YAKITORI CHICKEN ★

THESE ARE JAPANESE-STYLE KEBABS. THEY ARE EASY TO EAT AND IDEAL FOR BARBECUES OR PARTIES.
THE YAKITORI SAUCE IS SO TASTY THAT YOU WILL WANT TO MAKE EXTRA TO SERVE WITH THE KEBABS.

SERVES 4

INGREDIENTS
  6 skinless boneless
    chicken thighs
  bunch of spring onions (scallions)
  shichimi togarashi (seven-flavour
    spice), to serve (optional)
For the yakitori sauce
  60ml/4 tbsp sake
  75ml/5 tbsp shoyu
  15ml/1 tbsp mirin
  15ml/1 tbsp caster
    (superfine) sugar
  2.5ml/½ tsp cornflour (cornstarch)
    blended with 5ml/1 tsp water

1 Soak 12 bamboo skewers in water for at least 30 minutes.

2 In a small pan, mix the ingredients for the sauce, except the cornflour liquid.

3 Bring the sauce to the boil, then reduce the heat and simmer for about 10 minutes, or until the sauce has reduced slightly.

4 Add the cornflour liquid and stir the mixture over the heat until the sauce is thick. Transfer to a small bowl.

5 Cut each chicken thigh into bite-size pieces and set aside.

6 Cut the spring onions into 3cm/1¼in pieces. Preheat the grill or light the barbecue.

7 Thread the chicken and spring onions alternately on to the drained skewers. Grill under medium heat or cook on the barbecue, brushing several times with the sauce. Allow 5–10 minutes, until the chicken is cooked but moist.

8 Serve with a little extra yakitori sauce, offering *shichimi* (seven-flavour spice) with the kebabs if available.

COOK'S TIP
Paprika can be used instead of *shichimi togarashi*, if that is difficult to obtain.

Energy 129Kcal/545kJ; Protein 24.7g; Carbohydrate 5.1g, of which sugars 5g; Fat 1.2g, of which saturates 0.3g; Cholesterol 70mg; Calcium 16mg; Fibre 0.3g; Sodium 596mg.

GRILLED CHICKEN BALLS ON SKEWERS ★

THESE LITTLE MORSELS MAKE A GREAT LOW-FAT SNACK. HAVING THE CHICKEN BALLS ON SKEWERS MAKES THEM EASY TO EAT IN THE HAND, SO THEY ARE PERFECT FOR SERVING WITH DRINKS.

SERVES 4

INGREDIENTS
300g/11oz skinless chicken,
    minced (ground)
2 eggs
2.5ml/½ tsp salt
10ml/2 tsp plain (all-purpose) flour
10ml/2 tsp cornflour (cornstarch)
90ml/6 tbsp dried breadcrumbs
2.5cm/1in piece fresh root
    ginger, grated
shichimi togarashi (seven-flavour
    spice), to serve (optional)
For the yakitori sauce
60ml/4 tbsp sake
75ml/5 tbsp shoyu
15ml/1 tbsp mirin
15ml/1 tbsp caster
    (superfine) sugar
2.5ml/½ tsp cornflour
    (cornstarch) blended with
    5ml/1 tsp water

1 Soak eight bamboo skewers for about 30 minutes in water. Put all the ingredients for the chicken balls, except the ginger, in a food processor and process to blend well.

2 Wet your hands and scoop about a tablespoonful of the mixture into your palm. Shape it into a small ball about half the size of a golf ball. Make a further 30–32 balls in the same way, wetting your hands as necessary.

3 Squeeze the juice from the grated ginger into a small mixing bowl. Discard the pulp. Preheat the grill (broiler) or light the barbecue.

4 Add the ginger juice to a small pan of boiling water. Add the chicken balls, and boil for about 7 minutes, or until the colour of the meat changes and the balls float to the surface. Scoop the balls out using a slotted spoon and drain on kitchen paper.

5 In a small pan, mix all the ingredients for the yakitori sauce, except the cornflour liquid. Bring to the boil, then reduce the heat and simmer for about 10 minutes, or until the sauce has reduced slightly. Add the cornflour liquid and stir over the heat until the sauce is thick. Transfer to a small bowl.

6 Drain the skewers and thread 3–4 balls on each. Cook under a medium grill (broiler) or on a barbecue, keeping the skewer handles away from the fire. Turn them frequently for a few minutes, or until the balls start to brown. Brush with sauce and return to the heat. Repeat the process twice. Serve, sprinkled with *shichimi togarashi*, if you like.

Energy 217Kcal/917kJ; Protein 24.2g; Carbohydrate 22.3g, of which sugars 1.2g; Fat 4.1g, of which saturates 1g; Cholesterol 148mg; Calcium 53mg; Fibre 0.6g; Sodium 787mg.

GRILLED VEGETABLE STICKS ★★

FOR THIS TASTY DISH, MADE WITH TOFU, KONNYAKU AND AUBERGINE, YOU WILL NEED 40 BAMBOO SKEWERS, SOAKED IN WATER TO PREVENT THEM FROM BURNING WHILE BEING COOKED.

SERVES 4

INGREDIENTS
  1 × 285g/10¼oz packet firm tofu
  1 × 250g/9oz packet *konnyaku*
  2 small aubergines (eggplants)
  25ml/1½ tbsp toasted sesame oil
For the yellow and green sauces
  45ml/3 tbsp *shiro miso*
  15ml/1 tbsp caster (superfine) sugar
  5 young spinach leaves
  2.5ml/½ tsp *sansho*
  salt
For the red sauce
  15ml/1 tbsp *aka miso*
  5ml/1 tsp caster (superfine) sugar
  5ml/1 tsp mirin
To garnish
  pinch of white poppy seeds
  15ml/1 tbsp toasted sesame seeds

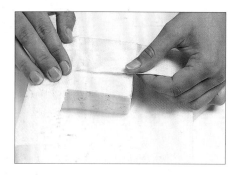

1 Drain the liquid from the tofu packet and wrap the tofu in three layers of kitchen paper.

2 Set a plate on top to press out the remaining liquid. Leave for 30 minutes until the excess liquid has been absorbed by the kitchen paper. Cut into eight 7.5 × 2 × 1cm/3 × ¾ × ½in slices.

3 Drain the liquid from the *konnyaku*. Cut it in half and put in a small pan with enough water to cover. Bring to the boil and cook for about 5 minutes. Drain and cut it into eight 6 × 2 × 1cm/ 2½ × ¾ × ½in slices.

4 Halve the aubergines lengthways, then halve the thickness to make four flat slices. Soak in cold water for 15 minutes. Drain and pat dry.

5 To make the yellow sauce, mix the *shiro miso* and the sugar in a pan, then cook over a low heat, stirring to dissolve the sugar. Remove the pan from the heat. Place half the sauce in a small bowl.

6 Blanch the spinach leaves in rapidly boiling water with a pinch of salt for 30 seconds and drain, then cool under running water. Squeeze out as much of the water as possible and chop finely.

7 Transfer the chopped spinach to a mortar and pound to a paste using a pestle. Mix the paste and *sansho* pepper into the bowl of yellow sauce to make the green sauce.

8 Put all the red sauce ingredients in a small pan and cook over a low heat, stirring constantly, until the sugar has dissolved. Remove from the heat.

9 Pierce the slices of tofu, *konnyaku* and aubergine with two bamboo skewers each. Heat the grill (broiler) to high. Brush the aubergine slices with sesame oil and grill (broil) for 7–8 minutes each side. Turn several times.

10 Grill the konnyaku and tofu slices for 3–5 minutes each side, or until lightly browned. Remove them from the heat but keep the grill hot.

11 Spread the red miso sauce on the aubergine slices. Spread one side of the tofu slices with green sauce and one side of the *konnyaku* with the yellow miso sauce from the pan. Grill the slices for 1–2 minutes. Sprinkle the aubergines with poppy seeds. Sprinkle the *konnyaku* with sesame seeds and serve all together.

Energy 132Kcal/549kJ; Protein 11.8g; Carbohydrate 6.5g, of which sugars 5.8g; Fat 6.7g, of which saturates 0.9g; Cholesterol 0mg; Calcium 711mg; Fibre 1.3g; Sodium 291mg.

NORI-ROLLED SUSHI ★

YOU WILL NEED A MAKISU (A SUSHI ROLLING MAT) TO MAKE THESE TWO TYPES OF SUSHI. THERE ARE TWO TYPES: HOSO-MAKI IS THIN-ROLLED SUSHI, WHILE FUTO-MAKI IS THE THICK-ROLLED TYPE.

SERVES 6–8

FUTO-MAKI (THICK-ROLLED SUSHI)
MAKES 16 PIECES

INGREDIENTS
For the vinegared rice
  200g/7oz/1 cup sushi rice soaked
    for 20 minutes in water to cover
  45ml/3 tbsp rice vinegar
  30ml/2 tbsp sugar
  5ml/1 tsp coarse salt
For the omelette
  2 eggs, beaten
  25ml/1½ tbsp water mixed with
    5ml/1 tsp dashi powder
  10ml/2 tsp sake
  2.5ml/½ tsp salt
  vegetable oil, for frying
For the fillings
  4 dried shiitake mushrooms, soaked
    in water for 30 minutes
  120ml/4fl oz/½ cup water mixed with
    7.5ml/1½ tsp dashi powder
  15ml/1 tbsp shoyu
  7.5ml/1½ tsp caster (superfine) sugar
  5ml/1 tsp mirin
  6 raw large prawns (shrimp), heads
    and shells removed, tails intact
  2 sheets nori seaweed
  4 asparagus spears, steamed for
    1 minute
  10 chives, about 23cm/9in long,
    ends trimmed

1 Drain the rice. Put it in a pan with 290ml/9fl oz/1⅓ cups water. Bring to the boil, then cover and simmer for about 15 minutes, or until all the water has been absorbed. Meanwhile, heat the vinegar, sugar and salt, stir well and cool. Add to the hot rice, then cover the pan and set aside for 20 minutes.

2 To make the omelette, mix the beaten eggs, dashi stock, sake and salt in a bowl. Heat a little oil in a frying pan on a medium-low heat. Pour in just enough egg mixture to thinly cover the base of the pan. As soon as the mixture sets, fold the omelette in half towards you and wipe the space left with a little oil.

3 With the first omelette still in the pan, repeat this process of frying and folding to make more omelettes. Each new one is laid on to the previous omelette, to form one multi-layered omelette. When all the mixture is used, slide the layered omelette on to a chopping board. Cool, then cut into 1cm/½in wide strips.

4 Put the shiitake mushrooms, dashi stock, shoyu, sugar and mirin in a small pan. Bring to the boil then reduce the heat. Cook for 20 minutes until half of the liquid has evaporated. Drain, remove the mushroom stems, and slice the caps thinly. Squeeze out any excess liquid, then dry on kitchen paper.

5 Make three cuts in the belly of each of the prawns to stop them curling up, and boil in salted water for 1 minute, or until they turn bright pink. Drain and cool, then remove the vein from each.

6 Place a nori sheet at the front edge of the *makisu*. Scoop up half of the rice and spread it on the nori sheet. Leave a 1cm/½in margin at the side nearest you, and 2cm/¾in at the side furthest from you.

7 Make a shallow depression horizontally across the centre of the rice. Fill this with a row of omelette strips, then put half the asparagus and prawns on top. Place five chives alongside, and then put half the shiitake slices on to the chives.

8 Lift the *makisu* with your thumbs while pressing the fillings with your fingers and roll up gently.

9 When completed, gently roll the *makisu* on the chopping board to firm it up. Unwrap and set the *futo-maki* aside. Repeat the process to make another roll.

HOSO-MAKI (THIN-ROLLED SUSHI)
MAKES 24 PIECES

INGREDIENTS
  2 sheets nori seaweed, cut in
    half crossways
  1 quantity vinegared rice
    (see recipe left)
  45ml/3 tbsp wasabi paste, plus
    extra for serving
For the fillings
  90g/3½oz very fresh tuna steak
  10cm/4in cucumber
  5ml/1 tsp roasted sesame seeds
  6cm/2½in *takuan* [daikon (mooli)
    pickle], cut into long strips
    1cm/½in thick

1 For the fillings, cut the tuna with the grain into 1cm/½in wide strips. Cut the cucumber into 1cm/½in thick strips.

2 Place the *makisu* on the work surface, then place a nori seaweed sheet on it horizontally, rough-side up. Spread a quarter of the vinegared rice over the nori to cover evenly, leaving a 1cm/½in margin on the side furthest from you. Press firmly to smooth the surface.

3 Spread a little wasabi paste across the rice and arrange some of the tuna strips horizontally in a row across the middle. Cut off any excess tuna which may be overhanging the edge of the rice.

Energy 71Kcal/296kJ; Protein 2.3g; Carbohydrate 12g, of which sugars 2.1g; Fat 1.5g, of which saturates 0.3g; Cholesterol 30mg; Calcium 10mg; Fibre 0g; Sodium 204mg.

4 Hold the *makisu* with both hands and carefully roll it up, wrapping the tuna in the middle, and rolling away from the side closest to you. Hold the rolled *makisu* with both hands and squeeze gently to firm the roll.

5 Slowly unwrap the *makisu*, remove the rolled tuna *hoso-maki* and set aside. Make another tuna *hoso-maki* with the remaining ingredients.

6 Repeat the same process using only the cucumber strips with the green skin on. Sprinkle sesame seeds on the cucumber before rolling.

7 Repeat with the *takuan* strips, but omit the wasabi paste. Keep the sushi on a slightly damp chopping board, covered with clear film (plastic wrap) during preparation. When finished, you should have two *hoso-maki* of tuna, and one each of cucumber and takuan.

To serve the sushi

1 Cut each *futo-maki* roll into eight pieces, using a very sharp knife. Wipe the knife with a dish towel dampened with rice vinegar after each cut. Cut each *hoso-maki* into six pieces in the same way.

2 Line up all the *maki* on a large tray. Serve with small dishes of wasabi, *gari* (pickled ginger) and shoyu for dipping.

COOK'S TIP

Half-fill a small bowl with water and add 30ml/2 tbsp rice vinegar. Use this to wet your hands to prevent the rice sticking when rolling sushi.

Energy 52Kcal/217kJ; Protein 2.1g; Carbohydrate 8g, of which sugars 1.4g; Fat 1.3g, of which saturates 0.2g; Cholesterol 17mg; Calcium 7mg; Fibre 0g; Sodium 90mg.

SEAWEED-WRAPPED PRAWN AND WATER CHESTNUT ROLLS ★

JAPANESE NORI SEAWEED IS USED TO ENCLOSE THE FRAGRANT FILLING OF PRAWNS, WATER CHESTNUTS AND FRESH HERBS AND SPICES IN THESE STEAMED ROLLS WHICH ARE VIRTUALLY FAT-FREE.

2 Lay the nori sheets rough-side up on a clean, dry surface and spread the prawn mixture over each sheet, leaving a 2cm/¾in border at one end. Roll up to form tight rolls, wrap in clear film (plastic wrap) and chill for 2–3 hours.

3 Unwrap the rolls and place on a board. Using a sharp knife, cut each roll into 2cm/¾in lengths.

4 Cut several pieces of baking parchment to fit the tiers of a bamboo steamer. Cut a few holes in each piece of parchment to allow the steam to circulate.

5 Place the rolls in the steamer, cover and place over a wok of simmering water (making sure the water does not touch the steamer). Steam for 6–8 minutes. Serve warm or at room temperature with the shoyu.

SERVES 4

INGREDIENTS
675g/1½lb raw tiger prawns (jumbo shrimp), peeled and deveined
1 fresh red chilli, seeded and chopped
5ml/1 tsp finely grated garlic
5ml/1 tsp finely grated fresh root ginger
5ml/1 tsp finely grated lime rind
60ml/4 tbsp very finely chopped fresh coriander (cilantro)
1 egg white, lightly beaten
30ml/2 tbsp chopped water chestnuts
4 sheets nori seaweed
salt and ground black pepper
shoyu, to serve

1 Place the prawns in a food processor with the red chilli, garlic, ginger, lime rind and coriander. Process until smooth, add the egg white and water chestnuts, season and process until combined. Scrape the mixture into a bowl, cover and chill in the refrigerator for 3–4 hours.

Energy 138Kcal/581kJ; Protein 31g; Carbohydrate 0.9g, of which sugars 0.3g; Fat 1.1g, of which saturates 0.2g; Cholesterol 329mg; Calcium 137mg; Fibre 0.3g; Sodium 337mg.

SASHIMI ★★★

THE SATURATED FAT LEVELS ARE LOW IN THIS JAPANESE SPECIALITY. SASHIMI LOOKS EXQUISITE AND IS VERY GOOD FOR YOU, BUT IT IS VITAL TO USE GOOD QUALITY FISH THAT IS EXTREMELY FRESH.

SERVES 4

INGREDIENTS
  2 fresh salmon fillets, skinned and
    any stray bones removed, total
    weight about 400g/14oz
  shoyu and wasabi paste, to serve
For the garnish
  50g/2oz daikon (mooli), peeled
  shiso leaves

1 Put the salmon fillets in a freezer for 10 minutes to make them easier to cut, then lay them on a board skinned side up with the thick end to your right and facing away from you.

2 Tilt a long sharp knife to the left, and slice carefully towards you, starting the cut from the point of the knife. Once you have sliced the whole length of the salmon fillet, slide the slice of fish away to the right. Always slice from the far side towards you.

3 Finely shred or grate the daikon, using a mandolin if you have one, and place it in a bowl of cold water. Leave the daikon to soak for 5 minutes, then drain well.

4 Arrange the salmon slices on a serving platter, fanning them out so that they look as attractive as possible, or divide among four serving plates.

5 Garnish the large platter or individual plates with shredded or grated daikon, heaped on shiso leaves. The fish is dipped in soy sauce and wasabi paste before being eaten.

COOK'S TIP
When buying salmon or any other fish for sashimi, use a reputable supplier and explain what the fish is for. Ask the fishmonger to cut the fillets from a large salmon. Do not use pre-cut pieces.

VARIATIONS
Tuna, turbot or swordfish can be used instead of salmon, if you prefer.

Energy 183Kcal/763kJ; Protein 20.4g; Carbohydrate 0.6g, of which sugars 0.5g; Fat 11g, of which saturates 1.9g; Cholesterol 50mg; Calcium 24mg; Fibre 0.1g; Sodium 314mg.

CUBED AND MARINATED RAW TUNA ★

TUNA IS A ROBUST, MEATY FISH. IT MAKES GREAT SASHIMI, ESPECIALLY IF YOU MARINATE IT BRIEFLY IN A MIXTURE OF SHOYU, WASABI PASTE AND FINELY CHOPPED SPRING ONIONS.

SERVES 4

INGREDIENTS

    400g/14oz very fresh tuna, skinned
    1 carton mustard and cress or
      land cress (optional)
    20ml/4 tsp wasabi paste
    60ml/4 tbsp shoyu
    8 spring onions (scallions), green
      part only, finely chopped
    4 shiso leaves, cut into thin
      slivers lengthways

COOK'S TIP
As the tuna is not cooked, make sure that you use very fresh fish from a reputable supplier.

1 Chill the tuna briefly so that it becomes firmer and easier to slice.

2 Cut the tuna into 2cm/¾in cubes. If using mustard and cress or land cress, tie into pretty bunches or arrange as a bed in four small serving bowls or plates.

3 Just 5–10 minutes before serving, blend the wasabi paste with the shoyu in a bowl, then add the tuna and spring onions. Mix well and leave to marinate for 5 minutes. Divide among the bowls and add a few slivers of shiso leaves on top. Serve immediately.

Energy 149Kcal/627kJ; Protein 24.5g; Carbohydrate 1.9g, of which sugars 1.7g; Fat 4.9g, of which saturates 1.3g; Cholesterol 28mg; Calcium 27mg; Fibre 0.4g; Sodium 783mg.

LEMON SOLE AND FRESH OYSTER SALAD ★★★

OYSTERS, WITH A RICE-VINEGAR DRESSING, TASTE WONDERFUL WITH LEMON SOLE SASHIMI. THIS SALAD IS A TYPICAL EXAMPLE OF HOW A JAPANESE CHEF WOULD PRESENT THE CATCH OF THE DAY.

SERVES 4

INGREDIENTS

1 very fresh lemon sole, skinned and
  filleted into 4 pieces
105ml/7 tbsp rice vinegar
dashi-konbu (dried kelp for stock), in 4
  pieces, big enough to cover the fillets
50g/2oz Japanese cucumber, ends
  trimmed, or ordinary salad
  cucumber with seeds removed
50g/2oz celery sticks,
  strings removed
450g/1lb large broad (fava)
  beans, podded
1 lime, ½ thinly sliced
60ml/4 tbsp walnut oil
  seeds from ½ pomegranate
  salt
For the oysters
15ml/1 tbsp rice vinegar
30ml/2 tbsp shoyu
15ml/1 tbsp sake or dry sherry
12 large fresh oysters, opened
25g/1oz daikon (mooli), peeled
  and very finely grated
8 chives

1 Sprinkle salt on the sole fillets. Cover and cool in the refrigerator for 1 hour.

2 Mix the rice vinegar and a similar amount of water in a bowl. Wash the fish fillets in the mixture, then drain well. Cut each fillet in half lengthways.

3 Lay one piece of *dashi-konbu* on a work surface. Place a pair of sole fillets, skinned sides together, on to it, then lay another piece of *konbu* on top. Cover all the fillets like this and chill for 3 hours.

4 Halve the cucumber crossways and slice thinly lengthways. Then slice again diagonally into 2cm/¾in wide pieces. Do the same for the celery. Sprinkle the cucumber with salt and leave to soften for 30–60 minutes. Gently squeeze to remove the moisture. Rinse if it tastes too salty, but drain well.

5 Boil the broad beans in lightly salted water for 15 minutes, or until soft. Drain and cool under running water, then peel off the skins to reveal the bright green beans inside. Sprinkle with salt.

6 Mix the rice vinegar, shoyu and sake for the oysters in a small bowl.

7 Slice the sole very thinly with a sharp knife. Remove the slightly chewy *dashi-konbu* first, if you prefer.

8 Place pieces of cucumber and celery in a small mound in the centre of four serving plates, then lay lime slices on top. Garnish with some chopped chives.

9 Place the oysters to one side of the cucumber, topped with a few broad beans, then season with 5ml/1 tsp of the vinegar mix and 10ml/2 tsp grated daikon. Arrange the sole sashimi on the other side and drizzle walnut oil and lime juice on top. Add pomegranate seeds and serve.

Energy 248Kcal/1036kJ; Protein 20g; Carbohydrate 14.1g, of which sugars 1.9g; Fat 12.7g, of which saturates 1.3g; Cholesterol 41mg; Calcium 108mg; Fibre 7.6g; Sodium 167mg.

SCALLOPS SASHIMI IN MUSTARD SAUCE ★

THANKS TO THEIR SUBTLE SWEETNESS AND APPEALING TEXTURE, SCALLOPS MAKE THE MOST SUPERB SUSHI. SERVE THIS LAUDABLY LOW-FAT DISH AS A SNACK OR WITH OTHER APPETIZERS.

2 Put the dried chrysanthemum or the flower petals in a sieve (strainer). Pour hot water from a kettle all over, and leave to drain for a while. When cool, gently squeeze the excess water out. Set aside and repeat with the watercress.

3 Mix together all the ingredients for the dressing in a bowl. Add the scallops 5 minutes before serving and mix well without breaking them.

4 Add the flower petals and the watercress, then transfer to four small bowls. Serve cold. Add a little more shoyu, if required.

COOK'S TIPS
- Any white fish sashimi can be used in this dish.
- Substitute the watercress with the finely chopped green part of spring onions (scallions).
- Do not pick the chrysanthemums for this recipe from your garden, as the edible species are different to ornamental ones. Fresh edible flowers are now increasingly available at specialist Japanese stores, or look for dried ones in Asian stores.

SERVES 4

INGREDIENTS
  8 scallops or 16 queen scallops, cleaned and coral removed
  ¼ dried sheet chrysanthemum petals (sold as *kiku nori*) or a handful of edible flower petals such as yellow nasturtium
  leaves from 4 bunches of watercress
For the dressing
  30ml/2 tbsp shoyu
  5ml/1 tsp sake or dry sherry
  10ml/2 tsp English (hot) mustard

1 Slice the scallops in three horizontally then cut them in half crossways. If you use queen scallops, slice them in two horizontally.

Energy 73Kcal/311kJ; Protein 13.3g; Carbohydrate 2.5g, of which sugars 0.8g; Fat 1.2g, of which saturates 0.4g; Cholesterol 24mg; Calcium 101mg; Fibre 0.8g; Sodium 649mg.

RICE IN GREEN TEA WITH SALMON ★

ACCORDING TO A CHINESE PROVERB, IT IS BETTER TO BE DEPRIVED OF FOOD FOR THREE DAYS THAN TEA FOR ONE. THIS RECIPE ENABLES YOU TO HAVE BOTH, AND VERY DELICIOUS IT IS TOO.

SERVES 4

INGREDIENTS

    150g/5oz salmon fillet
    ¼ sheet nori seaweed
    250g/9oz/1¼ cups Japanese short
      grain rice cooked using 350ml/
      12fl oz/1½ cups water
    15ml/1 tbsp *sencha* leaves
    5ml/1 tsp wasabi paste (optional)
    20ml/4 tsp shoyu
    salt

1 Thoroughly salt the salmon fillet and leave for 30 minutes. If the salmon fillet is thicker than 2.5cm/1in, slice it in half and salt both halves.

2 Wipe the salt off the salmon with kitchen paper and grill (broil) the fish under a preheated grill (broiler) for about 5 minutes until cooked through. Remove the skin and any bones, then roughly flake the salmon with a fork.

3 Using scissors, cut the nori into short, narrow strips about 20 x 5mm/¾ x ¼in long, or leave as long narrow strips, if you prefer.

4 If the cooked rice is warm, put equal amounts into individual rice bowls or soup bowls.

5 If the rice is cold, put it in a sieve (strainer) and pour hot water from a kettle over it to warm it up. Drain, then spoon it into the bowls. Place the salmon pieces on top of the rice.

6 Put the *sencha* leaves in a teapot. Bring 600ml/1 pint/2½ cups water to the boil, remove from the heat and allow to cool slightly.

7 Pour into the teapot and wait for 45 seconds. Strain the tea gently and evenly over the top of the rice and salmon. Add some nori and wasabi, if using, to the top of the rice, then trickle shoyu over and serve.

COOK'S TIPS
The word "*sencha*" simply means "commonplace" or "ordinary" in Japanese, and *sencha* leaves are what the popular Japanese green tea is made from. They are often packaged simply as loose green tea leaves.

Energy 294Kcal/1229kJ; Protein 12.4g; Carbohydrate 50.3g, of which sugars 0.4g; Fat 4.5g, of which saturates 0.7g; Cholesterol 19mg; Calcium 21mg; Fibre 0g; Sodium 373mg.

VEGETARIAN MAIN COURSES

Catering for vegetarian and vegan guests can prove challenging,

so this chapter explores the alternatives and introduces some

unusual ingredients that are well worth getting to know.

Vegetarians are well catered for in China and Far East Asia,

but it is important to ask precisely what a dish contains as

some stocks and sauces may not be suitable. Recipes like

Mushrooms with Garlic and Chilli Sauce and Mixed Vegetables

Monk-style are excellent choices and they are also low in fat.

NOODLE, TOFU AND SPROUTED BEAN SALAD ★

THIS CRISP, REFRESHING SALAD IS QUICK AND EASY TO MAKE AND IS BURSTING WITH THE GOODNESS OF FRESH VEGETABLES AND THE FRAGRANT FLAVOUR OF HERBS, RICE VINEGAR AND CHILLI OIL.

SERVES 4

INGREDIENTS

25g/1oz cellophane noodles
500g/1¼lb mixed sprouted beans
   and legumes (aduki, chickpea,
   mung, red lentil)
4 spring onions (scallions),
   finely shredded
115g/4oz firm tofu, diced
1 ripe plum tomato, seeded
   and diced
½ cucumber, peeled, seeded
   and diced
60ml/4 tbsp chopped fresh
   coriander (cilantro)
45ml/3 tbsp chopped fresh mint
60ml/4 tbsp rice vinegar
10ml/2 tsp caster (superfine) sugar
10ml/2 tsp sesame oil
5ml/1 tsp chilli oil
salt and ground black pepper

1 Place the cellophane noodles in a bowl and pour over enough boiling water to cover. Leave to soak for 12–15 minutes and then drain and refresh under cold, running water and drain again.

COOK'S TIP

Fresh sprouted beans are available from most supermarkets, but you can easily sprout them at home yourself.

2 Using a pair of scissors, cut the noodles roughly into 7.5cm/3in lengths and put them in a bowl.

3 Fill a wok one-third full of boiling water and place over a high heat. Add the sprouted beans and legumes and blanch for 1 minute.

4 Drain well, then add to the noodles with the spring onions, tofu, tomato, cucumber and herbs.

5 Thoroughly combine the rice vinegar and sugar in a small bowl. Whisk in the sesame oil and chilli oil and add to the noodle mixture.

6 Toss lightly to combine, then transfer the mixure to a salad bowl and chill for 30 minutes before serving.

Energy 114Kcal/476kJ; Protein 7.3g; Carbohydrate 11.6g, of which sugars 4.3g; Fat 4.4g, of which saturates 0.6g; Cholesterol 0mg; Calcium 206mg; Fibre 3g; Sodium 15mg.

MUSHROOMS WITH GARLIC AND CHILLI SAUCE ★

THE AMOUNT OF SATURATED FAT IN THIS DELICIOUS MUSHROOM DISH IS NEGLIGIBLE AND EVEN THE TOTAL FAT LEVELS ARE VERY LOW INDEED, SO YOU CAN ENJOY IT WITH A CLEAR CONSCIENCE.

SERVES 4

INGREDIENTS
   12 large field (portabello),
      chestnut or oyster mushrooms
      or a mixture
   4 garlic cloves,
      roughly chopped
   6 coriander (cilantro) roots,
      roughly chopped
   15ml/1 tbsp sugar
   30ml/2 tbsp light soy sauce
   ground black pepper
For the dipping sauce
   15ml/1 tbsp sugar
   90ml/6 tbsp rice vinegar
   5ml/1 tsp salt
   1 garlic clove, crushed
   1 small fresh red chilli, seeded
      and finely chopped

1 If using wooden skewers, soak eight of them in cold water for at least 30 minutes to prevent them from burning when exposed to direct heat.

2 Make the dipping sauce by heating the sugar, rice vinegar and salt in a small pan, stirring occasionally until the sugar and salt have dissolved.

3 Add the garlic and chilli to the mixture, pour into a serving dish and keep warm.

4 In a mortar or spice grinder pound or blend the garlic and coriander roots.

5 Scrape the mixture into a bowl and mix with the sugar, soy sauce and a little pepper.

6 Trim and wipe the mushrooms and cut them in half.

7 Thread three mushroom halves on to each skewer. Lay the filled skewers side by side in a shallow dish.

8 Brush the soy sauce mixture over the mushrooms and leave to marinate for 15 minutes.

9 Prepare the barbecue or preheat the grill (broiler) and cook the mushrooms for 2–3 minutes on each side. Serve with the dipping sauce.

Energy 51Kcal/215kJ; Protein 2.5g; Carbohydrate 9.7g, of which sugars 8.7g; Fat 0.5g, of which saturates 0.1g; Cholesterol 0mg; Calcium 12mg; Fibre 1.3g; Sodium 1031mg.

SPICED VEGETABLES WITH COCONUT ★

THIS SPICY AND SUBSTANTIAL DISH MAKES A DELICIOUS VEGETARIAN MAIN COURSE FOR TWO. SERVE IT WITH PLENTY OF PLAIN BOILED RICE FOR MOPPING UP THE DELICIOUS COCONUT AND GINGER STOCK.

SERVES 2

INGREDIENTS

    1 fresh red chilli
    6 celery stalks
    2 large carrots
    1 bulb fennel
    15ml/1 tbsp vegetable oil
    2.5cm/1in piece fresh root ginger,
       peeled and grated
    1 garlic clove, crushed
    3 spring onions (scallions), sliced
    200ml/7fl oz/scant 1 cup
       reduced-fat coconut milk
    200ml/7fl oz/scant 1 cup
       vegetable stock
    15ml/1 tbsp fresh coriander
       (cilantro), chopped
    salt and ground black pepper
    coriander (cilantro) sprigs,
       to garnish

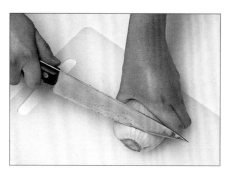

3 Trim the fennel and cut it into slices or chunks, using a sharp knife.

4 Heat the wok, then add the oil. When the oil is hot, add the ginger and garlic, chilli, carrots, celery, fennel and spring onions and stir-fry for 2 minutes.

5 Add the coconut milk and vegetable stock. Stir with a large spoon to mix well, then bring to the boil.

6 Stir in the chopped coriander with salt and pepper to taste, and serve straight from the wok, garnished with coriander sprigs.

1 Cut the chilli in half lengthways, remove the seeds and chop it finely. If necessary, wear rubber gloves to protect your hands.

2 Slice the celery stalks and the carrots on the diagonal using a sharp knife or cleaver, if you have one.

Energy 59Kcal/248kJ; Protein 2.2g; Carbohydrate 11.3g, of which sugars 10.9g; Fat 0.9g, of which saturates 0.3g; Cholesterol 0mg; Calcium 105mg; Fibre 4.8g; Sodium 175mg.

HERB AND CHILLI AUBERGINES ★★★

PLUMP AND JUICY AUBERGINES TASTE SENSATIONAL STEAMED UNTIL TENDER AND THEN TOSSED IN A FRAGRANT MINT AND CORIANDER DRESSING WITH CRUNCHY WATER CHESTNUTS.

SERVES 4

INGREDIENTS
500g/1¼lb firm baby
   aubergines (eggplants)
30ml/2 tbsp vegetable oil
6 garlic cloves, very
   finely chopped
15ml/1 tbsp very finely
   chopped fresh root ginger
8 spring onions (scallions), cut
   diagonally into 2.5cm/1in lengths
2 red chillies, seeded
   and thinly sliced
45ml/3 tbsp light soy sauce
15ml/1 tbsp Chinese rice wine
15ml/1 tbsp golden caster
   (superfine) sugar or palm sugar
a large handful of mint leaves
30–45ml/2–3 tbsp roughly chopped
   coriander (cilantro) leaves
115g/4oz water chestnuts
50g/2oz roasted peanuts,
   roughly chopped
steamed egg noodles or rice,
   to serve

1 Cut the aubergines in half lengthways and place them on a heatproof plate.

2 Place a steamer rack in a wok and add 5cm/2in of water. Bring the water to the boil over high heat, then carefully lower the plate on to the rack and reduce the heat to low.

3 Cover the plate and steam the aubergines for 25–30 minutes, until they are cooked through. Remove the plate from on top of the steamer and set the aubergines aside to cool.

4 Place the oil in a clean, dry wok and place over medium heat. When hot, add the garlic, ginger, spring onions and chillies and stir-fry for 2–3 minutes.

5 Remove from the heat and stir in the soy sauce, rice wine and sugar.

6 Add the mint leaves, chopped coriander, water chestnuts and peanuts to the cooled aubergine and toss.

7 Pour the garlic-ginger mixture evenly over the vegetables, toss gently and serve with steamed egg noodles or rice.

COOK'S TIP
When steaming the aubergines, check the water level frequently and top up with extra water if needed.

Energy 170Kcal/709kJ; Protein 5.8g; Carbohydrate 10.6g, of which sugars 8.9g; Fat 12g, of which saturates 1.9g; Cholesterol 0mg; Calcium 37mg; Fibre 4g; Sodium 540mg.

MIXED VEGETABLES MONK-STYLE ★

CHINESE MONKS EAT NEITHER MEAT NOR FISH, SO "MONK-STYLE" DISHES ARE FINE FOR VEGETARIANS. THIS SUBSTANTIAL DISH IS CHOLESTEROL-FREE AND VERY LOW IN FAT.

SERVES 4

INGREDIENTS

- 50g/2 oz dried tofu sticks
- 115g/4oz fresh lotus root, or 50g/2oz dried
- 10g/¼oz dried cloud ear (wood ear) mushrooms
- 8 dried Chinese mushrooms
- 6 golden needles (lily buds) (optional)
- 15ml/1 tbsp vegetable oil
- 75g/3oz/¾ cup drained, canned straw mushrooms
- 115g/4oz/1 cup baby corn cobs, cut in half
- 30ml/2 tbsp light soy sauce
- 15ml/1 tbsp sake or dry sherry
- 10ml/2 tsp caster (superfine) sugar
- 150ml/¼ pint/⅔ cup vegetable stock
- 75g/3oz mangetouts (snow peas)
- 5ml/1 tsp cornflour (cornstarch)
- 15ml/1 tbsp cold water
- salt

1 Put the tofu sticks in a bowl. Cover them with hot water and leave to soak for 1 hour.

2 If using fresh lotus root, peel it and slice it; if using dried lotus root, place it in a bowl of hot water and leave it to soak for 1 hour.

COOK'S TIP
The flavour of this tasty vegetable mix improves on keeping, so any leftovers would taste even better next day. Simply reheat in a wok or large pan until it is piping hot.

3 Prepare the wood ears and dried Chinese mushrooms by soaking them in separate bowls of hot water for 20 minutes.

4 Drain the wood ears, trim off and discard the hard base from each and cut the rest into bite-size pieces.

5 Drain the soaked Chinese mushrooms in a sieve (strainer), trim off and discard the stems and slice the caps roughly. If using golden needles, tie them into a bundle with kitchen string.

6 Drain the tofu sticks. Cut them into 5cm/2in long pieces, discarding any hard pieces. If using dried lotus root, drain well.

7 Heat the oil in a non-stick frying pan or wok. Stir-fry the wood ears, Chinese mushrooms and lotus root with the golden needles, if using, for about 30 seconds.

8 Add the pieces of tofu, straw mushrooms, baby corn cobs, soy sauce, sherry, caster sugar and stock. Bring to the boil, then cover, lower the heat and simmer for about 20 minutes.

9 Trim the mangetouts and cut them in half. Add to the vegetable mixture, with salt to taste, and cook, uncovered, for 2 minutes more. Mix the cornflour to a paste with the water and add to the pan or wok. Cook, stirring, until the sauce thickens. Serve immediately.

Energy 95Kcal/399kJ; Protein 3.3g; Carbohydrate 12g, of which sugars 4.6g; Fat 3.6g, of which saturates 0.4g; Cholesterol 0mg; Calcium 91mg; Fibre 1.4g; Sodium 885mg.

STIR-FRIED RICE AND VEGETABLES ★★

THE GINGER GIVES THIS MIXED RICE AND VEGETABLE DISH A WONDERFUL FLAVOUR. SERVE IT AS A VEGETARIAN MAIN COURSE FOR TWO OR AS AN UNUSUAL VEGETABLE ACCOMPANIMENT.

SERVES 2–4

INGREDIENTS

115g/4oz/generous ½ cup brown
   basmati rice, rinsed and drained
350ml/12fl oz/1½ cups
   vegetable stock
2.5cm/1in piece fresh root ginger
1 garlic clove, halved
5cm/2in piece pared lemon rind
115g/4oz/1½ cups
   shiitake mushrooms
15ml/1 tbsp vegetable oil
175g/6oz baby carrots, trimmed
225g/8oz baby courgettes
   (zucchini), halved
175–225g/6–8oz/about 1½ cups
   broccoli, broken into florets
6 spring onions (scallions),
   diagonally sliced
15ml/1 tbsp light soy sauce
10ml/2 tsp toasted sesame oil

1 Put the rice in a pan and pour in the vegetable stock.

2 Thinly slice the ginger and add it to the pan with the garlic and lemon rind. Slowly bring to the boil, then lower the heat, cover and cook very gently for 20–25 minutes until the rice is tender.

3 Discard the flavourings and keep the pan covered so that the rice stays warm.

4 Slice the mushrooms, discarding the stems. Heat the oil in a wok and stir-fry the carrots for 4–5 minutes until partially tender.

5 Add the mushrooms and courgettes, stir-fry for 2–3 minutes, then add the broccoli and spring onions and cook for 3 minutes more, by which time all the vegetables should be tender but should still retain a bit of "bite".

6 Add the cooked rice to the vegetables, and toss briefly over the heat to mix and heat through. Toss with the soy sauce and sesame oil. Spoon into a bowl and serve immediately.

COOK'S TIP
Keep fresh root ginger in the freezer. It can be sliced or grated and thaws very quickly.

Energy 190Kcal/792kJ; Protein 6.3g; Carbohydrate 29.1g, of which sugars 5.6g; Fat 5.4g, of which saturates 0.8g; Cholesterol 0mg; Calcium 63mg; Fibre 3.2g; Sodium 285mg.

NUTTY RICE AND MUSHROOM STIR-FRY ★★

THIS DELICIOUS AND SUBSTANTIAL SUPPER DISH CAN BE EATEN HOT OR COLD WITH SALADS. ONLY A FEW NUTS ARE ADDED, BUT THEY MAKE A SIGNIFICANT CONTRIBUTION TO THE FLAVOUR.

SERVES 4–6

INGREDIENTS

350g/12oz/1½ cups long grain
  rice, rinsed
1 small onion, roughly chopped
250g/9oz/3½ cups field (portabello)
  mushrooms, sliced
40g/1½oz/⅓ cup mixed nuts (such
  as cashews, peanuts and almonds)
15ml/1 tbsp vegetable oil
60ml/4 tbsp fresh coriander
  (cilantro), chopped
salt and ground black pepper

1 Put the rice in a pan. Add 750ml/
1¼ pints/3 cups of water and bring to
the boil. Cover the pan with a tight-
fitting lid, lower the heat and cook the
rice for 12–14 minutes until just tender.
Drain and refresh under cold water.

2 Heat a wok, then add half the oil.
When the oil is hot, stir-fry the rice for
2–3 minutes. Remove from the heat
and set aside.

3 Add the remaining oil to the pan and
stir-fry the onion for 2 minutes until it
has softened.

4 Mix in the field mushrooms and stir-
fry for 2 minutes. Keep tossing the
mixture, using two spoons or a pair
of chopsticks, until well mixed.

5 Add all the nuts to the wok and stir-fry
for 1 minute. Return the rice to the wok
and stir-fry for 3 minutes. Season and
stir in the parsley. Serve immediately.

Energy 278Kcal/1160kJ; Protein 6.8g; Carbohydrate 48.9g, of which sugars 1.2g; Fat 5.8g, of which saturates 0.9g; Cholesterol 0mg; Calcium 32mg; Fibre 1.2g; Sodium 24mg.

VEGETABLE CHOW MEIN ★★★

THE OVERALL FAT CONTENT OF THIS RECIPE IS FAIRLY HIGH, BUT THERE'S ONLY A RELATIVELY SMALL AMOUNT OF SATURATED FAT SO IT IS A PERFECTLY ACCEPTABLE CHOICE FOR AN OCCASIONAL TREAT.

SERVES 4

INGREDIENTS

   30ml/2 tbsp vegetable oil
   50g/2oz/½ cup cashew nuts
   2 carrots, cut into thin strips
   3 celery sticks, cut into thin strips
   1 green (bell) pepper, seeded
     and cut into thin strips
   225g/8oz/1 cup beansprouts
   225g/8oz/4 cups dried medium or
     thin egg noodles
   15ml/1 tbsp toasted sesame seeds,
     to garnish
For the lemon sauce
   30ml/2 tbsp light soy sauce
   15ml/1 tbsp Chinese rice wine
     or dry sherry
   150ml/¼ pint/⅔ cup vegetable stock
   finely grated rind and juice of 2 lemons
   15ml/1 tbsp sugar
   10ml/2 tsp cornflour (cornstarch)

1 Mix together the soy sauce, Chinese rice wine or dry sherry, stock, lemon rind and juice, sugar and cornflour in a jug (pitcher). Bring a large pan of lightly salted water to the boil.

2 Heat the oil in a wok or large heavy frying pan. Add the cashew nuts, toss quickly over high heat until golden, then remove with a slotted spoon, and set aside.

3 Add the carrots and celery to the pan and stir-fry for 4–5 minutes. Add the pepper and beansprouts and stir-fry for 2–3 minutes more.

4 Meanwhile, cook the noodles in the boiling water for 3 minutes, or according to the instructions on the packet. Drain well and set aside in a warmed serving dish while you make the sauce.

5 Remove the vegetables from the pan with a slotted spoon. Pour in the sauce mixture and cook for 2 minutes, stirring until thick.

6 Return the vegetables to the pan, add the cashew nuts and stir quickly to coat everything in the sauce.

7 Spoon the vegetables and sauce over the noodles. Sprinkle the chow mein with sesame seeds and serve.

VARIATION
You can ring the changes in this recipe by using unsalted peanuts and alternative vegetables such as red or yellow (bell) peppers, courgettes (zucchini), mangetouts (snow peas) or baby corn.

Energy 212Kcal/882kJ; Protein 4.2g; Carbohydrate 16.5g, of which sugars 9.9g; Fat 14.4g, of which saturates 2.3g; Cholesterol 0mg; Calcium 50mg; Fibre 2.2g; Sodium 591mg.

MUSHROOMS ᴡɪᴛʜ CELLOPHANE NOODLES ★★

RED FERMENTED TOFU, WHICH IS BRICK RED IN COLOUR, ADDS EXTRA INTEREST TO THIS HEARTY
VEGETARIAN DISH. ITS DISTINCTIVE CHEESE-LIKE FLAVOUR GOES WELL WITH THE MUSHROOMS.

SERVES 3–4

INGREDIENTS

115g/4oz dried Chinese mushrooms
25g/1oz dried cloud ear (wood
  ear) mushrooms
115g/4oz dried tofu
30ml/2 tbsp vegetable oil
2 garlic cloves, finely chopped
2 slices fresh root ginger,
  finely chopped
10 Sichuan peppercorns, crushed
15ml/1 tbsp red fermented tofu
½ star anise
pinch of sugar
15–30ml/1–2 tbsp dark soy sauce
50g/2oz cellophane noodles, soaked
  in hot water until soft
salt

1 Soak the Chinese mushrooms and cloud ears separately in bowls of hot water for 30 minutes. Break the dried tofu into pieces and soak in water according to the packet instructions.

2 Strain the mushrooms, squeezing as much liquid from them as possible. Reserve the liquid. Discard the stems and cut the caps in half if they are large. Drain the cloud ears, rinse and drain again. Cut off any gritty parts, then cut each cloud ear into two or three pieces.

COOK'S TIP
Red fermented tofu, sometimes called red fermented beancurd or just beancurd cheese, is fermented with rice wine and salt. It is sold in small cans or jars and tastes like salty cheese.

3 Heat the oil in a heavy pan and quickly fry the chopped garlic, ginger and Sichuan peppercorns for a few seconds. Add the mushrooms and red fermented tofu, toss to mix and stir-fry for 5 minutes.

4 Add the reserved mushroom liquid to the pan, with sufficient water to cover the mushrooms completely. Add the star anise, sugar and soy sauce, then cover the pan and simmer for 30 seconds. Add the chopped cloud ears and reconstituted tofu pieces to the pan. Cover and cook for about 10 minutes.

5 Drain the cellophane noodles, add them to the mixture and cook for a further 10 minutes until tender, adding more liquid if necessary. Add salt to taste and serve.

Energy 128Kcal/533kJ; Protein 4.9g; Carbohydrate 10.3g, of which sugars 0.9g; Fat 7.7g, of which saturates 0.8g; Cholesterol 0mg; Calcium 153mg; Fibre 0.9g; Sodium 360mg.

SICHUAN NOODLES WITH SESAME SAUCE ★★★

NOODLES DRESSED WITH A RICH SESAME PASTE AND CHILLI SAUCE ARE MORE THAN A MATCH FOR THE CRISP AND COLOURFUL RADISH AND DAIKON SALAD THAT TRADITIONALLY ACCOMPANIES THEM.

3 Coarsely grate the daikon using a mandolin or a food processor. Cut the spring onions into fine shreds.

4 Cut the radishes in half and slice finely. Add all the vegetables to the cucumber and toss gently. Set aside.

5 Heat the wok, then add the vegetable oil. When the oil is hot, fry the garlic for about 2 minutes to flavour the oil. Lift out the garlic, using a slotted spoon, and throw it away.

6 Remove the wok from the heat and stir in the sesame paste, with the sesame oil, soy and chilli sauces, vinegar and stock or water. Add a little sugar and season to taste.

7 Warm the mixture through over a gentle heat. Do not overheat the sauce or it will thicken too much.

8 Add the noodles to the sauce and toss together to thoroughly combine.

9 Tip the mixture into a serving dish, garnish with peanuts or cashew nuts, if you like, and serve with the vegetables.

SERVES 3–4

INGREDIENTS
 450g/1lb fresh or 225g/8oz dried
  egg noodles
 ½ cucumber, sliced lengthways,
  seeded and diced
 225g/8oz daikon (mooli), peeled
 4–6 spring onions (scallions)
 a bunch of radishes, about 115g/4oz
 115g/4oz/2 cups beansprouts, rinsed
  then left in iced water and drained
 10ml/2 tsp vegetable oil
 2 garlic cloves, halved
 45ml/3 tbsp toasted sesame paste
 5ml/1 tsp sesame oil
 15ml/1 tbsp light soy sauce
 5–10ml/1–2 tsp chilli sauce, to taste
 15ml/1 tbsp rice vinegar
 120ml/4fl oz/½ cup vegetable stock
  or water
 5ml/1 tsp sugar, or to taste
 salt and ground black pepper
 25g/1oz/3 tbsp roasted peanuts or
  cashew nuts, to garnish (optional)

1 If using fresh noodles, cook them in boiling water for 1 minute, then drain well. Rinse the noodles in fresh water and drain again. Cook dried noodles according to the instructions on the packet, draining and rinsing them as for fresh noodles.

2 Sprinkle the diced cucumber with salt and leave for 15 minutes for the salt to draw out the water. Put the cucumber in a colander or sieve (strainer), rinse well, then drain and pat dry on kitchen paper. Place in a large salad bowl.

Energy 480Kcal/2029kJ; Protein 15.6g; Carbohydrate 84.6g, of which sugars 5.4g; Fat 11.1g, of which saturates 2.9g; Cholesterol 34mg; Calcium 65mg; Fibre 4.8g; Sodium 482mg.

STIR-FRIED TOFU WITH NOODLES ★★★

TOFU DOES NOT HAVE MUCH FLAVOUR OF ITS OWN, BUT COMBINES WONDERFULLY WELL WITH MIXED VEGETABLES AND A SPICY SAUCE. THIS IS A VERY GOOD WAY OF SERVING IT.

SERVES 4

INGREDIENTS

   225g/8oz firm tofu
   15ml/1 tbsp vegetable oil
   175g/6oz medium egg noodles
   5ml/1 tsp cornflour (cornstarch)
   10ml/2 tsp dark soy sauce
   30ml/2 tbsp Chinese rice wine
   5ml/1 tsp sugar
   5ml/1 tsp sesame oil
   6–8 spring onions (scallions),
     cut diagonally into short lengths
   3 garlic cloves, sliced
   1 fresh green chilli, seeded
     and sliced
   115g/4oz Chinese leaves
     (Chinese cabbage),
     coarsely shredded
   50g/2oz/1 cup beansprouts
   25g/1oz/¼ cup cashew nuts

1 If the tofu is in water, drain it and pat it dry with kitchen paper. Cut it into 2.5cm/1in cubes.

2 Heat the oil in a wok until it is very hot, then stir-fry the tofu for 1–2 minutes until it is crisp and golden.

3 Remove the tofu with a slotted spoon and drain on kitchen paper. Set aside and keep warm.

4 Cook the egg noodles, following the instructions on the packet. Rinse them thoroughly under cold water in a sieve (strainer), drain well and set aside.

5 In a bowl, blend together the cornflour, soy sauce, rice wine, sugar and sesame oil.

6 Reheat the oil remaining in the wok and, when hot, add the spring onions, garlic, chilli, Chinese leaves and beansprouts. Stir-fry for 1–2 minutes.

7 Meanwhile, toast the cashew nuts in a dry frying pan over medium heat.

8 Add the tofu, noodles and soy sauce mixture to the wok. Cook, stirring, for about 1 minute, until all the ingredients are well mixed. Sprinkle over the toasted cashew nuts. Serve immediately.

Energy 335Kcal/1408kJ; Protein 12.3g; Carbohydrate 40.6g, of which sugars 7.5g; Fat 14.9g, of which saturates 2.6g; Cholesterol 13mg; Calcium 328mg; Fibre 2.6g; Sodium 104mg.

SIMMERED TOFU WITH VEGETABLES ★

A TYPICAL JAPANESE DINNER AT HOME GENERALLY CONSISTS OF A SOUP, THREE DIFFERENT DISHES AND A BOWL OF RICE. ONE OF THE THREE DISHES IS ALWAYS A SIMMERED ONE LIKE THIS MUSHROOM MIXTURE.

SERVES 4

INGREDIENTS

    4 dried shiitake mushrooms
    450g/1lb daikon (mooli)
    350g/12oz firm tofu
    115g/4oz/¾ cup green beans,
    5ml/1 tsp rice (any except for
      fragrant Thai or white basmati)
    115g/4oz carrot, peeled and cut
      into 1cm/½in thick slices
    300g/11oz baby potatoes, unpeeled
    750ml/1¼ pints/3 cups
      vegetable stock
    30ml/2 tbsp caster
      (superfine) sugar
    75ml/5 tbsp shoyu
    45ml/3 tbsp sake
    15ml/1 tbsp mirin

1 Put the dried shiitake in a bowl. Add 250ml/8fl oz/1 cup water and soak for 2 hours. Drain, discarding the liquid. Remove and discard the stems.

2 Peel the daikon and slice it into 1cm/½in discs. Shave the edge off the daikon discs to ensure they will cook evenly. Put the slices in cold water to prevent them from discolouring.

3 Drain and rinse the tofu, then pat dry with kitchen paper. Cut the tofu into pieces of about 2.5 × 5cm/1 × 2in.

4 Bring a pan of lightly salted water to the boil. Meanwhile, top and tail the beans, then cut them in half.

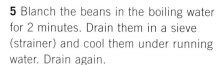

5 Blanch the beans in the boiling water for 2 minutes. Drain them in a sieve (strainer) and cool them under running water. Drain again.

6 Put the daikon slices in the clean pan. Pour in water to cover and add the rice. Bring to the boil, then reduce the heat and simmer for 15 minutes. Drain off the liquid and the rice.

7 Add the drained mushrooms, carrot and potatoes to the daikon in the pan.

8 Pour in the vegetable stock, bring the liquid to the boil, then reduce the heat to low and simmer.

9 Skim off any scum that comes to the surface of the liquid. Add the sugar, shoyu and sake and shake the pan gently to mix the ingredients thoroughly.

10 Cut a piece of baking parchment to a circle 1cm/½in smaller than the pan lid. Place the paper inside the pan, over the ingredients within.

11 Cover the pan with the lid and simmer for 30 minutes, or until the sauce has reduced by at least half.

12 Add the tofu and green beans and warm through for 2 minutes.

13 Remove the paper and add the mirin. Taste the sauce and adjust with shoyu if required. Serve immediately in warmed bowls.

COOK'S TIP
Once you have opened a packet of tofu, any that is unused should be rinsed and put in a bowl with fresh water to cover. Change the water every day and use the tofu within 5 days.

Energy 181Kcal/762kJ; Protein 10.3g; Carbohydrate 26.8g, of which sugars 14.8g; Fat 4.4g, of which saturates 0.7g; Cholesterol 0mg; Calcium 496mg; Fibre 3.1g; Sodium 833mg.

BRAISED TOFU WITH MUSHROOMS ★

THE SHIITAKE AND OYSTER MUSHROOMS FLAVOUR THE TOFU BEAUTIFULLY TO MAKE THIS THE PERFECT VEGETARIAN MAIN COURSE. IT CONTAINS VERY LITTLE SATURATED FAT.

SERVES 4

INGREDIENTS

350g/12oz tofu
2.5ml/½ tsp sesame oil
10ml/2 tsp light soy sauce
15ml/1 tbsp vegetable oil
2 garlic cloves, finely chopped
2.5ml/½ tsp grated fresh root ginger
115g/4oz/1 cup fresh shiitake
  mushrooms, stems removed
175g/6oz/2½ cups fresh
  oyster mushrooms
115g/4oz/1½ cups drained, canned
  straw mushrooms
115g/4oz/1½ cups button
  mushrooms, cut in half
15ml/1 tbsp dry sherry
15ml/1 tbsp dark soy sauce
90ml/6 tbsp vegetable stock
5ml/1 tsp cornflour (cornstarch)
15ml/1 tbsp cold water
salt and ground white pepper
2 spring onions (scallions), shredded

4 Mix the cornflour to a paste with the water. Stir into the pan or wok and cook, stirring, until thickened.

VARIATION
If fresh shiitake mushrooms are not available, use dried Chinese mushrooms soaked in hot water.

5 Carefully add the pieces of tofu, toss gently to coat thoroughly and simmer for 2 minutes.

6 Sprinkle the shredded spring onions over the top of the mixture, then transfer to a warm serving dish and serve immediately.

1 Put the tofu in a dish and sprinkle with the sesame oil, light soy sauce and a large pinch of pepper. Leave to marinate for 10 minutes, then drain. Use a sharp knife to cut the tofu into 2.5 x 1cm/1 x ½in pieces.

2 Heat the vegetable oil in a non-stick frying pan or wok. When it is very hot, fry the garlic and ginger for a few seconds. Add all the mushrooms and stir-fry for 2 minutes.

3 Stir in the sherry, soy sauce and stock, with salt, if needed, and pepper. Simmer for 4 minutes.

Energy 92Kcal/386kJ; Protein 9.6g; Carbohydrate 2.9g, of which sugars 1g; Fat 4.3g, of which saturates 0.6g; Cholesterol 0mg; Calcium 456mg; Fibre 1.4g; Sodium 456mg.

TERIYAKI SOBA NOODLES WITH TOFU ★★★

YOU CAN, OF COURSE, BUY READY-MADE TERIYAKI SAUCE, BUT IT IS EASY TO PREPARE AT HOME USING INGREDIENTS THAT ARE NOW READILY AVAILABLE IN SUPERMARKETS AND ASIAN SHOPS.

SERVES 4

INGREDIENTS
    350g/12oz soba noodles
    250g/9oz asparagus
    15ml/1 tbsp toasted sesame oil
    30ml/2 tbsp vegetable oil
    225g/8oz block firm tofu
    2 spring onions (scallions),
      cut diagonally
    1 carrot, cut into matchsticks
    2.5ml/½ tsp chilli flakes
    15ml/1 tbsp sesame seeds
    salt and ground black pepper
For the teriyaki sauce
    60ml/4 tbsp dark soy sauce
    60ml/4 tbsp sake or dry sherry
    60ml/4 tbsp mirin
    5ml/1 tsp caster
      (superfine) sugar

1 Cook the soba noodles according to the instructions on the packet, then drain and rinse under cold running water. Drain again and set aside.

2 Trim the asparagus, discarding the woody ends.

3 Lay the asparagus in a grill (broiler) pan, brush lightly with sesame oil, then grill (broil) under medium heat for 8–10 minutes, turning frequently, until they are tender and browned. Set aside.

VARIATIONS
Use dried egg or rice noodles instead of soba noodles, if you prefer. The asparagus could be steamed for just a couple of minutes instead of being grilled (broiled).

4 Meanwhile, heat the vegetable oil in a wok or large frying pan until it is very hot. Add the tofu to the pan and fry for 8–10 minutes until it is golden, turning it occasionally, using tongs or two wooden spoons, to crisp all sides.

5 Carefully remove the tofu from the wok or pan and leave to drain and cool slightly on kitchen paper. When is has cooled sufficiently, cut the tofu into 1cm/½in slices.

6 To make the teriyaki sauce, mix the soy sauce, sake or dry sherry, mirin and sugar together, then heat the mixture in the wok or frying pan.

7 Toss in the noodles and stir to coat in the sauce. Heat for 1–2 minutes, then spoon into warmed individual serving bowls with the tofu and asparagus. Sprinkle with the spring onions and carrot and sprinkle with the chilli flakes and sesame seeds. Serve immediately.

Energy 476Kcal/2007kJ; Protein 17g; Carbohydrate 71.6g, of which sugars 6.5g; Fat 13.7g, of which saturates 1g; Cholesterol 0mg; Calcium 332mg; Fibre 4.1g; Sodium 1081mg.

FISH AND SHELLFISH

Fish is an excellent source of protein, vitamins and minerals,

has very little carbohydrate and contains oils that can have

a positive impact on health. Some of our finest fish recipes

come from China and Far East Asia, from luxurious Chilli-

seared Scallops on Pak Choi to lightly cooked dishes like

Chinese-style Steamed Fish. Grills include the delicious

Salmon Teriyaki and Japanese Sweet Soy Salmon, and there

are plenty of superb stir-fries and salads.

GONG BOA PRAWNS ★

THERE'S SOMETHING DECADENT ABOUT TIGER PRAWNS, BUT WITH A TOTAL FAT CONTENT OF WELL UNDER 5 GRAMS AND A LOW SATURATED FAT CONTENT, THIS RECIPE CAN BE ENJOYED REGULARLY.

SERVES 4

INGREDIENTS

350g/12oz raw tiger prawns
    (jumbo shrimp)
½ cucumber, about 75g/3oz
300ml/½ pint/1¼ cups fish stock
15ml/1 tbsp vegetable oil
2.5ml/½ tsp crushed dried chillies
½ green (bell) pepper, seeded and
    cut into 2.5cm/1in strips
1 small carrot, thinly sliced
30ml/2 tbsp tomato ketchup
45ml/3 tbsp rice vinegar
15ml/1 tbsp caster sugar
150ml/¼ pint/⅔ cup vegetable stock
50g/2oz/½ cup drained canned
    pineapple chunks
10ml/2 tsp cornflour (cornstarch)
15ml/1 tbsp cold water
salt

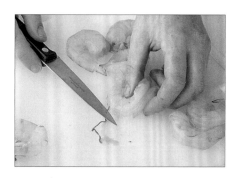

1 Peel and devein the prawns. Rub them gently with 2.5ml/½ tsp salt; leave them for a few minutes and then wash and dry thoroughly.

2 Using a narrow peeler or cannelle knife, pare strips of skin off the cucumber to give a stripy effect. Cut the cucumber in half lengthways and scoop out the seeds with a teaspoon. Cut the flesh into 5mm/¼in crescents.

3 Bring the fish stock to the boil in a pan. Add the prawns, lower the heat and poach the prawns for 2 minutes until they turn pink, then lift them out using a slotted spoon and set aside.

4 Heat the oil in a non-stick frying pan or wok over a high heat. Fry the chillies for a few seconds, then add the pepper strips and carrot slices and stir-fry for 1 minute more.

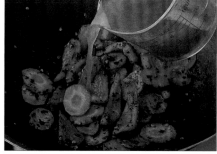

5 Spoon the tomato ketchup into a jug (pitcher) and stir in the vinegar, sugar and vegetable stock, with 1.5ml/¼ tsp salt. Pour into the pan and cook for 3 minutes more.

6 Add the prawns, cucumber and pineapple to the pan and cook for 2 minutes more. Mix the cornflour to a paste with the water.

7 Add the mixture to the pan and cook, stirring constantly, until the sauce thickens. Serve immediately.

COOK'S TIP
Omit the chillies if you like, or increase the quantity for a spicier dish.

Energy 147Kcal/617kJ; Protein 16.3g; Carbohydrate 13.2g, of which sugars 10.7g; Fat 3.5g, of which saturates 0.5g; Cholesterol 171mg; Calcium 88mg; Fibre 1.1g; Sodium 296mg.

STIR-FRIED PRAWNS WITH MANGETOUTS ★

MANGETOUT MEANS "EAT ALL" AND YOU CAN SAFELY DO JUST THAT WHEN A RECIPE IS AS LOW IN FAT AS THIS ONE IS. THE PRAWNS REMAIN BEAUTIFULLY SUCCULENT AND THE SAUCE IS DELICIOUS.

SERVES 4

INGREDIENTS

- 300ml/½ pint/1¼ cups fish stock
- 350g/12oz raw tiger prawns (jumbo shrimp), peeled and deveined
- 15ml/1 tbsp vegetable oil
- 1 garlic clove, finely chopped
- 225g/8oz/2 cups mangetouts (snow peas)
- 1.5ml/¼ tsp salt
- 15ml/1 tbsp mirin or dry sherry
- 15ml/1 tbsp oyster sauce
- 5ml/1 tsp cornflour (cornstarch)
- 5ml/1 tsp caster (superfine) sugar
- 15ml/1 tbsp cold water
- 1.5ml/¼ tsp sesame oil

1 Bring the fish stock to the boil in a frying pan. Add the prawns. Cook gently for 2 minutes until the prawns have turned pink, then lift them out on a slotted spoon and set aside.

2 Heat the vegetable oil in a non-stick frying pan or wok. When the oil is very hot, add the chopped garlic and cook for a few seconds, then add the mangetouts. Sprinkle with the salt. Stir-fry for 1 minute.

3 Add the prawns and mirin or sherry to the pan or wok. Toss the ingredients together over the heat for a few seconds, then add the oyster sauce and toss again.

4 Mix the cornflour and sugar to a paste with the water. Add to the pan and cook, stirring constantly, until the sauce thickens slightly. Drizzle with sesame oil.

Energy 125Kcal/524kJ; Protein 17.6g; Carbohydrate 5.2g, of which sugars 3.6g; Fat 3.4g, of which saturates 0.4g; Cholesterol 171mg; Calcium 96mg; Fibre 1.3g; Sodium 436mg.

SWEET AND SOUR PRAWNS ★

HEALTHIER THAN CONVENTIONAL SWEET AND SOUR PRAWNS, THESE ARE NOT DEEP-FRIED BUT RATHER JUST HEATED THROUGH IN THE TASTY SAUCE. COOKED THIS WAY, THEY STAY SUCCULENT.

SERVES 4–6

INGREDIENTS
  1 small cos or romaine lettuce
  350g/11oz cooked tiger prawns
    (jumbo shrimps) in their shells
For the sauce
  15ml/1 tbsp vegetable oil
  15ml/1 tbsp finely chopped
    spring onions (scallions)
  10ml/2 tsp finely chopped fresh
    root ginger
  30ml/2 tbsp light soy sauce
  30ml/2 tbsp soft light
    brown sugar
  45ml/3 tbsp rice vinegar
  15ml/1 tbsp Chinese rice wine or
    dry sherry
  about 120ml/4fl oz/½ cup chicken
    or vegetable stock
  15ml/1 tbsp cornflour
    (cornstarch) paste
  few drops sesame oil

1 Separate the lettuce leaves and rinse them under cold running water. Arrange them on a platter.

2 Pull the soft legs off the cooked prawns without removing the shells. Dry the peeled prawns well with kitchen paper and set aside.

VARIATION
It is not essential to use tiger prawns (jumbo shrimp). The smaller common prawns are not as luxurious, but still work well.

3 To make the sauce, heat the oil in a preheated wok. Add the spring onions and ginger and toss to mix. Drizzle over the soy sauce, sugar, rice vinegar, Chinese rice wine or dry sherry. Add the stock, and bring to the boil.

4 Add the prawns to the sauce and toss over the heat to coat them thoroughly and heat them through. Thicken the sauce with the cornflour paste, stirring until smooth. Sprinkle with the sesame oil. Serve on a bed of lettuce.

Energy 49Kcal/208kJ; Protein 5.2g; Carbohydrate 2g, of which sugars 0.5g; Fat 2g, of which saturates 0.3g; Cholesterol 61mg; Calcium 27mg; Fibre 0g; Sodium 707mg.

GINGERED PRAWNS WITH NOODLES ★

DRIED PORCINI MUSHROOMS ARE OFTEN REGARDED BY MANY AS HAVING A BETTER FLAVOUR THAN CHINESE DRIED MUSHROOMS, SO THEY ARE THE PREFERRED CHOICE FOR THIS FUSION RECIPE.

SERVES 4–6

INGREDIENTS

   15g/½oz dried porcini mushrooms
   300ml/½ pint/1¼ cups
     hot water
   bunch of spring onions (scallions),
     cut into thick diagonal slices
   2.5cm/1in piece fresh root ginger,
     peeled and grated
   1 red (bell) pepper, seeded
     and diced
   225g/8oz can water chestnuts, sliced
   45ml/3 tbsp light soy sauce
   30ml/2 tbsp sherry
   350g/12oz large cooked prawns
     (shrimp), peeled
   225g/8oz egg noodles

4 Stir in the water chestnuts, then add the soy sauce and sherry. Toss in the prawns and mix them with the sauce. Cover and cook gently for 2 minutes.

5 Cook the egg noodles according to the instructions on the packet. Drain, heap on a warmed serving dish, spoon the hot prawns on top and serve immediately.

1 Put the dried porcini mushrooms into a bowl. Pour over the hot water and set aside to soak for 20 minutes.

2 Put the sliced spring onions, grated ginger and diced red pepper into a pan with the mushrooms and their liquid.

3 Bring to the boil, cover the pan and cook for about 5 minutes until the vegetables are tender.

Energy 224Kcal/947kJ; Protein 16.7g; Carbohydrate 31.3g, of which sugars 4.3g; Fat 3.8g, of which saturates 1g; Cholesterol 125mg; Calcium 73mg; Fibre 2.3g; Sodium 717mg.

TIGER PRAWNS WITH HAM, CHICKEN AND EGG NOODLES ★★★

THIS RECIPE COMBINES PRAWNS WITH HAM AND CHICKEN, WHICH MAY SEEM UNCONVENTIONAL UNTIL YOU REMEMBER THAN THE SPANISH DO SOMETHING VERY SIMILAR IN THEIR PAELLA.

SERVES 4–6

INGREDIENTS

30ml/2 tbsp vegetable oil
2 garlic cloves, sliced
5ml/1 tsp fresh root ginger, peeled and chopped
2 fresh red chillies, seeded and chopped
75g/3oz lean ham, thinly sliced (optional)
1 skinless chicken breast fillet, thinly sliced
16 uncooked tiger prawns (jumbo shrimp), peeled, tails left intact and deveined
115g/4oz green beans, trimmed
225g/8oz beansprouts
50g/2oz Chinese chives
450g/1lb egg noodles, cooked in boiling water until tender
30ml/2 tbsp dark soy sauce
15ml/1 tbsp oyster sauce
salt and ground black pepper
5ml/1 tsp sesame oil
2 spring onions (scallions), cut into strips, and fresh coriander (cilantro) leaves, to garnish

1 Heat 15ml/1 tbsp of the oil in a wok or large frying pan. When the oil is hot, fry the garlic, ginger and chillies for 2 minutes.

2 Add the prepared ham, chicken, prawns and green beans to the wok or frying pan.

3 Stir-fry the meat for about 2 minutes over high heat or until the chicken and prawns are thoroughly cooked. Transfer the mixture to a bowl and set aside.

4 Heat the remaining oil in the wok or frying pan. When the oil is hot, add the beansprouts and Chinese chives. Stir-fry for 1–2 minutes.

5 Add the noodles and toss and stir to mix. Season with soy sauce, oyster sauce, salt and pepper.

6 Return the prawn mixture to the wok. Reheat and mix well with the noodles. Sprinkle with the sesame oil.

7 Serve garnished with the spring onions and coriander leaves.

VARIATIONS
You could use lean bacon, trimmed of fat, in place of the ham; and skinless turkey breast fillet in place of the chicken. You could also add extra green beans, mangetouts (snow peas) or sugar snap peas in place of the ham and chicken, if you prefer.

COOK'S TIP
Chinese chives, sometimes called garlic chives, have a delicate garlic/onion flavour. If they are not available, use regular chives, the green parts of spring onions (scallions), or just substitute 2 finely chopped shallots and a crushed garlic clove.

Energy 397Kcal/1674kJ; Protein 21.3g; Carbohydrate 56.4g, of which sugars 3.2g; Fat 11.1g, of which saturates 2.4g; Cholesterol 89mg; Calcium 72mg; Fibre 3.3g; Sodium 567mg.

CHILLI-SEARED SCALLOPS ON PAK CHOI ★★

TENDER, SUCCULENT SCALLOPS ARE SIMPLY DIVINE MARINATED IN FRESH CHILLI, FRAGRANT MINT AND AROMATIC BASIL, THEN QUICKLY SEARED IN A PIPING HOT WOK AND SERVED ON WILTED GREENS.

3 Using a sharp knife, cut each pak choi lengthways into four pieces.

4 Heat a frying pan or wok over a high heat. When the pan or wok is hot, drain the scallops (reserving the marinade) and add to the wok. Cook the scallops for 1 minute on each side, or until cooked to your liking.

5 Pour the marinade over the scallops and heat through briefly, then remove the wok from the heat and cover to keep warm.

6 Cook the pak choi for 2–3 minutes in a steamer over a pan of simmering water until the leaves are wilted.

7 Divide the greens among four warmed serving plates, then top with the reserved scallops and their juices.

8 Add more chopped herbs as a garnish if you like, and serve immediately.

COOK'S TIP
If you can't find pak choi, you can use Chinese leaves or tender young spring greens in its place.

SERVES 4

INGREDIENTS
20–24 king scallops or 24 queen
  scallops, cleaned
30ml/2 tbsp vegetable oil
finely grated rind and juice of
  1 lemon
15ml/1 tbsp finely chopped
  fresh mint
15ml/1 tbsp finely chopped
  fresh basil
1 fresh red chilli, seeded and
  finely chopped
salt and ground black pepper
500g/1¼lb pak choi (bok choy)
extra chopped fresh mint and basil,
  to garnish (optional)

1 Place the scallops in a shallow, non-metallic bowl in a single layer. In a clean bowl, whisk together the oil, lemon rind and juice, chopped herbs and chilli and spoon over the scallops.

2 Season the scallops well with salt and black pepper, cover the bowl and set aside for 10 minutes to allow the flavours to blend.

Energy 199Kcal/833kJ; Protein 26.7g; Carbohydrate 5.4g, of which sugars 1.9g; Fat 7.9g, of which saturates 1.2g; Cholesterol 47mg; Calcium 242mg; Fibre 2.6g; Sodium 355mg.

ASPARAGUS WITH CRAB MEAT SAUCE ★★

THE SUBTLE FLAVOUR OF FRESH ASPARAGUS IS ENHANCED BY THE EQUALLY DELICATE TASTE OF THE CRAB MEAT IN THIS CLASSIC DISH, WHICH IS RELATIVELY LOW IN SATURATED FAT.

SERVES 4

INGREDIENTS

- 450g/1lb asparagus, trimmed
- 15ml/1 tbsp vegetable oil
- 4 thin slices of fresh root ginger
- 2 garlic cloves, finely chopped
- 115g/4oz/²⁄₃ cup fresh or thawed frozen white crab meat
- 5ml/1 tsp sake or dry sherry
- 150ml/¼ pint/²⁄₃ cup semi-skimmed (low-fat) milk
- 15ml/1 tbsp cornflour (cornstarch)
- 45ml/3 tbsp cold water
- salt and ground white pepper
- 1 spring onion (scallion), thinly shredded, to garnish

1 Bring a large pan of lightly salted water to the boil. Poach the asparagus for about 5 minutes until just crisp-tender. Drain well and keep hot in a shallow serving dish.

2 Bruise the slices of ginger with a rolling pin. Heat the oil in a non-stick frying pan or wok. Add the ginger and garlic for 1 minute and cook to release their flavour, then lift them out with a slotted spoon and discard them.

3 Add the crab meat to the flavoured oil and toss to mix. Drizzle over the sherry, then pour in the milk. Cook, stirring often, for 2 minutes.

4 Meanwhile, put the cornflour in a small bowl with the water and mix to a smooth paste.

5 Add the cornflour paste to the pan, stirring constantly, then cook the mixture, continuing to stir, until it forms a thick and creamy sauce.

6 Season to taste with salt and pepper, spoon over the asparagus, garnish with shreds of spring onion and serve.

Energy 199Kcal/833kJ; Protein 26.7g; Carbohydrate 5.4g, of which sugars 1.9g; Fat 7.9g, of which saturates 1.2g; Cholesterol 47mg; Calcium 242mg; Fibre 2.6g; Sodium 355mg.

SPICY SQUID SALAD ★★

THE GENERAL RULE WITH SQUID IS THAT IT MUST EITHER BE COOKED VERY QUICKLY OR SIMMERED VERY SLOWLY. FOR THIS SUPERB SALAD THE FORMER METHOD IS USED WITH SPECTACULAR SUCCESS.

3 Cut the body open lengthways and wash thoroughly. Score criss-cross patterns on the inside, taking care not to cut through the squid, then cut into 7.5 x 5cm/3 x 2in pieces.

4 Bring the fish stock to the boil in a wok or pan. Add the squid, lower the heat and cook for about 2 minutes until they are tender and have curled. Drain.

5 In a separate pan of lightly salted boiling water, cook the beans for 3–4 minutes over medium heat until crisp-tender. Drain, refresh under cold water, then drain again. Mix the squid and beans in a serving bowl, and set aside.

6 In a small bowl or jug (pitcher), mix the coriander leaves, sugar, rice vinegar, sesame oil and soy sauce. Pour the mixture over the squid and beans.

7 Heat the vegetable oil in a wok or small pan until very hot. Stir-fry the garlic, ginger and chilli for a few seconds, then pour the dressing over the squid mixture. Toss gently and leave for at least 5 minutes. Add salt to taste and serve warm or cold.

SERVES 4

INGREDIENTS

450g/1lb squid
300ml/½ pint/1¼ cups fish stock
175g/6oz green beans, trimmed
  and halved
45ml/3 tbsp fresh coriander
  (cilantro) leaves
10ml/2 tsp caster (superfine) sugar
30ml/2 tbsp rice vinegar
5ml/1 tsp sesame oil
15ml/1 tbsp light soy sauce
15ml/1 tbsp vegetable oil
2 garlic cloves, finely chopped
10ml/2 tsp finely chopped fresh
  root ginger
1 fresh chilli, seeded and chopped
salt

1 Prepare the squid. Holding the body in one hand, gently pull the head and tentacles away from the body with the other hand. Discard the head; trim and reserve the tentacles.

2 Remove the transparent "quill" from inside the body and peel off the purplish skin on the outside.

Energy 121Kcal/507kJ; Protein 10.4g; Carbohydrate 7.5g, of which sugars 3.9g; Fat 5.6g, of which saturates 1.1g; Cholesterol 23mg; Calcium 84mg; Fibre 1.9g; Sodium 126mg.

SQUID WITH BROCCOLI ★★

THE SLIGHTLY CHEWY SQUID CONTRASTS BEAUTIFULLY WITH THE CRISP CRUNCH OF THE BROCCOLI TO GIVE THIS DISH THE PERFECT COMBINATION OF TEXTURES SO BELOVED BY THE CHINESE.

SERVES 4

INGREDIENTS

300ml/½ pint/1¼ cups fish stock
350g/12oz prepared squid, cut into
  large pieces
225g/8oz broccoli
15ml/1 tbsp vegetable oil
2 garlic cloves, finely chopped
15ml/1 tbsp Chinese rice wine
  or dry sherry
10ml/2 tsp cornflour (cornstarch)
2.5ml/½ tsp caster (superfine) sugar
45ml/3 tbsp cold water
15ml/1 tbsp oyster sauce
2.5ml/½ tsp sesame oil
noodles, to serve

3 Heat the vegetable oil in a wok or non-stick frying pan. When the oil is hot, add the garlic, stir-fry for a few seconds, then add the squid, broccoli and sherry. Stir-fry the mixture over medium heat for about 2 minutes.

4 Mix the cornflour and sugar to a paste with the water. Stir the mixture into the wok or pan, with the oyster sauce. Cook, stirring, until the sauce thickens slightly. Just before serving, stir in the sesame oil. Serve with noodles.

1 Bring the fish stock to the boil in a wok or pan. Add the squid pieces and cook for 2 minutes over medium heat until they are tender and have curled. Drain the squid pieces and set aside until required.

2 Trim the broccoli and cut it into small florets. Bring a pan of lightly salted water to the boil, add the broccoli and cook for 2 minutes until crisp-tender. Drain thoroughly.

Energy 143Kcal/602kJ; Protein 18.2g; Carbohydrate 5.4g, of which sugars 3.6g; Fat 5.6g, of which saturates 0.9g; Cholesterol 253mg; Calcium 32mg; Fibre 1g; Sodium 124mg.

CLAY POT OF CHILLI SQUID ★★★

THIS DISH IS DELICIOUS IN ITS OWN RIGHT, OR SERVED AS PART OF A LARGER CHINESE MEAL, WITH OTHER MEAT OR FISH DISHES AND RICE. DON'T OVERCOOK THE SQUID OR IT WILL TOUGHEN.

SERVES 2–4

INGREDIENTS

675g/1½lb fresh squid
30ml/2 tbsp vegetable oil
3 slices fresh root ginger,
  finely chopped
2 garlic cloves, finely chopped
1 red onion, thinly sliced
1 carrot, thinly sliced
1 celery stick, sliced diagonally
50g/2oz sugar snap peas
5ml/1 tsp sugar
15ml/1 tbsp chilli bean paste
2.5ml/½ tsp chilli powder
75g/3oz cellophane noodles, soaked
  in hot water until soft
120ml/4fl oz/½ cup chicken stock
  or water
15ml/1 tbsp light soy sauce
15ml/1 tbsp oyster sauce
5ml/1 tsp sesame oil
pinch of salt
fresh coriander (cilantro) leaves,
  to garnish

1 Prepare the squid. Holding the body in one hand, pull away the head and tentacles with the other hand. Discard the head; trim and reserve the tentacles.

2 Remove the "quill" from inside the body of the squid. Peel off the brown skin on the outside. Rub salt into the squid and wash under water.

COOK'S TIP
To vary the flavour of this dish, the vegetables can be altered according to what is available.

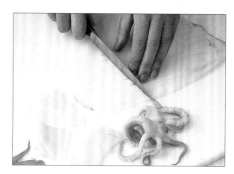

3 Cut the body into rings or split it open lengthways, score criss-cross patterns on the inside of the body and cut it into 5 x 4cm/2 x 1½in pieces.

4 Heat the oil in a large, flameproof casserole or wok. Add the ginger, garlic and onion and fry for 1–2 minutes. Add the squid, carrot, celery and sugar snap peas. Fry until the squid curls up. Season with salt and sugar and then stir in the chilli bean paste and powder. Transfer to a bowl and set aside.

5 Drain the soaked noodles and add to the casserole or wok. Stir in the chicken stock or water, light soy sauce and oyster sauce. Cover and cook over medium heat for 10 minutes or until the noodles are tender.

6 Return the squid and vegetable mixture to the pot. Cover and cook for a further 5–6 minutes, until all the flavours are combined. Season to taste.

7 Spoon the mixture into a warmed clay pot and drizzle with the sesame oil. Sprinkle with the coriander leaves and serve immediately.

Energy 292Kcal/1229kJ; Protein 29.1g; Carbohydrate 21.2g, of which sugars 5.1g; Fat 10.8g, of which saturates 1.9g; Cholesterol 385mg; Calcium 45mg; Fibre 1.5g; Sodium 762mg.

SEAFOOD CHOW MEIN ★★★

CHOW MEIN IS A CHINESE-AMERICAN DISH MEANING SIMPLY "STIR-FRIED NOODLES". IT IS USUALLY MEAT-BASED BUT TASTES MARVELLOUS WHEN MADE WITH SQUID, PRAWNS AND SCALLOPS.

SERVES 4

INGREDIENTS
  75g/3oz fresh squid, cleaned
  75g/3oz raw prawns (shrimp)
  3–4 fresh scallops, prepared
  ½ egg white
  15ml/1 tbsp cornflour paste
   (see Cook's Tip)
  250g/9oz egg noodles
  30ml/2 tbsp vegetable oil
  50g/2oz mangetouts (snow peas)
  2.5ml/½ tsp salt
  2.5ml/½ tsp light brown sugar
  15ml/1 tbsp Chinese rice wine
  30ml/2 tbsp light soy sauce
  2 spring onions (scallions), shredded
  vegetable stock, (optional)
  few drops sesame oil

1 Open up the squid and score the inside in a criss-cross pattern. Cut the squid into pieces, each about the size of a postage stamp. Soak the squid in a bowl of boiling water until all the pieces curl up. Rinse in cold water and drain.

2 Peel and devein the prawns, then cut each of them in half lengthways.

3 Cut each scallop into 3–4 slices. Mix the scallops and prawns with the egg white and cornflour paste and set aside.

4 Cook the noodles in boiling water according to the packet instructions.

COOK'S TIP
To make cornflour paste, mix 4 parts dry cornflour with about 5 parts cold water until smooth.

5 Meanwhile, heat the oil in a preheated wok until hot. Stir-fry the mangetouts, squid, prawns and scallops for about 2 minutes, then add the salt, sugar, rice wine, half of the soy sauce and about half the spring onions. Blend well and add a little stock, if necessary. Transfer to a bowl and keep warm.

6 Drain the noodles and toss with the remaining soy sauce.

7 Place the noodles in a large serving dish, pour the seafood topping on top, garnish with the remaining spring onions and sprinkle with sesame oil. Serve hot or cold.

Energy 359Kcal/1515kJ; Protein 19.5g; Carbohydrate 47.6g, of which sugars 2.9g; Fat 11.4g, of which saturates 2.3g; Cholesterol 106mg; Calcium 53mg; Fibre 2.3g; Sodium 1101mg.

FIVE-SPICE SQUID WITH BLACK BEAN SAUCE ★★

SQUID IS PERFECT FOR STIR-FRYING AS COOKING IT QUICKLY PREVENTS IT FROM BECOMING TOUGH.
THIS SPICY BLACK BEAN AND MUSHROOM SAUCE IS THE IDEAL ACCOMPANIMENT.

SERVES 6

INGREDIENTS

450g/1lb cleaned small squid
30ml/2 tbsp vegetable oil
2.5cm/1in piece fresh root
  ginger, grated
1 garlic clove, crushed
8 spring onions (scallions), cut
  diagonally into 2.5cm/1in lengths
1 red (bell) pepper, seeded and
  cut into strips
1 fresh green chilli, seeded and
  thinly sliced
6 fresh shiitake mushrooms, stems
  removed, caps sliced
5ml/1 tsp five-spice powder
30ml/2 tbsp black bean sauce
30ml/2 tbsp soy sauce
5ml/1 tsp granulated sugar
15ml/1 tbsp rice wine or dry sherry

1 Prepare the squid. Holding the body in one hand, gently pull away the head and tentacles with the other hand. Discard the head; trim and reserve the tentacles.

2 Peel off the brown skin on the outside of the squid. Remove the "quill" from inside the body. Rub salt into the squid and wash under water.

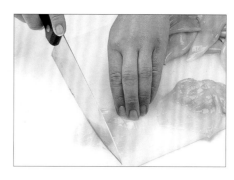

3 Slit the squid open and score the outside into diamonds with a sharp knife. Cut the squid into strips.

4 Heat the oil in a wok until hot. Stir-fry the squid quickly. Remove the squid from the wok with a slotted spoon; set aside. Add the ginger, garlic, spring onions, red pepper, chilli and mushrooms to the oil remaining in the wok and toss over the heat for 2 minutes.

5 Return the squid to the wok and stir in the five-spice powder using chopsticks. Stir in the black bean sauce, soy sauce, sugar and rice wine or sherry. Bring to the boil and cook, stirring, for 1 minute. Serve in heated bowls, with steamed rice or egg noodles.

Energy 112Kcal/469kJ; Protein 12.6g; Carbohydrate 4g, of which sugars 2.9g; Fat 5.2g, of which saturates 0.8g; Cholesterol 169mg; Calcium 20mg; Fibre 0.8g; Sodium 797mg.

SEA BASS WITH CHINESE CHIVES ★★

THIS SIMPLE TREATMENT IS JUST RIGHT FOR SEA BASS, ENHANCING THE FISH'S EXCELLENT FLAVOUR WITHOUT OVERWHELMING IT. IT IS IMPORTANT TO KEEP THE CHUNKS OF FISH FAIRLY LARGE.

SERVES 4

INGREDIENTS
    450g/1lb sea bass
    5ml/1 tsp cornflour (cornstarch)
    30ml/2 tbsp vegetable oil
    175g/6oz Chinese chives
    15ml/1 tbsp Chinese rice wine or
        dry sherry
    5ml/1 tsp caster (superfine) sugar
    salt and ground pepper
    Chinese chives with flowerheads,
        to garnish

1 Remove the scales from the bass by scraping the fish with the back of a knife, working from the tail end to the head end.

2 Cut the fish into large chunks and dust them lightly with cornflour, salt and pepper.

COOK'S TIP
Chinese chives are widely available in Asian supermarkets but if you are unable to buy them, use half a large Spanish (Bermuda) onion, finely sliced, instead.

3 Heat the wok, then add the oil. When the oil is hot, toss in the chunks of fish briefly to seal, remove the fish with a slotted spoon and set aside.

4 Cut the Chinese chives into 5cm/2in lengths and discard the flowers. Add the Chinese chives to the wok and stir-fry for 30 seconds.

5 Return the fish to the wok and add the rice wine, then stir in the sugar. Lower the heat and cook the fish for a futher 2–3 minutes.

6 Spoon the fish into heated bowls, garnish with some flowering Chinese chives, and serve with a side dish of crisp mixed lettuce salad.

Energy 180Kcal/754kJ; Protein 23g; Carbohydrate 2.7g, of which sugars 1.7g; Fat 8.7g, of which saturates 1.1g; Cholesterol 90mg; Calcium 221mg; Fibre 0.9g; Sodium 140mg.

THREE SEA FLAVOURS STIR-FRY ★

THIS DELECTABLE SEAFOOD COMBINATION CONTAINS VERY LITTLE SATURATED FAT AND IS IDEAL FOR A SPECIAL OCCASION MEAL. FRESH ROOT GINGER AND SPRING ONIONS ENHANCE THE FLAVOUR.

3 Remove the seafood, using a slotted spoon, and set aside. Reserve about 60ml/4 tbsp of the stock.

4 Heat the oil in a non-stick frying pan or wok over a high heat until very hot. Stir-fry the garlic, ginger and spring onions for a few seconds.

5 Add the seafood and wine. Stir-fry for 1 minute, then add the reserved stock and simmer for 2 minutes.

6 Mix the cornflour to a paste with the water. Add the mixture to the pan or wok and cook, stirring gently just until the sauce thickens.

7 Season the stir-fry with salt and pepper to taste. Serve immediately, with noodles or rice.

VARIATION

For a more economical version of this dish, substitute 275g/10oz smoked haddock for the scallops and white fish.

COOK'S TIP

Do not overcook the seafood or it will become rubbery.

SERVES 4

INGREDIENTS
    4 large scallops, with the corals
    225g/8oz firm white fish fillet, such
        as monkfish or cod
    115g/4oz raw tiger prawns
        (jumbo shrimp)
    300ml/½ pint/1¼ cups fish stock
    15ml/1 tbsp vegetable oil
    2 garlic cloves, roughly chopped
    5cm/2in piece of fresh root ginger,
        thinly sliced
    8 spring onions (scallions), cut into
        4cm/1½in pieces
    30ml/2 tbsp dry white wine
    5ml/1 tsp cornflour (cornstarch)
    15ml/1 tbsp cold water
    salt and ground white pepper
    noodles or rice, to serve

1 Separate the corals and slice each scallop in half horizontally. Cut the fish into chunks. Peel and devein the prawns.

2 Bring the fish stock to the boil in a pan. Add the seafood, lower the heat and poach gently for 1–2 minutes until the fish, scallops and corals are just firm and the prawns have turned pink.

Energy 159Kcal/668kJ; Protein 26.2g; Carbohydrate 3.3g, of which sugars 0.6g; Fat 4.1g, of which saturates 0.6g; Cholesterol 103mg; Calcium 50mg; Fibre 0.3g; Sodium 172mg.

JAPANESE SWEET SOY SALMON ★★★

TERIYAKI SAUCE FORMS THE MARINADE FOR THE SALMON IN THIS RECIPE. SERVED WITH SOFT-FRIED NOODLES, IT MAKES A STUNNING DISH, WHICH PEOPLE OF ALL AGES WILL ENJOY.

SERVES 4

INGREDIENTS
- 350g/12oz salmon fillet
- 30ml/2 tbsp shoyu
- 30ml/2 tbsp sake
- 60ml/4 tbsp mirin or sweet sherry
- 5ml/1 tsp soft light brown sugar
- 10ml/2 tsp grated fresh root ginger
- 3 garlic cloves, 1 crushed and
  2 sliced into rounds
- 15ml/1 tbsp vegetable oil
- 225g/8oz dried egg noodles,
  cooked and drained
- 50g/2oz/1 cup alfalfa sprouts
- 10ml/2 tsp sesame seeds,
  lightly toasted

1 Chill the salmon briefly in the freezer, if you have time, to make it easier to slice. Using a sharp chopping knife, cut the salmon away from you into thin slices. Place the slices of fish in a shallow dish.

2 In a measuring jug (pitcher), mix together the soy sauce, sake, mirin or sherry, sugar, ginger and crushed garlic. Pour the mixture over the salmon, cover and leave for 30 minutes.

3 Preheat the grill (broiler). Drain the salmon, and scrape off and reserve the marinade. Place the salmon in a single layer on a baking sheet. Cook under the grill for 2–3 minutes without turning.

4 Meanwhile, heat a wok until hot, add the oil and swirl it around. Add the garlic rounds and cook until golden brown but not burnt.

5 Add the cooked noodles and reserved marinade to the wok and stir-fry for 3–4 minutes, until the marinade has reduced slightly to a syrupy glaze and coats the noodles.

6 Toss in the alfalfa sprouts, then remove immediately from the heat. Transfer to warmed serving plates and top with the salmon. Sprinkle with the toasted sesame seeds. Serve immediately.

Energy 392Kcal/1649kJ; Protein 19.3g; Carbohydrate 43.6g, of which sugars 4g; Fat 15.0g, of which saturates 2.9g; Cholesterol 45mg; Calcium 50mg; Fibre 2g; Sodium 664mg.

SIMMERED SQUID AND DAIKON ★

*THE SECRET OF HOW TO MAKE THIS DISH USED TO BE HANDED DOWN FROM MOTHER TO DAUGHTER.
IT IS SERVED IN RESTAURANTS THESE DAYS BUT IS EASY TO MAKE AT HOME.*

SERVES 4

INGREDIENTS
    450g/1lb squid, cleaned, body
        and tentacles separated
    900ml/1½ pints/3¾ cups water and
        5ml/1 tsp instant dashi powder
    about 1kg/2¼lb daikon
        (mooli), peeled
    60ml/4 tbsp shoyu
    45ml/3 tbsp sake or dry sherry
    15ml/1 tbsp caster (superfine) sugar
    30ml/2 tbsp mirin
    grated rind of ½ lime, to garnish

COOK'S TIP
When buying daikon look for one that is
at least 7.5cm/3in in diameter, with a
shiny, undamaged skin, and that sounds
dense and heavy when you pat it.

1 Separate the two triangular flaps from
the body of the squid, then cut the body
into 1cm/½in thick rings. Cut the
triangular flaps into 1cm/½in strips.

2 Cut off and discard 2.5cm/1in from
the thin end of the tentacles and chop
them into 4cm/1½in lengths. Make the
dashi stock.

3 Cut the daikon into 3cm/1¼in thick
rounds and shave off the edges with a
sharp knife. Plunge the slices into cold
water. Drain just before cooking.

4 Put the daikon and squid in a heavy
pan and pour on the stock. Bring to the
boil, and cook for 5 minutes, skimming
constantly. Reduce the heat and add the
shoyu, sake or sherry, sugar and mirin.

5 Cover the surface with a circle of
baking parchment cut 2.5cm/1in
smaller than the lid of the pan, and
simmer for 45 minutes, shaking the pan
occasionally. The liquid will reduce by
almost half.

6 Leave to stand for 5 minutes and
serve in small bowls with the lime rind.

Energy 153Kcal/643kJ; Protein 19.6g; Carbohydrate 11.8g, of which sugars 10.3g; Fat 2.4g, of which saturates 0.7g; Cholesterol 253mg; Calcium 67mg; Fibre 2.3g; Sodium 1221mg.

SALMON TERIYAKI ★★★

*FOR THIS POPULAR DISH A SWEET SAUCE IS USED FOR MARINATING AS WELL AS FOR GLAZING THE FISH
AND VEGETABLES, GIVING THEM A SHINY GLOSS.*

SERVES 4

INGREDIENTS
    4 small salmon fillets with skin, each
        weighing about 115g/4oz
    50g/2oz/¼ cup beansprouts, washed
    50g/2oz mangetouts (snow peas),
        ends trimmed
    20g/¾oz carrot, cut into thin strips
    salt

For the teriyaki sauce
    45ml/3 tbsp shoyu
    45ml/3 tbsp sake
    45ml/3 tbsp mirin
    15ml/1 tbsp plus 10ml/2 tsp
        caster (superfine) sugar

1 Mix all the ingredients for the teriyaki
sauce except for the 10ml/2 tsp sugar,
in a pan. Heat to dissolve the sugar.
Remove and cool for 1 hour.

2 Place the salmon fillets in a shallow
glass or china dish and pour over the
teriyaki sauce. Leave to marinate for
30 minutes.

3 Meanwhile, blanch the vegetables
in lightly salted water. First add the
beansprouts, then after 1 minute,
the mangetouts. Leave for 1 minute
again, and then add the thin carrot
strips. Remove the pan from the heat
after 1 minute, then drain the
vegetables and keep warm.

4 Preheat the grill (broiler) to medium.
Take the salmon fillet out of the sauce
and pat dry with kitchen paper. Reserve
the sauce.

5 Lightly oil a grill (broiling) pan. Grill
(broil) the salmon for 6 minutes, turning
once, until golden on both sides.

6 Pour the sauce into the pan. Add the
remaining sugar and heat until dissolved.
Remove from the heat. Brush the
salmon with the sauce, then grill until
the surface of the fish bubbles. Turn
over and repeat on the other side.

7 Heap the vegetables on to four heated
serving plates. Place the salmon on top
and spoon over the rest of the sauce.
Serve immediately.

Energy 239Kcal/995kJ; Protein 24.8g; Carbohydrate 2.1g, of which sugars 1.7g; Fat 13.3g, of which saturates 2.3g; Cholesterol 58mg; Calcium 93mg; Fibre 0.3g; Sodium 323mg.

FRESH TUNA SHIITAKE TERIYAKI ★★

TUNA IS A ROBUST FISH, WELL ABLE TO COPE WITH THE STRONG FLAVOURS IN THE TERIYAKI SAUCE.
SHIITAKE MUSHROOMS ARE AN INSPIRED ADDITION, TURNING A SIMPLE DISH INTO A RARE TREAT.

SERVES 4

INGREDIENTS

    4 x 175g/6oz fresh tuna or yellowfin
      tail steaks
    175g/6oz shiitake mushrooms, sliced
    225g/8oz daikon (mooli), peeled
    2 large carrots, peeled
    salt
    boiled rice, to serve
For the teriyaki sauce
    45ml/3 tbsp shoyu
    45ml/3 tbsp sake
    45ml/3 tbsp mirin
    15ml/1 tbsp plus 10ml/2 tsp
      caster (superfine) sugar

1 Season the tuna steaks with a
sprinkling of salt, then set aside for
20 minutes. Meanwhile, make the
teriyaki sauce by mixing the shoyu,
sake, mirin and sugar in a small pan.
Heat gently, stirring until the sugar has
dissolved. Pour into a bowl and cool.

2 Mix together the fish and sliced
mushrooms, pour the teriyaki sauce
over them and set aside to marinate for
a further 20–30 minutes, or longer if
you have the time.

3 Drain the tuna steaks, reserving
the marinade and mushrooms. Cook
the tuna under a preheated moderate
grill (broiler) or on a barbecue for
8 minutes, turning once.

4 Transfer the sliced mushrooms and
the marinade to a stainless-steel pan
and simmer the mixture over a medium
heat for 3–4 minutes.

5 Slice the daikon and carrots thinly,
then shred finely with a chopping knife.
Arrange in heaps on four serving plates
and add the fish.

6 Spoon over the mushrooms and the
sauce. Serve with plain boiled rice.

VARIATION
If you don't like – or have trouble
locating – daikon, use celeriac instead,
but make sure you toss it in lemon juice
to prevent discoloration.

Energy 277Kcal/1165kJ; Protein 43.4g; Carbohydrate 7.2g, of which sugars 6.7g; Fat 8.5g, of which saturates 2.2g; Cholesterol 49mg; Calcium 57mg; Fibre 2g; Sodium 1883mg.

STEAMED FISH WITH CHILLI SAUCE ★

STEAMING IS ONE OF THE BEST METHODS OF COOKING FISH WITHOUT ADDITIONAL FAT. BY LEAVING THE FISH WHOLE AND ON THE BONE, ALL THE DELICIOUS FLAVOUR AND MOISTNESS IS RETAINED.

SERVES 6

INGREDIENTS

1 large or 2 medium firm fish such as bass or grouper, scaled and cleaned
a fresh banana leaf or large piece of foil
30ml/2 tbsp rice wine
3 fresh red chillies, seeded and finely sliced
2 garlic cloves, finely chopped
2cm/¾in piece of fresh root ginger, finely shredded
2 lemon grass stalks, crushed and finely chopped
2 spring onions (scallions), chopped
30ml/2 tbsp Thai fish sauce
juice of 1 lime

For the chilli sauce

8–10 fresh red chillies, seeded and chopped
4 garlic cloves, chopped
60ml/4 tbsp Thai fish sauce
15ml/1 tbsp sugar
75ml/5 tbsp lime juice

2 Place the fish on the banana leaf or foil. Mix the rice wine, sliced chillies, garlic, ginger, lemon grass and spring onions in a bowl. Stir in the fish sauce and lime juice and spread over the fish.

3 Place a small upturned plate in the bottom of a wok or large frying pan, and add about 5cm/2in boiling water. Lay the banana leaf or foil with the fish on top on the plate and cover with a lid. Steam for 10–15 minutes or until the fish is fully cooked.

4 Meanwhile, put all the chilli sauce ingredients in a food processor and process until smooth. You may need to add a little cold water.

5 Serve the fish hot, on the banana leaf if you like, with the sweet chilli sauce to spoon over the top.

1 Rinse the fish under cold running water. Pat dry with kitchen paper. With a sharp knife, slash the skin of the fish a few times on both sides.

COOK'S TIP
Leaving the fish whole and on the bone conserves the flavour and keeps the flesh moist, but you can cook this dish in individual parcels if you prefer.

Energy 134Kcal/563kJ; Protein 22.8g; Carbohydrate 4g, of which sugars 3.9g; Fat 3g, of which saturates 0.5g; Cholesterol 93mg; Calcium 156mg; Fibre 0.3g; Sodium 260mg.

CHINESE-STYLE STEAMED FISH ★★

THIS IS A CLASSIC CHINESE WAY OF COOKING WHOLE FISH, WITH GARLIC, SPRING ONIONS, GINGER AND BLACK BEANS. THE FISH MAKES A SPLENDID CENTREPIECE FOR A CHINESE MEAL.

SERVES 4–6

INGREDIENTS

2 sea bass, grey mullet or trout,
  each weighing about 675–800g/
  1½–1¾lb, cleaned
25ml/1½ tbsp salted black beans
2.5ml/½ tsp sugar
30ml/2 tbsp finely shredded
  fresh root ginger
4 garlic cloves, thinly sliced
30ml/2 tbsp Chinese rice wine
  or dry sherry
30ml/2 tbsp light soy sauce
4–6 spring onions (scallions), finely
  shredded or sliced diagonally
10ml/2 tsp sesame oil

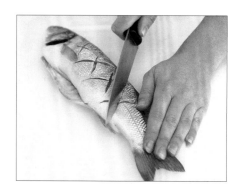

1 Wash the fish inside and out under cold running water, then pat them dry on kitchen paper. Using a sharp knife, slash three or four deep cross shapes on each side of each fish, taking care not to cut right through.

2 Mash half the black beans with the sugar in a small bowl and then stir in the remaining whole beans.

3 Place a little ginger and garlic inside the cavity of each fish and then lay them on a plate or dish that will fit inside a large steamer.

4 Rub the bean mixture into the fish, especially into the slashes, then sprinkle the remaining ginger and garlic over the top.

5 Cover the fish with clear film (plastic wrap) and chill for 30 minutes.

6 Place the steamer over a pan of simmering water. Sprinkle the rice wine or sherry and half the soy sauce over the fish, place them in the steamer and steam them for 15–20 minutes, or until just cooked.

7 Sprinkle the steamed fish with the remaining soy sauce and the sesame oil, then scatter with the spring onions. Serve immediately.

Energy 260Kcal/1095kJ; Protein 41.9g; Carbohydrate 1.5g, of which sugars 1g; Fat 9.1g, of which saturates 2g; Cholesterol 171mg; Calcium 69mg; Fibre 0.2g; Sodium 512mg.

FISH CAKES AND VEGETABLES ★★★

THIS IS A SIMPLE DISH BUT YOU WILL NEED TO MAKE THE FISH BALLS AND CAKES OR BUY THEM FROM AN ASIAN FOOD STORE. YOU WILL BE ABLE TO GET THE OTHER UNUSUAL INGREDIENTS THERE TOO.

SERVES 4

INGREDIENTS

  30 × 7.5cm/12 × 3in *dashi-konbu*
  675g/1½lb daikon (mooli), peeled
    and cut into 4cm/1½in lengths
  12–20 ready-made fish balls and
    cakes (4 of each kind)
  1 *konnyaku*
  1 piece *atsu-age*
  8 small shiitake mushrooms,
    stems removed
  4 medium potatoes, unpeeled,
    soaked in a bowl of water (to
    remove some of the starch)
  4 hard-boiled eggs, unshelled
  285g/10½oz packet tofu block,
    cut into 8 cubes
  English (hot) mustard, to serve
For the soup stock
  1.5 litres/2¼ pints/6½ cups
    water and 10ml/2 tsp instant
    dashi powder
  75ml/5 tbsp sake
  15ml/1 tbsp salt
  40ml/8 tsp shoyu

1 Wrap the *dashi-konbu* in a wet, clean dish towel and leave for 5 minutes, or until it is soft enough to bend easily by hand without breaking.

2 Snip the softened *dashi-konbu* in half crossways with a pair of scissors, then cut each piece lengthways into four ribbons. Tie a loose knot in the centre of each "ribbon".

COOK'S TIP
Konnyaku is a dense, gelatinous cake made from a yam-like plant.

3 Slightly shave the edges of each of the pieces of daikon. Place all the fish balls and cakes, *konnyaku* and *atsu-age* in a large pan. Add enough hot water to cover the ingredients, then drain.

4 Cut the *konnyaku* in quarters, then cut each quarter in half diagonally to make eight triangles. Cut large fish cakes in half. Put two shiitake mushrooms on to each of four bamboo skewers.

5 Mix all the ingredients for the soup stock, but only fill the pot or casserole by two-thirds. Add the daikon and potatoes and bring to the boil. Add the hard-boiled eggs.

6 Reduce the heat to low and simmer for an hour, uncovered, skimming off any scum occasionally.

7 Increase the heat to medium and add the other ingredients except for the mustard. Cover and cook for 30 minutes. Transfer to a casserole or pot that can be kept hot at the table on a hot tray or burner. Serve with the mustard.

VARIATIONS
Prawn Balls Combine 200g/7oz raw peeled small prawns (shrimp), 50g/2oz pork fat, 15ml/1 tbsp grated ginger juice, 1 egg white, 15ml/1 tbsp salt and 15ml/1 tbsp cornflour in a food processor, and shape into balls.
Squid and Ginger Balls Blend 200g/7oz chopped squid, 1 egg white, 15ml/1 tbsp cornflour, 10ml/2 tsp grated ginger juice and 15ml/1 tbsp salt in a food processor. Mix with 10ml/2 tsp chopped ginger, and shape into balls.

Energy 370Kcal/1555kJ; Protein 37.2g; Carbohydrate 28.8g, of which sugars 5.8g; Fat 10.4g, of which saturates 2.4g; Cholesterol 237mg; Calcium 452mg; Fibre 3.1g; Sodium 1926mg.

VEGETABLES AND SALMON IN A PARCEL ★★★

IN THIS RECIPE, THE VEGETABLES AND SALMON ARE WRAPPED AND STEAMED WITH SAKE IN THEIR OWN MOISTURE. WHEN YOU OPEN THE PARCEL, YOU'LL FIND A COLOURFUL AUTUMN GARDEN INSIDE.

4 Slice the carrot very thinly, then with a Japanese vegetable cutter or sharp knife, cut out 8–12 maple-leaf or flower shapes. Carefully slice the spring onions in half lengthways with a sharp knife. Trim the mangetouts.

5 Cut four sheets of foil, each about 29 × 21cm/11½ × 8½in wide. Place the long side of one sheet facing towards you. Arrange the salmon and *shimeji* mushrooms in the centre, then place a spring onion diagonally across them. Put two shiitake on top, three to four mangetouts in a fan shape and then sprinkle with a few carrot leaves.

6 Sprinkle the marinade and a good pinch of salt over the top. Fold the two longer sides of the foil together, then fold the shorter sides to seal. Repeat to make four parcels.

7 Place the parcels on a baking sheet and bake for 15–20 minutes in the middle of the preheated oven. When the foil has expanded into a balloon, the dish is ready to serve. Serve the parcels unopened with a little extra shoyu, if required.

SERVES 4

INGREDIENTS
  450g/1lb salmon fillet, skinned
  30ml/2 tbsp sake or dry sherry
  15ml/1 tbsp shoyu, plus extra to
    serve (optional)
  about 250g/9oz/3 cups fresh
    shimeji mushrooms
  8 fresh shiitake mushrooms
  2.5cm/1in carrot
  2 spring onions (scallions)
  115g/4oz mangetouts (snow peas)
  salt

1 Cut the salmon into bitesize pieces. Marinate in the sake and shoyu for about 15 minutes, then drain and reserve the marinade. Preheat the oven to 190°C/375°F/Gas 5.

2 Clean the *shimeji* mushrooms and chop off the hard root. Remove and discard the stems from the shiitake.

3 Carve a shallow slit on the top of each shiitake with a sharp knife inserted at a slant. Repeat from the other side to cut out a notch about 4cm/1½in long, then rotate the shiitake 90° and carefully carve another notch to make a small white cross in the brown top.

Energy 231Kcal/964kJ; Protein 25.2g; Carbohydrate 3.9g, of which sugars 3.3g; Fat 12.9g, of which saturates 2.2g; Cholesterol 56mg; Calcium 49mg; Fibre 2g; Sodium 328mg.

STEAMED RED SNAPPER ★

ORIGINALLY, THIS ELEGANT DISH FEATURED A WHOLE RED SNAPPER WRAPPED IN LAYERED JAPANESE HANDMADE PAPER SOAKED IN SAKE AND TIED WITH RIBBONS. THIS VERSION IS A LITTLE EASIER.

SERVES 4

INGREDIENTS

4 small red snapper fillets, no
greater than 18 × 6cm/7 × 2½in,
or whole snapper, 20cm/8in long,
gutted but with head, tail and
fins intact
1 lime
8 asparagus spears, hard
ends snapped off
4 spring onions (scallions)
60ml/4 tbsp sake
5ml/1 tsp shoyu (optional)
salt

1 Sprinkle the red snapper fillets with salt on both sides and leave in the refrigerator for 20 minutes.

2 Preheat the oven to 180°C/350°F/ Gas 4. Cut the lime in half. Grate one half and thinly slice the other.

3 To make the parcels, lay baking parchment measuring 38 × 30cm/ 15 × 12in on a work surface. Use two pieces for extra strength. Fold up one-third of the paper and turn back 1cm/½in from one end to make a flap.

4 Fold 1cm/½in in from the other end to make another flap. Fold the top edge down to fold over the first flap. Interlock the two flaps to form a long rectangle.

VARIATION
You could use any firm fish you like, such as salmon, trout, tuna or swordfish, in place of the red snapper in this quick and easy recipe.

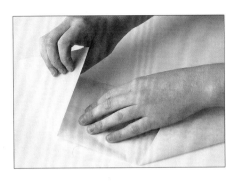

5 At each end, fold the top corners down diagonally, then fold the bottom corners up to meet the opposite folded edge to make a triangle. Press flat with your palm. Repeat the process to make four parcels.

6 Cut 2.5cm/1in from the tip of the asparagus, and slice in half lengthways. Slice the asparagus stems and spring onions diagonally into thin ovals. Par-boil the tips for 1 minute in a small pan of lightly salted water and drain. Set aside.

7 Open the paper parcels. Place the asparagus slices and the spring onions inside. Sprinkle with salt and place the fish on top. Add more salt and some sake, then sprinkle in the lime rind. Refold the parcels.

8 Pour hot water from a kettle into a deep roasting pan fitted with a wire rack to 1cm/½in below the rack. Place the parcels on the rack. Cook in the centre of the preheated oven for 20 minutes. Check that the fish is cooked by carefully unfolding a parcel from one triangular side. The fish should have changed from translucent to white.

9 Transfer the parcels on to individual plates. Unfold both triangular ends on the plate and lift open the middle a little. Insert a thin slice of lime and place two asparagus tips on top. Serve immediately, asking the guests to open their own parcels. Add a little shoyu, if you like.

Energy 112Kcal/471kJ; Protein 20.6g; Carbohydrate 1g, of which sugars 0.9g; Fat 1.5g, of which saturates 0.3g; Cholesterol 37mg; Calcium 52mg; Fibre 0.6g; Sodium 79mg.

MARINATED AND GRILLED SWORDFISH ★★

THERE'S A TENDENCY FOR SWORDFISH TO TASTE RATHER DRY, SO FOR THIS RECIPE IT IS MARINATED IN A MISO MIXTURE WHICH KEEPS IT SUCCULENT EVEN WHEN COOKED ON THE BARBECUE.

SERVES 4

INGREDIENTS
  4 × 175g/6oz swordfish steaks
  2.5ml/½ tsp salt
  300g/11oz *shiro miso*
  45ml/3 tbsp sake
For the asparagus
  25ml/1½ tbsp shoyu
  25ml/1½ tbsp sake or
    dry sherry
  8 asparagus spears, the hard ends
    snapped off, each spear cut
    into three

1 Place the swordfish in a shallow dish. Sprinkle evenly with the salt on both sides and leave for 2 hours. Drain and wipe the fish with kitchen paper.

2 Mix the miso and sake, then spread half across the bottom of the cleaned dish. Cover with a sheet of muslin or cheesecloth the size of a dish towel, folded in half, then open the fold.

3 Place the swordfish, side by side, on top, and cover with the muslin. Spread the rest of the miso mixture on the muslin. Make sure the muslin is touching the fish. Marinate for 2 days in the coolest part of the refrigerator.

4 Preheat the grill (broiler) to medium. Oil the wire rack and grill (broil) the fish slowly for about 8 minutes on each side, turning every 2 minutes. If the steaks are thin, check them frequently to see if they are ready.

5 Mix the shoyu and sake in a bowl. Grill the asparagus for 2 minutes on each side, then dip into the mixture. Return to the grill for 2 minutes more on each side. Dip in the sauce again and set aside.

6 Serve the fish hot on four individual serving plates. Garnish with the drained, grilled asparagus.

Energy 203Kcal/851kJ; Protein 32g; Carbohydrate 0.7g, of which sugars 0.6g; Fat 7.3g, of which saturates 1.6g; Cholesterol 72mg; Calcium 12mg; Fibre 0.2g; Sodium 495mg.

SWORDFISH WITH CITRUS DRESSING ★★★

FOR THIS BEAUTIFULLY PRESENTED SALAD, FRESH FISH IS SEARED OR MARINATED AND SLICED THINLY, THEN SERVED WITH SALAD LEAVES AND VEGETABLES.

SERVES 4

INGREDIENTS
  75g/3oz daikon (mooli), peeled
  50g/2oz carrot, peeled
  1 cucumber
  10ml/2 tsp vegetable oil
  300g/11oz skinned fresh swordfish
    steak, cut against the grain
  2 cartons mustard and cress
    (fine curled cress)
  15ml/1 tbsp toasted sesame seeds
For the dressing
  105ml/7 tbsp shoyu
  105ml/7 tbsp water and 5ml/1 tsp
    instant dashi powder
  30ml/2 tbsp toasted sesame oil
  juice of ½ lime
  rind of ½ lime, shredded into
    thin strips

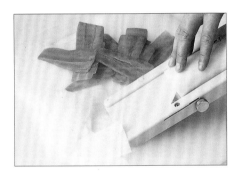

1 Make the vegetable garnishes first. Use a very sharp knife, mandoline or vegetable slicer with a julienne blade to make very thin (about 4cm/1½in long) strands of daikon, carrot and cucumber.

2 Soak the daikon and carrot in ice-cold water for 5 minutes, then drain well and keep in the refrigerator.

3 Mix together all the ingredients for the dressing and stir well, then chill.

4 Heat the oil in a small frying pan until smoking hot. Sear the fish for 30 seconds on all sides.

5 Plunge the fish into cold water to stop the cooking. Dry on kitchen paper and wipe off as much oil as possible.

6 Cut the swordfish steak in half lengthways before slicing it into 5mm/¼in thick pieces in the other direction, against the grain.

7 Arrange the fish slices into a ring on individual plates. Mix the vegetable strands, mustard and cress (fine curled cress) and sesame seeds.

8 Shape the vegetable strands into a sphere. Gently place it on the swordfish. Pour the dressing around the plate's edge and serve immediately.

COOK'S TIP
If you cannot locate mustard and cress or fine curled cress, serve on a pile of wild rocket (arugula) leaves. You could also add grapefruit segments.

Energy 182Kcal/758kJ; Protein 15.2g; Carbohydrate 2.4g, of which sugars 2.3g; Fat 12.5g, of which saturates 2g; Cholesterol 31mg; Calcium 63mg; Fibre 1.1g; Sodium 645mg.

STEAMED FISH <u>WITH</u> FIVE WILLOW SAUCE ★★

A FISH KETTLE WILL COME IN USEFUL FOR THIS RECIPE. CARP IS TRADITIONALLY USED, BUT ANY CHUNKY FISH THAT CAN BE COOKED WHOLE CAN BE GIVEN THIS TREATMENT.

SERVES 4

INGREDIENTS

    1–2 carp or similar whole fish, total
       weight about 1kg/2¼lb, cleaned
       and scaled
    2.5cm/1in piece fresh root ginger,
       peeled and thinly sliced
    4 spring onions (scallions), cut
       into thin strips
    2.5ml/½ tsp salt

For the five willow sauce

    375g/13oz jar *chow chow* (Chinese
       sweet mixed pickles)
    300ml/½ pint/1¼ cups water
    30ml/2 tbsp rice vinegar
    25ml/1½ tbsp sugar
    25ml/1½ tbsp
       cornflour (cornstarch)
    15ml/1 tbsp light soy sauce
    15ml/1 tbsp rice wine or
       medium-dry sherry
    1 small green (bell) pepper,
       seeded and diced
    1 carrot, peeled and cut
       into matchsticks
    1 tomato, peeled, seeded
       and diced

1 Rinse the fish under running cold water inside and out. Pat dry with kitchen paper.

2 Thoroughly mix the ginger, spring onions and salt in a small bowl, then tuck the mixture into the body cavity of each fish.

3 Create a support for each fish by folding one or two broad strips of foil to make a long wide strip.

4 Place the fish on the foil and then lift the fish on to the trivet. Lower the trivet into the fish kettle and tuck the ends of the foil over the fish.

5 Pour boiling water into the fish kettle to a depth of 2.5cm/1in. Bring to a rolling boil, then lower the heat and cook until the flesh flakes, topping with boiling water as necessary. Allow about 20–25 minutes for a 1kg/2¼ lb fish; 15–20 minutes for a 675g/1½ lb fish.

6 Meanwhile, prepare the sauce. Tip the *chow chow* into a sieve (strainer) placed over a bowl. Reserve the liquid. Cut each of the pickles in half. Pour 250ml/8fl oz/ 1 cup of the water into a pan and bring to the boil. Add the vinegar and sugar and stir until dissolved.

COOK'S TIP
If using one large fish that is too long to fit in a fish kettle, cut it in half and cook it on a rack placed over a large roasting tin. Pour in a similar quantity of boiling water as for the fish kettle, cover with foil and cook on top of the stove. Reassemble the halved fish before coating it with the sauce.

7 In a small bowl, mix the cornflour to a paste with the remaining water. Stir in the soy sauce and rice wine or sherry and combine thoroughly.

8 Add the cornflour mixture to the sauce and bring to the boil, stirring until it thickens and becomes quite glossy. Add all the vegetables, the chopped pickles and the pickle liquid and cook over a gentle heat for 2 minutes.

9 Using the foil strips as a support, carefully transfer the cooked fish to a platter, then ease the foil away. Spoon the warm sauce over the fish and serve.

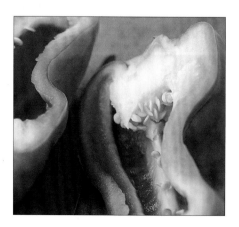

Energy 231Kcal/973kJ; Protein 25.8g; Carbohydrate 20.3g, of which sugars 13g; Fat 5.8g, of which saturates 0.1g; Cholesterol 0mg; Calcium 126mg; Fibre 2.3g; Sodium 912mg.

TEPPAN YAKI ★★

THIS IS NOT JUST A RECIPE, IT IS MORE OF AN EXPERIENCE. A FEAST OF FLAVOURS GIVES EVERY GUEST THE CHANCE TO GRILL HIS OR HER OWN FOOD AND DIP IT INTO ANY OF THE SAUCES PROVIDED.

SERVES 4

INGREDIENTS
275g/10oz monkfish tail
4 large scallops, cleaned and
  corals separated
250g/9oz squid body, cleaned
  and skinned
12 raw king or tiger prawns
  (jumbo shrimp), shells and heads
  removed, tails intact
115g/4oz/½ cup beansprouts, washed
1 red (bell) pepper, seeded and cut
  into 2.5cm/1in wide strips
8 fresh shiitake mushrooms,
  stems removed
1 red onion, cut into 5mm/¼in
  thick rounds
1 courgette (zucchini), cut into
  1cm/½in thick rounds
3 garlic cloves, thinly
  sliced lengthways
15ml/1 tbsp vegetable oil,
  for frying
Sauce A, radish and chilli sauce
8 radishes, finely grated
1 dried chilli, seeded and crushed
15ml/1 tbsp toasted sesame oil
½ onion, finely chopped
90ml/6 tbsp shoyu
30ml/2 tbsp caster
  (superfine) sugar
15ml/1 tbsp toasted
  sesame seeds
juice of ½ orange or 30ml/2 tbsp
  unsweetened orange juice
Sauce B, wasabi mayonnaise
60ml/4 tbsp reduced-fat mayonnaise
15ml/1 tbsp wasabi paste
5ml/1 tsp shoyu
Sauce C, lime and soy sauce
juice of 1 lime
grated rind and juice of 1 lime
20ml/4 tsp sake
90ml/6 tbsp shoyu
1 bunch chives, finely chopped

1 Sauce A In a small bowl, mix the grated radish, with its juice and with the chilli until it is thoroughly combined. Heat the sesame oil in a frying pan and fry the onion until soft.

2 Pour in the shoyu and add the sugar and sesame seeds, removing the pan from the heat just as it starts to boil.

3 Tip the mixture over the radish into the bowl and add the orange juice. Stir well and leave to cool.

4 Sauce B and C Mix the ingredients separately in small bowls, cover with clear film (plastic wrap) and set aside.

5 Cut the monkfish tail into 5mm/¼in slices. Halve the scallops horizontally.

6 With a small sharp knife, make neat shallow criss-cross slits in the skinned side of the squid. Slice into 2.5 × 4cm/1 × 1½in pieces.

7 Place all the seafood on half of a serving platter, and arrange all the prepared vegetables (apart from the garlic) on the other half. Divide sauces A and C among eight small dishes; these are for dipping. Put the wasabi mayonnaise in a small bowl with a teaspoon. Prepare serving plates as well.

8 Heat the griddle at the table and lightly oil it with a brush or kitchen paper. First, fry the garlic slices until crisp and golden. Remove the garlic chips to a small dish to mix with any sauces you like.

9 Guests cook ingredients on the griddle and either dip them into the sauces or eat them with the wasabi mayonnaise.

Energy 292Kcal/1232kJ; Protein 43.2g; Carbohydrate 9.6g, of which sugars 5.6g; Fat 8.8g, of which saturates 1.6g; Cholesterol 274mg; Calcium 87mg; Fibre 1.8g; Sodium 913mg.

GREY MULLET <u>WITH</u> PORK ★★

THIS ASIAN ANSWER TO SURF AND TURF COMBINATION MAKES A SPECTACULAR MAIN DISH AND TAKES VERY LITTLE EFFORT. THERE'S ONLY A SMALL AMOUNT OF PORK SO FAT LEVELS ARE NOT TOO HIGH.

SERVES 4

INGREDIENTS

   1 grey mullet, red snapper
     or ponpano, about 900g/2lb,
     gutted and cleaned
   50g/2oz lean pork
   3 dried Chinese mushrooms, soaked
     in hot water until soft
   2.5ml/½ tsp cornflour (cornstarch)
   30ml/2 tbsp light soy sauce
   15ml/1 tbsp vegetable oil
   15ml/1 tbsp finely shredded fresh
     root ginger
   15ml/1 tbsp shredded spring
     onion (scallions)
   salt and ground black pepper
   rice, to serve
   sliced spring onion (scallion),
     to garnish

1 Make four diagonal cuts on either side of the fish and rub with a little salt; place the fish on a large shallow heatproof serving dish.

2 Cut the pork into thin strips. Place in a bowl. Drain the mushrooms, remove the stems and slice the caps thinly.

3 Add the mushrooms to the pork, with the cornflour and half the soy sauce. Stir in 5ml/1 tsp of the oil and plenty of black pepper. Arrange the pork mixture along the length of the fish. Sprinkle the ginger shreds over the top.

COOK'S TIP
If the fish is too big to fit into the steamer whole, cut the fish in half for cooking, then reassemble it later.

4 Set a trivet in a roasting pan that is large enough to hold the serving dish in which the pork stands.

5 Put the dish on the trivet and place the roasting pan on the stovetop. Pour boiling water into the roasting pan to a depth of about 5cm/2in. Cover and steam the fish.

6 Remove the foil and test the fish by pressing the flesh gently. If it comes away from the bone with a slight resistance, then the fish is cooked.

7 Lift the dish out of the pan and carefully pour away any excess liquid.

8 Heat the remaining oil in a small pan. Fry the shredded spring onion for a few seconds, then pour it over the fish, taking care as it will splatter. Drizzle over the remaining soy sauce, garnish with spring onion and serve with rice.

Energy 228Kcal/960kJ; Protein 34.7g; Carbohydrate 0.7g, of which sugars 0.6g; Fat 9.8g, of which saturates 2.3g; Cholesterol 62mg; Calcium 46mg; Fibre 0g; Sodium 647mg.

CHICKEN AND DUCK

*Poultry is popular in China and Far East Asia. In China,
where thrift is highly prized, cooks tend to buy whole birds,
whereas in Japan it is the breast fillets that are preferred. From
a low-fat perspective, chicken is a more sensible choice than
duck. Remove the skin and any obvious fat and use a
low-fat cooking method like steaming, stir-frying or cooking
in vegetable stock. Chicken Teriyaki and Kabocha Squash
with Chicken are excellent options.*

SICHUAN CHICKEN WITH KUNG PO SAUCE ★★★

ONE OF THE BEST WAYS OF ADDING FLAVOUR TO LOW-FAT DISHES IS BY SKILFUL USE OF SPICES, SOMETHING FOR WHICH SICHUAN COOKING IS FAMOUS. THIS IS A POPULAR CHICKEN RECIPE.

SERVES 4

INGREDIENTS

3 skinless chicken breast fillets,
   about 500g/1¼lb
1 egg white
10ml/2 tsp cornflour (cornstarch)
2.5ml/½ tsp salt
30ml/2 tbsp yellow salted beans
15ml/1 tbsp hoisin sauce
5ml/1 tsp light brown sugar
15ml/1 tbsp rice wine or
   medium-dry sherry
15ml/1 tbsp wine vinegar
4 garlic cloves, crushed
150ml/¼ pint/⅔ cup chicken stock
30ml/2 tbsp vegetable oil
2–3 dried chillies, broken into
   small pieces
50g/2oz/2½ cups roasted cashew nuts
fresh coriander (cilantro), to garnish

1 Cut the chicken into neat pieces. Lightly whisk the egg white in a dish, whisk in the cornflour and salt, then add the chicken and stir until coated.

COOK'S TIP
Peanuts are the classic ingredient in this dish, but cashew nuts have an even better flavour and have become popular both in home cooking and in restaurants.

2 In a separate bowl, mash the beans with the back of a spoon. Stir in the hoisin sauce, brown sugar, rice wine or sherry, vinegar, garlic and stock.

3 Heat a wok, add the oil and when the oil is very hot, add the chicken and fry, turning constantly, for about 1 minute.

4 Add the chillies and continue to stir-fry for a further minute or until the chicken is tender.

5 Pour in the bean sauce mixture. Bring to the boil and then stir in the cashew nuts.

6 Spoon into a heated serving dish and garnish with fresh coriander leaves.

Energy 270Kcal/1131kJ; Protein 33.6g; Carbohydrate 4.3g, of which sugars 2.6g; Fat 13.2g, of which saturates 2.3g; Cholesterol 88mg; Calcium 14mg; Fibre 0.4g; Sodium 928mg.

BANG BANG CHICKEN ★★

DESPITE HAVING A RICH SAUCE BASED ON TOASTED SESAME PASTE, THIS CHICKEN DISH IS RELATIVELY LOW IN FAT, WITH SATURATED FAT LEVELS THAT ARE WELL WITHIN ACCEPTABLE LIMITS.

SERVES 4

INGREDIENTS
  3 skinless boneless chicken breast
    fillets, about 450g/1lb
  1 garlic clove, crushed
  2.5ml/½ tsp black peppercorns
  1 small onion, halved
  1 large cucumber
  salt and ground black pepper
For the sauce
  45ml/3 tbsp toasted sesame paste
  15ml/1 tbsp light soy sauce
  15ml/1 tbsp wine vinegar
  2 spring onions (scallions),
    finely chopped
  2 garlic cloves, crushed
  5cm/2½in fresh root ginger, peeled
    and cut into matchsticks
  15ml/1 tbsp Sichuan peppercorns,
    dry fried and crushed
  5ml/1 tsp light brown sugar
  15ml/1 tbsp chilli sauce, to serve

1 Place the chicken fillets in a pan. Just cover with water, add the garlic, peppercorns and onion and bring the water to the boil. Skim off any scum as it rises to the surface, stir in salt and pepper to taste, then cover the pan.

2 Cook for 25 minutes or until the chicken is just tender. Drain, reserving the stock in a bowl.

3 Make the sauce by mixing the toasted sesame paste with 45ml/3 tbsp of the chicken stock. Add the soy sauce, vinegar, spring onions, garlic, ginger and crushed peppercorns to the sesame mixture. Stir in sugar to taste.

4 Peel the cucumber, then cut in half lengthways and remove the seeds. Cut into batons. Spread on a platter. Cut the chicken fillets into pieces of about the same size as the cucumber and pile them on top. Pour over the sesame sauce, sprinkle over the chilli sauce and serve.

Energy 200Kcal/838kJ; Protein 29.5g; Carbohydrate 2.8g, of which sugars 2.4g; Fat 7.9g, of which saturates 1.3g; Cholesterol 79mg; Calcium 89mg; Fibre 1.2g; Sodium 338mg.

CHICKEN WITH MIXED VEGETABLES ★

FAR EAST ASIAN COOKS ARE EXPERTS IN MAKING DELICIOUS DISHES FROM A RELATIVELY SMALL AMOUNT OF MEAT AND A LOT OF VEGETABLES. GOOD NEWS FOR ANYONE TRYING TO EAT LESS FAT.

2 Bring the stock to the boil in a pan. Add the chicken fillets and cook for 12 minutes, or until tender. Drain and slice, reserving 75ml/5 tbsp of the chicken stock.

3 Heat the remaining oil in a non-stick frying pan or wok, add all the vegetables and stir-fry for 2 minutes. Stir in the sherry, oyster sauce, caster sugar and reserved stock. Add the chicken to the pan and cook for 2 minutes more.

4 Mix the cornflour to a paste with the water. Add the mixture to the pan and cook, stirring, until the sauce thickens slightly. Season to taste with salt and pepper and serve immediately.

SERVES 4

INGREDIENTS
  350g/12oz skinless chicken
    breast fillets
  20ml/4 tsp vegetable oil
  300ml/½ pint/1¼ cups
    chicken stock
  75g/3oz/¾ cup drained, canned
    straw mushrooms
  50g/2oz/½ cup sliced, drained,
    canned bamboo shoots
  50g/2oz/⅓ cup drained, canned
    water chestnuts, sliced
  1 small carrot, sliced
  50g/2oz/½ cup mangetouts (snow peas)
  15ml/1 tbsp dry sherry
  15ml/1 tbsp oyster sauce
  5ml/1 tsp caster (superfine) sugar
  5ml/1 tsp cornflour (cornstarch)
  15ml/1 tbsp cold water
  salt and ground white pepper

1 Put the chicken in a shallow bowl. Add 5ml/1 tsp of the oil, 1.5ml/¼ tsp salt and a pinch of pepper. Cover and set aside for 10 minutes in a cool place.

COOK'S TIP
Water chestnuts give a dish great texture as they remain crunchy, no matter how long you cook them for.

Energy 154Kcal/646kJ; Protein 22.2g; Carbohydrate 4.9g, of which sugars 3.4g; Fat 4.3g, of which saturates 0.7g; Cholesterol 61mg; Calcium 17mg; Fibre 1g; Sodium 61mg.

CHICKEN WITH LEMON SAUCE ★

TENDER CHICKEN WITH A REFRESHING CITRUS-BASED SAUCE IS A WINNER IN THE FLAVOUR STAKES, AND WITH JUST 2 GRAMS OF TOTAL FAT, IT ALSO GETS THE PRIZE FOR HELPING TO KEEP HEARTS HEALTHY.

SERVES 4

INGREDIENTS

  4 small skinless chicken
    breast fillets
  5ml/1 tsp sesame oil
  15ml/1 tbsp dry sherry
  1 egg white, lightly beaten
  30ml/2 tbsp cornflour (cornstarch)
  15ml/1 tbsp vegetable oil
  salt and ground white pepper
  chopped coriander (cilantro) leaves,
    spring onions (scallions) and lemon
    wedges, to garnish
For the sauce
  45ml/3 tbsp fresh lemon juice
  30ml/2 tbsp sweetened lime juice
  45ml/3 tbsp caster (superfine) sugar
  10ml/2 tsp cornflour (cornstarch)
  90ml/6 tbsp cold water

1 Arrange the chicken fillets in a single layer in a shallow bowl.

2 Mix the sesame oil with the sherry and add 2.5ml/½ tsp salt and 1.5ml/¼ tsp pepper. Pour the mixture over the chicken, cover with clear film (plastic wrap) and marinate for 15 minutes.

3 Mix the beaten egg white and cornflour in a bowl. Pour over the chicken and turn the fillets with tongs until they are thoroughly coated with the mixture.

4 Heat the vegetable oil in a non-stick frying pan or wok. When the oil is hot, add the chicken fillets and fry for about 15 minutes until they are golden brown on both sides.

5 Meanwhile, make the sauce. Combine all the ingredients in a small pan. Add 1.25ml/¼ tsp salt. Bring to the boil over a low heat, stirring constantly until the sauce is smooth and has thickened slightly.

6 Cut the chicken into pieces and arrange on a warm serving plate. Pour the sauce over so that it coats the pieces evenly, garnish with the coriander leaves, spring onions and lemon wedges and serve.

Energy 208Kcal/881kJ; Protein 24.9g; Carbohydrate 24.1g, of which sugars 10.1g; Fat 2g, of which saturates 0.4g; Cholesterol 70mg; Calcium 13mg; Fibre 0g; Sodium 84mg.

CHICKEN AND MUSHROOM DONBURI ★★

"DONBURI" IS A JAPANESE WORD, MEANING A ONE-DISH MEAL. THIS IS A SIMPLE VERSION, MIXING RICE AND SHIITAKE MUSHROOMS WITH PROTEIN IN THE FORM OF CHICKEN AND TOFU.

SERVES 4

INGREDIENTS

225–275g/8–10oz/generous
  1–1½ cups Japanese rice or
  Thai fragrant rice
30ml/2 tbsp vegetable oil
2 garlic cloves, crushed
2.5cm/1in piece fresh root
  ginger, grated
5 spring onions (scallions),
  diagonally sliced
1 fresh green chilli, seeded and
  finely sliced
3 skinless chicken breast fillets,
  cut into thin strips
150g/5oz tofu, cut into small cubes
115g/4oz/1¾ shiitake mushrooms,
  stems discarded and cups sliced
15ml/1 tbsp sake or dry sherry
30ml/2 tbsp light soy sauce
10ml/2 tsp granulated sugar
400ml/14fl oz/1⅔ cups chicken stock

1 Cook the rice in lightly salted boiling water following the instructions on the packet.

2 While the rice is cooking, heat the oil in a large frying pan. Stir-fry the garlic, ginger, spring onions and chilli for 1–2 minutes until slightly softened.

3 Add the strips of chicken and fry, in batches if necessary, until all the pieces are evenly browned.

4 Transfer the chicken mixture to a plate using a slotted spoon, and add the tofu to the pan.

5 Stir-fry the tofu for a few minutes, then add the mushrooms. Stir-fry for 2–3 minutes over medium heat until the mushrooms are tender.

6 Stir in the sake or sherry, soy sauce and sugar and cook the mixture briskly for 1–2 minutes, stirring all the time.

7 Return the chicken to the pan, toss over the heat for about 2 minutes, then pour in the stock. Stir well and cook over a gentle heat for 5–6 minutes until the sauce is bubbling.

8 Spoon the cooked rice into individual serving bowls and pile the chicken mixture on top, making sure that each portion gets a generous amount of chicken sauce.

COOK'S TIP
Once the rice is cooked, leave it covered until you are ready to serve. It will stay warm for about 30 minutes. Fork through lightly to fluff up just before serving.

Energy 408Kcal/1709kJ; Protein 35.2g; Carbohydrate 46.3g, of which sugars 1.1g; Fat 8.8g, of which saturates 1.2g; Cholesterol 79mg; Calcium 216mg; Fibre 0.5g; Sodium 605mg.

CHICKEN WITH CASHEW NUTS ★

BASED ON A CLASSIC DISH, BUT CONSIDERABLY LOWER IN FAT, THIS VERSION OF CASHEW NUT CHICKEN ADDS CUBES OF BAMBOO SHOOTS, CARROTS AND CUCUMBER TO THE SAVOURY SAUCE.

SERVES 4

INGREDIENTS

    350g/12oz skinless chicken
      breast fillets
    1.5ml/¼ tsp salt
    pinch of ground white pepper
    15ml/1 tbsp dry sherry
    300ml/½ pint/1¼ cups
      chicken stock
    5ml/1 tsp cornflour (cornstarch)
    15ml/1 tbsp light soy sauce
    5ml/1 tsp caster (superfine) sugar
    15ml/1 tbsp vegetable oil
    1 garlic clove, finely chopped
    1 small carrot, cut into cubes
    ½ cucumber, about 75g/3oz, cut
      into 1cm/½in cubes
    50g/2oz/½ cup drained canned
      bamboo shoots, cut into
      1cm/½in cubes
    25g/1oz/¼ cup dry roasted
      cashew nuts
    2.5ml/½ tsp sesame oil
    noodles, to serve

1 Cut the chicken fillets into 2cm/¾in cubes using a sharp knife or a cleaver, if you have one. Place the cubes in a bowl, stir in the salt, pepper and sherry, cover with clear film (plastic wrap) and marinate for 15 minutes.

2 Bring the stock to the boil in a large pan. Add the chicken and cook, stirring, for 3 minutes. Drain, reserving 90ml/ 6 tbsp of the stock, and set aside.

3 Mix the cornflour with the soy sauce and sugar in a small bowl. Stir until it forms a smooth paste.

4 Heat the vegetable oil in a non-stick frying pan until very hot, add the garlic and stir-fry for a few seconds. Add the carrot, cucumber and bamboo shoots and continue to stir-fry over medium heat for 2 minutes.

5 Stir the chicken into the pan with the reserved stock and cornflour paste. Cook, stirring, until the sauce thickens slightly. Add the cashew nuts and sesame oil. Toss to mix thoroughly, then serve with noodles.

Energy 153Kcal/645kJ; Protein 22.9g; Carbohydrate 5.1g, of which sugars 2.8g; Fat 4.3g, of which saturates 0.9g; Cholesterol 61mg; Calcium 14mg; Fibre 0.7g; Sodium 342mg.

SOY SAUCE AND STAR ANISE CHICKEN ★★

THE PUNGENT FLAVOUR OF STAR ANISE PENETRATES THE CHICKEN FILLETS AND ADDS A WONDERFUL
ANISEEDY KICK TO THE SMOKY FLAVOUR OF THE BARBECUE. SERVE WITH A REFRESHING SALAD.

SERVES 4

INGREDIENTS
    4 skinless chicken breast fillets
    2 whole star anise
    30ml/2 tbsp soy sauce
    30ml/2 tbsp vegetable oil
    ground black pepper

1 Lay the skinless chicken breast fillets side by side in a shallow, non-metallic dish and add both pieces of star anise, keeping them whole.

2 Place the soy sauce in a small bowl. Add the oil and whisk together with a fork until the mixture emulsifies. Season to taste with black pepper to make a simple marinade.

3 Pour the marinade over the chicken and stir to coat each breast fillet all over. Cover the dish with clear film (plastic wrap) and chill for up to 8 hours.

4 Prepare a barbecue. Cook the chicken fillets for 8–10 minutes on each side, spooning over the marinade from time to time, until the chicken is cooked through. Serve immediately.

COOK'S TIP
Star anise is the fruit of an evergreen tree native to south-west China. It has a distinct liquorice aroma and is the principal ingredient in five-spice powder. In China, the points of the star are sometimes snapped off and sucked as a breath freshener.

Energy 210Kcal/884kJ; Protein 36.1g; Carbohydrate 0.3g, of which sugars 0.3g; Fat 7.2g, of which saturates 1.2g; Cholesterol 105mg; Calcium 8mg; Fibre 0g; Sodium 357mg.

CHICKEN TERIYAKI ★

When you are short of time, this is the perfect recipe. It takes less than half an hour, including marinating the chicken, and has less fat than many alternative light meals.

SERVES 4

INGREDIENTS
    450g/1lb skinless chicken
      breast fillets
    orange segments and mustard
      and cress (fine curled cress),
      to garnish
For the marinade
    5ml/1 tsp sugar
    15ml/1 tbsp rice wine
    15ml/1 tbsp dry sherry
    30ml/2 tbsp dark
      soy sauce
    rind of 1 orange,
      finely grated

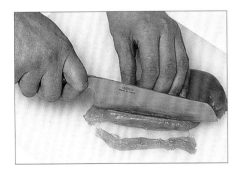

1 Lay the chicken portions on a board. Using a sharp knife, slice each breast into long, thin strips.

2 Combine the sugar, rice wine, dry sherry and dark soy sauce in a bowl.

3 Place the chicken in a separate, large bowl, pour over the marinade and cover with clear film (plastic wrap). Leave to marinate in the refrigerator for at least 15 minutes. If you have time, leave it to marinate overnight.

4 Heat a wok, and stir-fry the chicken and marinade for 4–5 minutes.

5 Serve garnished with orange segments and mustard and cress

COOK'S TIP
Make sure that the marinade is brought to the boil in the wok, and that it cooks for at least 5 minutes, because it has been in contact with raw chicken.

VARIATIONS
• Turkey can be substituted for chicken in this recipe. Buy turkey steaks, place them between pieces of clear film (plastic wrap) and flatten them with a rolling pin before cutting them into thin strips for cooking. Any white fish sashimi can also be used in this dish.
• You could also serve the chicken with steamed rice and a side serving of vegetables, such as shredded cabbage.

Energy 149Kcal/630kJ; Protein 27.4g; Carbohydrate 3.8g, of which sugars 3.8g; Fat 1.3g, of which saturates 0.4g; Cholesterol 79mg; Calcium 21mg; Fibre 0.5g; Sodium 70mg.

TABLE-TOP HOTPOT ★★★

COOKING YOUR OWN FOOD FROM A COMMUNAL POT ON THE TABLE IS GREAT FUN. IT IS A HEALTHY OPTION, TOO, IF YOU USE STOCK INSTEAD OF OIL FOR COOKING, AND USE LEAN MEAT AND FISH.

SERVES 4

INGREDIENTS

225g/8oz piece of white fish fillet, such as sea bream, cod, plaice or haddock

4 x 5cm/2in thick salmon steaks

300g/11oz skinless chicken thighs, cut into large chunks, with bones

4 leaves from the head of Chinese leaves (Chinese cabbage), base trimmed

115g/4oz spinach

1 large carrot

2 thin leeks, washed and cut diagonally into 5cm/2in lengths

8 fresh shiitake mushrooms, stalks removed, or 150g/5oz oyster mushrooms, base trimmed

285g/10¼oz packet firm tofu, drained and cut into 16 cubes

salt

For the hot-pot liquid

12 × 6cm/4½ × 2½in piece *dashi-konbu*

1.2 litres/2 pints/5 cups water

120ml/4fl oz/½ cup sake or dry sherry

For the condiments

90g/3½oz daikon (mooli), peeled

1 dried chilli, halved, seeded and cut into 2–3 strips

1 lemon, cut into 16 wedges

4 spring onions (scallions), chopped

2 × 5g/⅛oz packets *kezuri-bushi*

shoyu

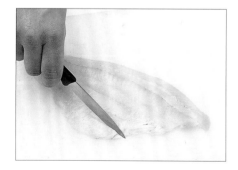

1 Trim the white fish fillet neatly, then cut it into four equal portions. Place the white fish, salmon steaks and the chunks of chicken in separate bowls.

2 Boil plenty of water in a large pan and cook the Chinese leaves for 3 minutes. Lift out and drain in a sieve (strainer) and leave to cool. Add a pinch of salt to the water and boil the spinach for 1 minute, then drain in a sieve under running water.

3 Squeeze the spinach and lay on a sushi rolling mat, then roll it up firmly. Leave to rest, then unwrap and take the cylinder out. Lay the Chinese leaves next to each other on the mat. Put the spinach cylinder in the middle and roll again firmly. Leave for 5 minutes, then unroll and cut into 5cm/2in long cylinders.

4 Using a sharp knife, cut the carrot into rounds, then into flowers.

5 Transfer the cabbage and spinach cylinders to the platter along with all the remaining vegetables and the tofu.

6 Lay the *dashi-konbu* on the bottom of a clay pot or flameproof casserole. Mix the water and sake or sherry in a bowl.

7 Cut the peeled daikon in half and insert a wooden skewer in two or three places. Insert the chilli pieces. Leave for 20 minutes, then grate finely. Drain in a fine-meshed sieve and squeeze the liquid out. Shape the grated daikon into a mound and put in a bowl. Put the other condiments into small bowls.

8 Fill the pot or casserole with two-thirds of the water and sake mixture. Bring to the boil, then reduce the heat.

9 Put the carrot, leeks and shiitake mushrooms into the pot and cook until the carrot is tender. Transfer the pot to a table-top burner. Add a batch of meat and fish to the pot, and, when they have changed colour, add some tofu.

10 Each guest pours a little soy sauce into a small bowl, squeezes in a little lemon juice, then mixes these with a condiment. The food is picked from the pot with chopsticks and dipped into the sauce. More ingredients can be cooked as needed and the water and sake can be topped up when necessary.

COOK'S TIP
Kezuri-bushi is ready-shaved, dried *katsuo* (skipjack tuna) flakes sold in packets for use in dashi fish stock.

Energy 283Kcal/1186kJ; Protein 41.7g; Carbohydrate 5.1g, of which sugars 4.2g; Fat 10.7g, of which saturates 1.8g; Cholesterol 89mg; Calcium 454mg; Fibre 2.3g; Sodium 940mg.

CUBED CHICKEN AND VEGETABLES ★

A POPULAR JAPANESE COOKING STYLE SIMMERS VEGETABLES OF DIFFERENT TEXTURES WITH A SMALL AMOUNT OF MEAT TOGETHER IN DASHI STOCK. THIS CHICKEN VERSION IS KNOWN AS IRIDORI.

SERVES 4

INGREDIENTS

 2 skinless chicken thighs, about
  200g/7oz, boned
 1 large carrot, trimmed
 1 *konnyaku*
 300g/11oz *satoimo* or small potatoes
 500g/1¼lb canned bamboo shoots
 30ml/2 tbsp vegetable oil
 300ml/½ pint/1¼ cups water and
  7.5ml/1½ tsp instant dashi powder
 salt
For the simmering seasonings
 75ml/5 tbsp shoyu
 30ml/2 tbsp sake or dry sherry
 30ml/2 tbsp caster (superfine) sugar
 30ml/2 tbsp mirin

1 Cut the chicken into bitesize pieces. Chop the carrot into 2cm/¾in triangular chunks by cutting it diagonally and turning it 90 degrees each time you cut.

2 Boil the *konnyaku* in rapidly boiling water for 1 minute, then drain in a sieve (strainer) under running water. Cool, then slice it crossways into 5mm/¼in thick rectangular strips.

3 Cut a 4cm/1½in slit down the centre of a strip of cooled *konnyaku* without cutting the ends. Carefully push the top of the strip through the slit to make a decorative tie. Repeat with all of the *konnyaku* strips.

4 Peel and halve the *satoimo* or the new potatoes, if using. Put the pieces in a colander and sprinkle with a generous amount of salt. Rub well and wash under running water. Drain.

5 Drain and halve the canned bamboo shoots, then cut them into the same shape as the carrot.

6 In a medium pan, heat the vegetable oil and stir-fry the chicken pieces until the surface of the meat turns white.

7 Add the carrot, *konnyaku* ties, *satoimo* or potato and bamboo shoots. Stir well to thoroughly combine each time you add a new ingredient.

8 Add the dashi stock and bring to the boil. Cook on a high heat for 3 minutes then reduce to medium-low.

9 Add the shoyu, sake, sugar and mirin, cover the pan, then simmer for 15 minutes, until most of the liquid has evaporated, shaking the pan from time to time.

10 When the *satoimo* or potato is soft, remove the pan from the heat and spoon the chicken and vegetables into a large serving bowl. Serve immediately.

COOK'S TIP
When you cut *satoimo*, it produces a sticky juice. Rinsing with salt and water is the best way of washing it off the surface of the *satoimo*, your hands and any other surfaces it may have come into contact with.

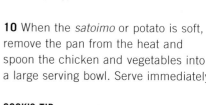

Energy 101Kcal/430kJ; Protein 8.4g; Carbohydrate 16.1g, of which sugars 4.8g; Fat 0.8g, of which saturates 0.2g; Cholesterol 18mg; Calcium 65mg; Fibre 2.7g; Sodium 906mg.

KABOCHA SQUASH <u>WITH</u> CHICKEN SAUCE ★

IN THIS LOW-FAT DISH, THE MILD SWEETNESS OF KABOCHA SQUASH, WHICH TASTES RATHER LIKE SWEET POTATO, GOES VERY WELL WITH THE CHICKEN AND SAKE SAUCE.

SERVES 4

INGREDIENTS

    1 kabocha squash, about 500g/1¼lb
    ½ lime
    20g/¾oz mangetouts (snow peas)
    salt
For the chicken sauce
    100ml/3½fl oz/scant ½ cup water
    30ml/2 tbsp sake or dry sherry
    300g/11oz lean chicken,
      minced (ground)
    60ml/4 tbsp caster (superfine) sugar
    60ml/4 tbsp shoyu
    60ml/4 tbsp mirin

1 Halve the kabocha, then remove the seeds and fibre around the seeds. Halve again to make four wedges. Trim the stem end of each kabocha wedge.

2 Partially peel each wedge, cutting off two strips lengthways about 1–2.5cm/ ½–1in wide. The kabocha wedges will now have green (skin) and yellow (flesh) stripes. This will help preserve the kabocha's most tasty part just beneath the skin, and also allows it to be cooked until soft as well as being decorative.

3 Chop each wedge into large bitesize pieces. Place them side by side in a pan. Pour in enough water to cover, then sprinkle with some salt. Cover and cook for 5 minutes over a medium heat, then lower the heat and simmer for 15 minutes until tender.

4 Test the kabocha by pricking with a skewer. When soft enough, remove from the heat, cover and leave for 5 minutes.

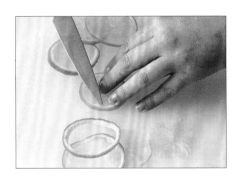

5 Slice the lime into thin discs, then hollow out the inside of the skin to make rings of peel. Cover with a sheet of clear film (plastic wrap) until needed. Blanch the mangetouts in lightly salted water. Drain and set aside.

6 To make the chicken sauce, bring the water and sake to the boil in a pan. Add the chicken, and when the colour of the meat has changed, add the sugar, shoyu and mirin. Whisk together until the liquid has almost all evaporated.

7 Pile up the kabocha on a large plate, then pour the hot meat sauce on top. Add the mangetouts and serve, garnished with lime rings.

VARIATION
Use tofu for a vegetarian sauce. Wrap in kitchen paper and leave for 30 minutes. Mash with a fork, then add instead of the chicken in step 6.

Energy 165Kcal/701kJ; Protein 19.2g; Carbohydrate 18.8g, of which sugars 18.1g; Fat 1.1g, of which saturates 0.4g; Cholesterol 53mg; Calcium 51mg; Fibre 1.4g; Sodium 47mg.

STIR-FRIED SWEET AND SOUR CHICKEN ★★★

AS WELL AS BEING QUICK AND VERY EASY TO MAKE, THIS ASIAN DISH IS DECIDEDLY TASTY AND YOU WILL FIND YOURSELF BEING ASKED TO MAKE IT AGAIN AND AGAIN.

SERVES 3–4

INGREDIENTS

    275g/10oz dried medium egg noodles
    30ml/2 tbsp vegetable oil
    3 spring onions (scallions), chopped
    1 garlic clove, crushed
    2.5cm/1in fresh root ginger, grated
    5ml/1 tsp paprika
    5ml/1 tsp ground coriander
    3 skinless chicken breast
      fillets, sliced
    225g/8oz sugar snap peas, trimmed
    115g/4oz baby corn cobs, halved
    225g/8oz/4 cups beansprouts
    15ml/1 tbsp cornflour (cornstarch)
    45ml/3 tbsp light soy sauce
    45ml/3 tbsp lemon juice
    15ml/1 tbsp sugar
    45ml/3 tbsp chopped fresh coriander
      (cilantro), to garnish

1 Bring a large pan of lightly salted water to the boil. Add the egg noodles and cook until they are just soft and pliable, following the instructions on the packet instructions. Tip into a colander and drain thoroughly, then cover and keep warm.

2 Heat the oil. Add the spring onions, garlic, ginger, paprika and coriander and stir-fry for 1 minute.

3 Stir in the chicken and stir-fry for 3–4 minutes. Add the sugar snap peas, corn cobs and beansprouts and cook briefly. Add the noodles and toss lightly to mix with the other ingredients.

4 Combine the cornflour, soy sauce, lemon juice and sugar in a small bowl. Add to the wok and simmer briefly to thicken. Serve garnished with chopped fresh coriander.

Energy 501Kcal/2116kJ; Protein 37.4g; Carbohydrate 63g, of which sugars 9.8g; Fat 12.8g, of which saturates 2.6g; Cholesterol 91mg; Calcium 70mg; Fibre 4.7g; Sodium 1319mg.

DUCK AND GINGER CHOP SUEY ★★★

CHICKEN CAN ALSO BE USED IN THIS RECIPE, AND WOULD BE LOWER IN FAT, BUT DUCK GIVES A RICHER RESULT AND IS GREAT FOR A SPECIAL TREAT. START MAKING THIS A DAY AHEAD, IF YOU CAN.

SERVES 4

INGREDIENTS

    2 duck breast fillets, about
       175g/6oz each
    30ml/2 tbsp vegetable oil
    1 egg, lightly beaten
    1 garlic clove
    175g/6oz beansprouts
    2 slices fresh root ginger, cut
       into matchsticks
    10ml/2 tsp oyster sauce
    2 spring onions (scallions), cut
       into matchsticks
    salt and ground black pepper
For the marinade
    15ml/1 tbsp clear honey
    10ml/2 tsp Chinese rice wine
    10ml/2 tsp light soy sauce
    10ml/2 tsp dark soy sauce

1 Remove the skin and fat from the duck, cut the breasts into thin strips and place in a bowl. Mix the marinade ingredients together, pour over the duck, cover with clear film (plastic wrap), and marinate in the refrigerator for 6–8 hours or overnight.

2 Next day, make an egg omelette. Heat a small frying pan and add 15ml/1 tbsp of the oil. When the oil is hot, pour in the egg and swirl around to make an omelette. Once cooked, leave it to cool and cut into strips. Drain the duck and discard the marinade.

COOK'S TIP

If you like the flavour of garlic, add 1–2 crushed cloves with the beansprouts instead of just using it to flavour the oil.

3 Bruise the garlic with the flat blade of a knife. Heat the wok, then add 10ml/ 2 tsp oil. When the oil is hot, add the garlic and fry for 30 seconds, pressing it to release the flavour. Discard. Add the beansprouts with seasoning and stir-fry for 30 seconds. Transfer to a heated dish, draining off any liquid.

4 Heat the wok and add the remaining oil. When the oil is hot, stir-fry the duck for 3 minutes until cooked. Add the ginger and oyster sauce and stir-fry for a further 2 minutes.

5 Add the beansprouts, egg strips and spring onions, stir-fry briefly and serve.

Energy 202Kcal/844kJ; Protein 20.3g; Carbohydrate 5.1g, of which sugars 4.3g; Fat 12.8g, of which saturates 2.2g; Cholesterol 144mg; Calcium 29mg; Fibre 0.7g; Sodium 384mg.

DUCK AND SESAME STIR-FRY ★★★

THIS RECIPE IS INTENDED FOR GAME BIRDS, AS FARMED DUCK WOULD USUALLY HAVE TOO MUCH FAT. IF YOU DO USE FARMED DUCK, YOU SHOULD REMOVE THE SKIN AND FAT LAYER.

SERVES 4

INGREDIENTS

   250g/9oz skinless wild duck
     breast fillets
   15ml/1 tbsp sesame oil
   15ml/1 tbsp vegetable oil
   4 garlic cloves, finely sliced
   2.5ml/½ tsp dried chilli flakes
   15ml/1 tbsp Thai fish sauce
   15ml/1 tbsp light soy sauce
   120ml/4fl oz/½ cup water
   1 head broccoli, cut into small florets
   coriander (cilantro) and 15ml/1 tbsp
     toasted sesame seeds, to garnish

VARIATIONS

This also works well with pheasant or partridge in place of the duck.

1 Cut the duck into bitesize pieces. Heat the oils in a wok or large frying pan and stir-fry the garlic over medium heat until it is golden brown – do not let it burn.

2 Add the duck pieces to the pan and stir-fry for a further 2 minutes, until the meat begins to brown.

3 Stir in the chilli flakes, fish sauce, soy sauce and water.

4 Add the broccoli florets and continue to stir-fry the mixture for about 2 minutes, until the duck pieces are just cooked through.

5 Serve immediately on warmed plates, garnished with sprigs of coriander and sesame seeds.

COOK'S TIP

Large wok lids are cumbersome and can be difficult to store in a small kitchen. If you need to cover a wok it may be easier to just place a circle of baking parchment against the food surface to keep cooking juices in.

Energy 156Kcal/651kJ; Protein 16.3g; Carbohydrate 1.9g, of which sugars 1.6g; Fat 10.4g, of which saturates 1.7g; Cholesterol 69mg; Calcium 58mg; Fibre 2.3g; Sodium 343mg.

DUCK WITH PLUM SAUCE ★★★

RIPE, JUICY PLUMS ARE THE PERFECT ACCOMPANIMENT FOR DUCK, PROVIDING A FRUITY COUNTERPOINT TO THE RICHNESS OF THE MEAT. THE COLOUR OF THE SAUCE LOOKS BEAUTIFUL, TOO.

SERVES 4

INGREDIENTS
    4 duck quarters
    1 large red onion, finely chopped
    500g/1¼lb ripe plums, stoned
      (pitted) and quartered
    30ml/2 tbsp redcurrant jelly
    salt and ground black pepper

1 Using a metal skewer or a fork, prick the duck skin all over to release the fat during cooking. Place the portions skin side down in a dry frying pan.

COOK'S TIP
The plums must be very ripe or the mixture will be dry and the sauce tart.

VARIATIONS
You can use a white onion instead of a red onion. Fine-cut orange marmalade is a great alternative to the redcurrant jelly.

2 Cook the duck pieces over a medium heat for 10 minutes on each side, or until they are golden brown and cooked right through.

3 Remove the duck from the frying pan using a slotted spoon, place on a plate and keep warm.

4 Pour away all but 30ml/2 tbsp of the duck fat, then stir-fry the onion for about 5 minutes, or until softened.

5 Add the plums to the wok or frying pan and cook for 5 minutes more, stirring frequently. Stir in the redcurrant jelly until dissolved.

6 Replace the duck portions and simmer gently for a further 5 minutes, or until the duck is thoroughly reheated.

7 Season to taste with salt and ground black pepper, before serving with plain egg noodles or boiled rice.

Energy 296Kcal/1250kJ; Protein 35.9g; Carbohydrate 20.1g, of which sugars 19g; Fat 11.6g, of which saturates 2.3g; Cholesterol 193mg; Calcium 51mg; Fibre 2.7g; Sodium 199mg.

FRUITY DUCK CHOP SUEY ★★★

SKINNING THE DUCK REDUCES THE FAT, BUT THIS IS STILL AN INDULGENT RECIPE. IF THIS WORRIES YOU, USE LESS DUCK AND MORE NOODLES. PINEAPPLE GIVES THE DISH A LOVELY FLAVOUR.

2 Meanwhile, heat a wok. Add the strips of duck and stir-fry for 2–3 minutes, Drain off all but 30ml/2 tbsp of the fat.

3 Add the spring onions and celery to the wok and stir-fry for 2 minutes more.

4 Use a slotted spoon to remove the ingredients from the wok and set them aside. Add the pineapple strips and mixed vegetables, and stir-fry for 2 minutes more.

5 Add the cooked noodles and plum sauce to the wok, then replace the duck, spring onion and celery mixture.

6 Stir-fry the duck mixture for about 2 minutes more, or until the noodles and vegetables are hot and the duck is cooked through. Serve immediately.

COOK'S TIP
Fresh sesame noodles can be bought from large supermarkets – you will usually find them in the chiller cabinets alongside fresh pasta. If they aren't available, then use fresh egg noodles instead and cook according to the instructions on the packet.

SERVES 4

INGREDIENTS
    250g/9oz fresh sesame noodles
    2 skinless duck breast fillets
    3 spring onions (scallions), cut
       into strips
    2 celery sticks, cut into strips
    1 fresh pineapple, peeled, cored
       and cut into strips
    300g/11oz mixed vegetables, such as
       carrots, peppers, beansprouts and
       cabbage, shredded or cut into strips
    90ml/6 tbsp plum sauce

1 Cook the noodles in a large pan of boiling water for 3 minutes. Drain. Slice the duck breast fillets into strips.

Energy 603Kcal/2553kJ; Protein 36.3g; Carbohydrate 93g, of which sugars 28.1g; Fat 14.2g, of which saturates 1.7g; Cholesterol 138mg; Calcium 96mg; Fibre 6.9g; Sodium 167mg.

DUCK WITH PINEAPPLE ★★

DUCK AND PINEAPPLE IS A FAVOURITE COMBINATION, BUT THE FRUIT MUST NOT BE ALLOWED TO DOMINATE. THESE PROPORTIONS ARE PERFECT AND THE DISH HAS A SUBTLE SWEET-SOUR FLAVOUR.

SERVES 4

INGREDIENTS

15ml/1 tbsp dry sherry
15ml/1 tbsp dark soy sauce
2 small skinless duck breast fillets
15ml/1 tbsp vegetable oil
2 garlic cloves, finely chopped
1 small onion, sliced
1 red (bell) pepper, seeded and cut
 into 2.5cm/1in squares
75g/3oz/½ cup drained, canned
 pineapple chunks
90ml/6 tbsp pineapple juice
15ml/1 tbsp rice vinegar
5ml/1 tsp cornflour (cornstarch)
15ml/1 tbsp cold water
5ml/1 tsp sesame oil
salt and ground white pepper
1 spring onion (scallion), shredded

1 Mix together the sherry and soy sauce. Stir in 2.5ml/½ tsp salt and 1.5ml/¼ tsp white pepper. Put the duck fillets in a bowl and add the marinade. Cover and leave in a cool place for 1 hour.

2 Drain the duck fillets and place them on a rack in a grill (broiler) pan. Cook under a medium to high heat for 10 minutes on each side. Leave to cool for 10 minutes, then cut the duck into bite-size pieces.

VARIATION
Another type of fruit that goes well with duck is physalis or Cape gooseberry. Release each berry from its papery jacket and add to the wok instead of the pineapple.

3 Heat the vegetable oil in a non-stick frying pan or wok and stir-fry the garlic and onion for 1 minute. Add the red pepper, pineapple chunks, duck, pineapple juice and vinegar and toss over the heat for 2 minutes.

4 Mix the cornflour to a paste with the water. Add the mixture to the pan with 1.5ml/¼ tsp salt. Cook, stirring, until the sauce thickens. Stir in the sesame oil and serve immediately, garnished with spring onion shreds.

Energy 171Kcal/715kJ; Protein 15.7g; Carbohydrate 10.1g, of which sugars 8.4g; Fat 8.6g, of which saturates 1.5g; Cholesterol 83mg; Calcium 21mg; Fibre 1g; Sodium 355mg.

DUCK WITH PANCAKES ★★

THIS HAS CONSIDERABLY LESS FAT THAN TRADITIONAL PEKING DUCK, BUT IS JUST AS DELICIOUS.
GUESTS SPREAD THEIR PANCAKES WITH SAUCE, ADD DUCK AND VEGETABLES, THEN ROLL THEM UP.

SERVES 4

INGREDIENTS
15ml/1 tbsp clear honey
1.5ml/¼ tsp five-spice powder
1 garlic clove, finely chopped
15ml/1 tbsp hoisin sauce
2.5ml/½ tsp salt
a large pinch of ground white pepper
2 small skinless duck breast fillets
½ cucumber
10 spring onions (scallions)
3 leaves from a head of Chinese
    leaves (Chinese cabbage)
12 Chinese pancakes (see Cook's Tip)
For the sauce
5ml/1 tsp vegetable oil
2 garlic cloves, chopped
2 spring onions (scallions), chopped
1cm/½in fresh root ginger, bruised
60ml/4 tbsp hoisin sauce
15ml/1 tbsp dry sherry
15ml/1 tbsp cold water
2.5ml/½ tsp sesame oil

4 Cut off and discard the green tops from the spring onions. Finely shred the white parts and place on a serving plate with the cucumber batons.

5 Make the sauce. Heat the oil in a small pan and fry the garlic gently for a few seconds without browning. Add the spring onions, ginger, hoisin sauce, sherry and water. Cook gently for 5 minutes, stirring often, then strain and mix with the sesame oil.

7 Line a bamboo steamer with the Chinese leaves and place the pancakes on top.

8 Pour boiling water into a large pan, to a depth of 5cm/2in. Cover the steamer and place it on a trivet in the pan of boiling water.

9 Steam for 2 minutes or until the pancakes are hot. Serve at once with the duck, cucumber, spring onions and the sauce.

COOK'S TIP
Chinese pancakes can be bought frozen from Chinese supermarkets. Leave to thaw before steaming.

1 Mix the honey, five-spice powder, garlic, hoisin sauce, salt and pepper in a shallow dish which is large enough to hold the duck fillets side by side. Add the duck fillets, and turn to coat them in the marinade.

2 Cover the dish with clear film (plastic wrap) and leave in a cool place to marinate for 2 hours, or overnight if you have the time.

3 Cut the cucumber in half lengthways. Using a teaspoon scrape out and discard the seeds. Cut the flesh into thin batons 5cm/2in long.

6 Remove the duck fillets from the marinade and drain. Grill (broil) under a medium heat for 8–10 minutes on each side. Leave to cool for 5 minutes before cutting into thin slices. Arrange on a serving platter, cover and keep warm.

Energy 241Kcal/1018kJ; Protein 19.1g; Carbohydrate 29.6g, of which sugars 7.5g; Fat 6.3g, of which saturates 1.1g; Cholesterol 83mg; Calcium 92mg; Fibre 2.6g; Sodium 462mg.

MEAT DISHES

Balancing relatively small amounts of meat with plenty of

vegetables and noodles or rice is standard practice in China and

Far East Asia, so recipes from the region are good for reducing

the amount of red meat you eat. Sizzling Beef with Celeriac

Straw and Beef Noodles with Orange and Ginger illustrate this

point perfectly. Sticky Pork Ribs sound wickedly indulgent but

are also acceptable, largely because what looks like a generous

plateful contains a small proportion of meat to bone.

ORIENTAL BEEF ★★

THIS SUMPTUOUSLY RICH BEEF MELTS IN THE MOUTH, AND IS PERFECTLY COMPLEMENTED BY THE COOL, CRUNCHY RELISH. USE VERY LEAN MEAT AND CUT OFF ANY OBVIOUS FAT.

SERVES 4

INGREDIENTS

   450g/1lb lean rump (round) steak, trimmed of fat
   4 whole radishes, to garnish
For the marinade
   15ml/1 tbsp vegetable oil
   2 garlic cloves, crushed
   60ml/4 tbsp dark soy sauce
   30ml/2 tbsp dry sherry
   10ml/2 tsp soft dark brown sugar
For the relish
   6 radishes
   10cm/4in piece cucumber
   1 piece preserved stem ginger

1 If you have time, place the steak in the freezer for 30 minutes. This firms it so it can be cut very thinly. Remove the steak from the freezer, cut it into thin strips and place it in a bowl.

2 To make the marinade, pour the oil into a bowl and stir in the garlic, soy sauce, sherry and sugar. Pour the mixture over the beef, cover and leave to marinate overnight.

3 To make the relish, use a sharp knife to chop the radishes and cucumber into matchsticks and the ginger into slivers. Mix well together in a bowl.

4 Heat a wok or large non-stick frying pan until it is very hot, then add the meat with the marinade, and stir-fry for 3–4 minutes.

5 Serve the beef immediately with the relish, and garnish each plate with a whole radish.

Energy 169Kcal/709kJ; Protein 25g; Carbohydrate 0.6g, of which sugars 0.6g; Fat 7.4g, of which saturates 2.3g; Cholesterol 66mg; Calcium 11mg; Fibre 0.3g; Sodium 70mg.

SIZZLING BEEF WITH CELERIAC STRAW ★★★

THE CRISP CELERIAC MATCHSTICKS LOOK LIKE FINE PIECES OF STRAW WHEN COOKED AND HAVE A MILD CELERY-LIKE FLAVOUR THAT IS QUITE DELICIOUS WITH THE STRIPS OF STEAK.

SERVES 4

INGREDIENTS
450g/1lb celeriac
30ml/2 tbsp vegetable oil
1 red (bell) pepper
6 spring onions (scallions)
450g/1lb lean rump (round) steak
60ml/4 tbsp beef stock
30ml/2 tbsp sherry vinegar
10ml/2 tsp Worcestershire sauce
10ml/2 tsp tomato purée (paste)
salt and ground black pepper

1 Peel the celeriac and then cut it into fine matchsticks, using a sharp knife or a cleaver, if you have one.

2 Heat the wok, then add 15ml/1 tbsp of the oil. When the oil is hot, fry the celeriac matchsticks until golden brown and crisp. Drain well.

3 Cut the red pepper in half lengthways, then remove and discard the core and seeds. Slice each half into 2.5cm/1in wide strips.

4 Trim the spring onions and cut them into similar lengths.

5 Trim any fat from the steak, then chop the lean beef into strips, across the grain of the meat.

6 Heat the wok and add the remaining oil. When the oil is hot, stir-fry the spring onions and pepper for 2–3 minutes.

7 Add the beef strips and stir-fry for a further 3–4 minutes until well browned. Pour in the stock, then add the vinegar, Worcestershire sauce and tomato purée. Stir well and heat through for 1–2 minutes. Season with salt and pepper and serve with the celeriac straw.

Energy 237Kcal/994kJ; Protein 26.7g; Carbohydrate 9.3g, of which sugars 8.9g; Fat 10.7g, of which saturates 2.6g; Cholesterol 66mg; Calcium 74mg; Fibre 3.7g; Sodium 123mg.

BEEF AND MUSHROOMS WITH BLACK BEANS ★★

THIS CLASSIC CHINESE DISH IS LOW IN FAT AND OFFERS A GOOD SUPPLY OF MINERALS NEEDED FOR OPTIMUM HEALTH, INCLUDING ZINC AND IRON. SERVE WITH STEAMED VEGETABLES SUCH AS BROCCOLI.

SERVES 4

INGREDIENTS
- 30ml/2 tbsp dark soy sauce
- 30ml/2 tbsp Chinese rice wine
- 10ml/2 tsp cornflour (cornstarch)
- 10ml/2 tsp sesame oil
- 450g/1lb fillet (beef tenderloin) or rump (round) steak, trimmed of fat
- 12 dried shiitake mushrooms
- 25ml/1½ tbsp salted black beans
- 5ml/1 tsp caster (superfine) sugar
- 30ml/2 tbsp vegetable oil
- 4 garlic cloves
- 2.5cm/1in fresh root ginger
- 200g/7oz open cap mushrooms, sliced
- 1 bunch spring onions (scallions), sliced diagonally
- 1 fresh red chilli, seeded and shredded
- salt and ground black pepper

1 In a large bowl, mix together half the dark soy sauce, half the Chinese rice wine, half the cornflour and all of the sesame oil with 15ml/1 tbsp fresh cold water until smooth and thoroughly combined. Add a generous pinch of salt and ground black pepper.

2 If you have time, place the beef in the freezer and leave it for 30 minutes. Cut it into very thin slices, no more than 5mm/¼in thick.

3 Add the slices of meat to the cornflour mixture and rub the mixture into the beef with your fingers. Cover the bowl and set the beef aside for 30 minutes at room temperature.

4 Meanwhile, pour boiling water over the dried mushrooms and leave them to soak for about 25 minutes.

5 Transfer 45ml/3 tbsp of the soaking water to a cup or small bowl. Lift the mushrooms out of the bowl and gently squeeze them to remove any excess soaking water.

6 Using a sharp knife, cut off the mushroom stems. Discard these, then cut the caps in half, and set them aside.

7 Peel the garlic cloves and slice them thinly, using a sharp knife. Peel the ginger and cut the flesh into thin strips.

8 Mash the salted black beans with the caster sugar. In another bowl, combine the remaining cornflour, soy sauce and Chinese rice wine.

9 Heat the oil in a wok, then stir-fry the beef for about 30–45 seconds, until just brown. Transfer it to a plate and set aside.

10 Add the sliced garlic and the strips of ginger to the remaining oil in the wok, stir-fry for 1 minute, then add all the mushrooms and stir-fry for 2 minutes more.

11 Set aside a few tablespoons of the sliced green part of the spring onions, then add the rest to the wok. Add the mashed black bean mixture and stir-fry for 1–2 minutes.

12 Stir in the beef, then add the shiitake soaking water. Add the cornflour mixture and simmer until the sauce thickens.

13 Sprinkle the shredded chilli and the reserved slices from the green part of the spring onions over the beef, and serve immediately.

Energy 208Kcal/873kJ; Protein 25.9g; Carbohydrate 4.7g, of which sugars 1.5g; Fat 8.8g, of which saturates 3.5g; Cholesterol 69mg; Calcium 20mg; Fibre 1.1g; Sodium 590mg.

BEEF NOODLES WITH ORANGE AND GINGER ★★

STIR-FRYING IS ONE OF THE BEST WAYS TO COOK WITH THE MINIMUM OF FAT. IT'S ALSO ONE OF THE QUICKEST WAYS TO COOK, BUT YOU DO NEED TO CHOOSE GOOD QUALITY TENDER MEAT.

SERVES 4

INGREDIENTS

450g/1lb lean beef, e.g. rump
  (round), fillet (beef tenderloin)
  or sirloin steak
finely grated rind and juice of
  1 orange
15ml/1 tbsp light soy sauce
5ml/1 tsp cornflour (cornstarch)
2.5cm/1in fresh root ginger,
  finely chopped
175g/6oz rice noodles
10ml/2 tsp sesame oil
15ml/1 tbsp vegetable oil
1 large carrot, cut into thin strips
2 spring onions (scallions),
  thinly sliced

1 If you have time, place the beef in the freezer and leave for 30 minutes, then cut it into very thin slices.

2 Place the beef in a bowl and sprinkle over the orange rind and juice. If possible, cover the bowl and leave the beef to marinate for at least 30 minutes.

3 Drain the liquid from the meat into a bowl and set aside, then mix the beef strips with the soy sauce, cornflour and ginger.

4 Cook the noodles according to the instructions on the packet. Drain well, toss with the sesame oil and keep warm.

5 Heat the vegetable oil in a wok or large frying pan. When the oil is very hot, add the beef strips and stir-fry for 1 minute until lightly coloured, then add the carrot and stir-fry for a further 2–3 minutes.

6 Stir in the spring onions and the reserved liquid from the meat, then cook, stirring, until the sauce boils and thickens. Serve immediately with the rice noodles.

COOK'S TIP
The citrus flavours that are such a success in this beef recipe work equally well with chicken or duck. Use thin strips from breast portions and toss in some orange segments just before serving.

Energy 353Kcal/1478kJ; Protein 27.2g; Carbohydrate 39.6g, of which sugars 2.6g; Fat 9g, of which saturates 2.5g; Cholesterol 66mg; Calcium 18mg; Fibre 0.6g; Sodium 80mg.

NOODLES WITH BEEF AND BLACK BEAN SAUCE ★★

THIS IS AN EXCELLENT COMBINATION OF FLAVOURS AND TEXTURES — TENDER BEEF WITH A CHILLI BLACK BEAN SAUCE TOSSED WITH SILKY-SMOOTH RICE NOODLES.

SERVES 4

INGREDIENTS

    450g/1lb fresh rice noodles
    30ml/2 tbsp vegetable oil
    1 onion, thinly sliced
    2 garlic cloves, finely chopped
    2 slices fresh root ginger,
      finely chopped
    225g/8oz mixed (bell) peppers,
      seeded and sliced
    350g/12oz rump (round) steak, thinly
      sliced against the grain
    45ml/3 tbsp fermented black beans,
      rinsed in warm water, drained
      and chopped
    30ml/2 tbsp dark soy sauce
    30ml/2 tbsp oyster sauce
    15ml/1 tbsp chilli black bean sauce
    15ml/1 tbsp cornflour (cornstarch)
    120ml/4fl oz/½ cup beef stock
      or water
    2 spring onions (scallions), finely
      chopped, and 2 red chillies, seeded
      and thinly sliced, to garnish

1 Rinse the noodles under hot water until soft, then drain well. Set aside.

2 Heat half the oil in a wok or frying pan, swirling it around. Add the onion, garlic, ginger and pepper slices. Stir-fry for 3–5 minutes, then remove all the ingredients from the wok or pan and keep warm.

3 Add the remaining oil to the wok or pan and swirl to coat. When hot, add the sliced beef and fermented black beans and stir-fry over a high heat for 5 minutes or until they are cooked.

4 In a small bowl, blend the soy sauce, oyster sauce and chilli black bean sauce with the cornflour and stock or water and stir until smooth. Add the mixture to the wok, together with the onion and pepper mixture and cook, stirring, for 1 minute.

5 Add the noodles and mix together lightly. Stir over a medium heat until the noodles are heated through. Taste and adjust the seasoning if necessary. Serve immediately, garnished with the chopped spring onions and thinly sliced chillies.

Energy 567Kcal/2376kJ; Protein 25.8g; Carbohydrate 100.4g, of which sugars 4.7g; Fat 5.5g, of which saturates 1.7g; Cholesterol 52mg; Calcium 29mg; Fibre 1.2g; Sodium 338mg.

SUKIYAKI-STYLE BEEF ★★

THIS JAPANESE DISH IS A MEAL IN ITSELF; THE RECIPE INCORPORATES ALL THE TRADITIONAL ELEMENTS — MEAT, VEGETABLES, NOODLES AND TOFU — IN A HIGHLY FLAVOURED MUSHROOM BROTH.

3 To make the stock, mix together the sugar, rice wine, soy sauce and water in a small bowl.

4 Heat the wok, then add the oil. When the oil is hot, stir-fry the beef for 2–3 minutes until it is cooked, but still pink in colour.

SERVES 4

INGREDIENTS
    450g/1lb lean rump (round) steak
    200g/7oz rice noodles
    15ml/1 tbsp vegetable oil
    200g/7oz firm tofu, cubed
    8 fresh shiitake mushrooms, wiped
      and trimmed
    2 medium leeks, sliced into
      2.5cm/1in lengths
    90g/3½oz baby spinach,
      to serve
For the stock
    15ml/1 tbsp caster (superfine) sugar
    90ml/6 tbsp rice wine
    45ml/3 tbsp dark soy sauce
    120ml/4fl oz/½ cup water

1 Trim off the fat from the beef. If you have time, place it in the freezer and leave for 30 minutes. Cut it into very thin slices.

2 Blanch the noodles in boiling water for 2 minutes. Drain well.

5 Pour the stock over the beef. Add the tofu, mushrooms and leeks. Toss together over the heat for 4 minutes, until the leeks are tender. Meanwhile, wash and thoroughly drain the baby spinach leaves.

6 Serve immediately with the baby spinach leaves, making sure that each person receives some beef and tofu.

Energy 418Kcal/1748kJ; Protein 32.4g; Carbohydrate 42.2g, of which sugars 1.1g; Fat 9.8g, of which saturates 2.5g; Cholesterol 66mg; Calcium 307mg; Fibre 0.7g; Sodium 377mg.

BEEF WITH TOMATOES ★★

BASED ON A SIMPLE KOREAN DISH, THIS COLOURFUL AND FRESH-TASTING MIXTURE IS THE PERFECT WAY OF SERVING SUN-RIPENED TOMATOES FROM THE GARDEN OR FARMERS' MARKET.

SERVES 4

INGREDIENTS

  350g/12oz lean rump (round) steak,
    trimmed of fat
  15ml/1 tbsp vegetable oil
  300ml/½ pint/1¼ cups beef stock
  1 garlic clove, finely chopped
  1 small onion, sliced into rings
  5 tomatoes, quartered
  15ml/1 tbsp tomato purée (paste)
  5ml/1 tsp caster (superfine) sugar
  15ml/1 tbsp dry sherry
  15ml/1 tbsp cold water
  salt and ground white pepper
  noodles, to serve

1 Slice the rump steak thinly. Place the steak slices in a bowl, add 5ml/1 tsp of the vegetable oil and stir to coat.

2 Bring the stock to the boil in a large pan. Add the beef and cook for 2 minutes, stirring constantly. Drain the beef and set it aside.

VARIATION
Add 5–10ml/1–2 tsp soy sauce to the tomato purée (paste). You will not need to add any extra salt.

3 Heat the remaining oil in a non-stick frying pan or wok until very hot. Stir-fry the garlic and onion for a few seconds.

COOK'S TIP
Use plum tomatoes or vine tomatoes from the garden, if you can. The store-bought ones are a little more expensive than standard tomatoes but have a far better flavour.

4 Add the beef to the pan or wok, then tip in the tomatoes. Stir-fry for 1 minute more over high heat.

5 Mix the tomato purée, sugar, sherry and water in a cup or small bowl. Stir into the pan or wok, add salt and pepper to taste and mix thoroughly. Cook for 1 minute until the sauce is hot. Serve in heated bowls, with noodles.

Energy 172Kcal/723kJ; Protein 20.5g; Carbohydrate 6.7g, of which sugars 6.4g; Fat 6.8g, of which saturates 1.9g; Cholesterol 52mg; Calcium 18mg; Fibre 1.6g; Sodium 74mg.

BEEF IN OYSTER SAUCE ★★

THE OYSTER SAUCE GIVES THE BEEF EXTRA RICHNESS AND DEPTH OF FLAVOUR. TO COMPLETE THE DISH, ALL YOU NEED IS PLAIN BOILED RICE OR NOODLES, AND PERHAPS SOME STEAMED GREENS.

SERVES 4

INGREDIENTS

350g/12oz lean rump (round) steak, trimmed of fat
15ml/1 tbsp vegetable oil
300ml/½ pint/1¼ cups beef stock
2 garlic cloves, finely chopped
1 small carrot, thinly sliced
3 celery sticks, sliced
15ml/1 tbsp dry sherry
5ml/1 tsp caster (superfine) sugar
45ml/3 tbsp oyster sauce
5ml/1 tsp cornflour
15ml/1 tbsp cold water
4 spring onions (scallions), cut into 2.5cm/1in lengths
ground white pepper
rice or noodles, to serve

1 Slice the steak thinly. Place the slices in a bowl, add 5ml/1 tsp of the vegetable oil and stir to coat.

2 Bring the stock to the boil in a large pan. Add the beef and cook, stirring, for 2 minutes.

3 Drain the beef, reserving 45ml/3 tbsp of the stock in a small bowl, and set the beef aside on a plate.

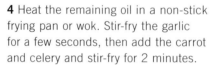

4 Heat the remaining oil in a non-stick frying pan or wok. Stir-fry the garlic for a few seconds, then add the carrot and celery and stir-fry for 2 minutes.

5 Stir in the sherry, caster sugar, oyster sauce and a large pinch of pepper. Add the steak to the pan with the reserved stock. Simmer for 2 minutes.

6 Mix the cornflour to a paste with the water. Add the mixture to the pan and cook, stirring, until thickened.

7 Stir in the spring onions, then serve immediately, with rice or noodles.

VARIATION
To increase the number of servings without upping the fat content of the dish, simply add more vegetables, such as (bell) peppers, mangetouts (snow peas), water chestnuts, baby corn cobs and mushrooms.

Energy 162Kcal/679kJ; Protein 19.9g; Carbohydrate 5.3g, of which sugars 5g; Fat 6.5g, of which saturates 1.8g; Cholesterol 52mg; Calcium 25mg; Fibre 1g; Sodium 260mg.

BEEF WITH PEPPERS AND BLACK BEAN SAUCE ★★

THE BLACK BEAN SAUCE GIVES THIS LOW-FAT DISH A LOVELY RICH FLAVOUR. THE BEEF IS FIRST SIMMERED IN STOCK AND THEN STIR-FRIED WITH GARLIC, GINGER, CHILLI AND GREEN PEPPER.

SERVES 4

INGREDIENTS

350g/12oz rump (round) steak, trimmed and thinly sliced
15ml/1 tbsp vegetable oil
300ml/½ pint/1¼ cups beef stock
2 garlic cloves, finely chopped
5ml/1 tsp grated fresh root ginger
1 fresh red chilli, seeded and finely chopped
15ml/1 tbsp black bean sauce
1 green (bell) pepper, seeded and cut into 2.5cm/1in squares
15ml/1 tbsp dry sherry
5ml/1 tsp cornflour (cornstarch)
5ml/1 tsp caster (superfine) sugar
45ml/3 tbsp cold water
salt
rice noodles, to serve

1 Place the sliced steak in a bowl. Add 5ml/1 tsp of the oil and stir to coat.

2 Bring the stock to the boil in a large pan. Add the sliced steak and cook for 2 minutes, stirring constantly to prevent the slices from sticking together. Strain the beef through a sieve (strainer) and set aside.

3 Heat the remaining oil in a non-stick frying pan or wok. Stir-fry the garlic, ginger and chilli with the black bean sauce for a few seconds.

4 Add the pepper and a little water. Cook for about 2 minutes more, then stir in the sherry. Add the beef slices to the pan and spoon the sauce over.

5 Mix the cornflour and sugar to a paste with the water. Pour the mixture into the pan. Cook, stirring, until the sauce has thickened. Season with salt. Serve immediately, with rice noodles.

COOK'S TIP
For extra colour, use half each of a green pepper and red pepper.

Energy 146Kcal/613kJ; Protein 19.3g; Carbohydrate 2.1g, of which sugars 1.1g; Fat 6.4g, of which saturates 1.8g; Cholesterol 52mg; Calcium 5mg; Fibre 0g; Sodium 115mg.

SIMMERED BEEF SLICES AND VEGETABLES ★★

THIS ONE-POT DISH IS A FAMILY FAVOURITE IN JAPAN. IT IS A GOOD EXAMPLE OF HOW A SMALL AMOUNT OF MEAT CAN BE STRETCHED WITH VEGETABLES TO MAKE A TASTY LOW-FAT MEAL.

SERVES 4

INGREDIENTS

    250g/9oz lean fillet (beef tenderloin)
      or rump (round) steak, trimmed of
      fat and very thinly sliced
    1 large onion
    15ml/1 tbsp vegetable oil
    450g/1lb small potatoes, halved
      then soaked in water
    1 carrot, cut into 5mm/¼in rounds
    45ml/3 tbsp frozen peas, thawed
      and blanched for 1 minute
For the seasonings
    30ml/2 tbsp caster (superfine) sugar
    75ml/5 tbsp shoyu
    15ml/1 tbsp mirin
    15ml/1 tbsp sake or dry sherry

1 Cut the thinly sliced beef slices into 2cm/¾in wide strips, and slice the onion lengthways into 5mm/¼in pieces.

2 Heat the vegetable oil in a pan and lightly fry the beef and onion slices. When the colour of the meat changes, drain the potatoes and add to the pan.

3 Once the potatoes are coated with the oil in the pan, add the carrot. Pour in just enough water to cover, then bring to the boil, skimming a few times.

4 Boil vigorously for 2 minutes, then rearrange the ingredients so that the potatoes are underneath the beef and vegetables. Reduce the heat to medium-low and add all the seasonings. Simmer for 20 minutes, partially covered, or until most of the liquid has evaporated.

5 Check if the potatoes are cooked. Add the peas and cook to heat through, then remove the pan from the heat. Serve the beef and vegetables immediately in four small serving bowls.

Energy 263Kcal/1110kJ; Protein 17.8g; Carbohydrate 34.7g, of which sugars 15.6g; Fat 6g, of which saturates 1.6g; Cholesterol 37mg; Calcium 37mg; Fibre 2.8g; Sodium 1393mg.

PAPER-THIN SLICED BEEF <u>IN</u> STOCK ★★★

THIS DISH IS GREAT FOR SHARING WITH FRIENDS, AS THE COOKING IS DONE AT THE TABLE. THE SESAME SAUCE THAT USUALLY ACCOMPANIES IT HAS BEEN OMITTED HERE BECAUSE IT IS HIGH IN FAT.

SERVES 4

INGREDIENTS
  600g/1⅓lb lean rump (round) steak
  2 thin leeks, trimmed and cut into
    thin strips
  4 spring onions (scallions), quartered
  8 shiitake mushrooms, minus stems
  175g/6oz/2 cups oyster mushrooms,
    base part removed, torn into
    small pieces
  ½ head Chinese leaves (Chinese
    cabbage), cut into 5cm/2in squares
  300g/11oz *shungiku*, halved
  275g/10oz firm tofu, halved
    and cut crossways in 2cm/¾in
    thick slices
  10 x 6cm/4 x 2½in *dashi-konbu*,
    wiped with a damp cloth
For the lime sauce
  1 lime
  20ml/4 tsp mirin
  60ml/4 tbsp rice vinegar
  120ml/4fl oz/½ cup shoyu
  4 x 6cm/1½ x 2½in *dashi-konbu*
  5g/1/8oz *kezuri-bushi*
For the pink daikon
  1 piece daikon (mooli), 6cm/2½in
    in length, peeled
  1 dried chilli, seeded and cut
    in strips

1 Make the lime sauce. Squeeze the lime into a liquid measure and make up to 120ml/4fl oz/½ cup with water.

2 Pour the lime juice into a small bowl and add the mirin, rice vinegar, shoyu, *dashi-konbu* and *kezuri-bushi*. Cover with clear film (plastic wrap) and leave to stand overnight.

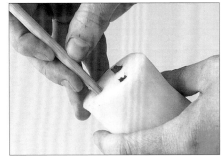

3 Make the pink daikon. Using a wooden skewer, pierce the daikon in several places and insert the chilli strips. Leave for 20 minutes, then grate finely into a sieve (strainer). Squeeze out the liquid and divide among four small bowls.

4 Slice the meat very thinly and arrange on a platter. Put the vegetables and tofu on another platter. Fill a flameproof casserole three-quarters full of water and add the dashi-konbu. Bring to the boil, then transfer to a table burner. Strain the citrus sauce and add 45ml/3 tbsp to each bowl of grated daikon.

5 Remove the konbu from the stock. Add some tofu and vegetables to the pot. Each guest picks up a slice of beef, holds it in the stock for a few seconds until cooked, then dips it in the sauce. As the tofu and vegetables are cooked, they are removed and dipped in the same way, and more are added to the pot.

Energy 311Kcal/1302kJ; Protein 40.7g; Carbohydrate 7.1g, of which sugars 6g; Fat 12.9g, of which saturates 4.7g; Cholesterol 92mg; Calcium 412mg; Fibre 3.8g; Sodium 887mg.

ROASTED AND MARINATED PORK ★★

JAPANESE COOKS OFTEN USE A SOY SAUCE AND CITRUS MARINADE TO FLAVOUR MEAT, ADDING IT BEFORE OR AFTER COOKING. IF POSSIBLE, LEAVE THE MEAT TO MARINATE OVERNIGHT.

SERVES 4

INGREDIENTS

600g/1⅓lb pork fillet (tenderloin)
1 garlic clove, crushed
generous pinch of salt
4 spring onions (scallions), trimmed,
  white part only
10g/¼oz dried wakame seaweed,
  soaked in water for 20 minutes
  and drained
10cm/4in celery stick, trimmed
  and cut in half crossways
1 carton mustard and cress
  (fine curled cress)
For the sauce
  105ml/7 tbsp shoyu
  45ml/3 tbsp sake
  60ml/4 tbsp mirin
  1 lime, sliced into thin rings

1 Preheat the oven to 200°C/400°F/ Gas 6. Rub the pork with crushed garlic and salt, and leave for 15 minutes.

2 Roast the pork for 20 minutes, then turn the meat over and reduce the oven temperature to 180°C/350°F/ Gas 4. Cook for a further 20 minutes, or until the pork is cooked and there are no pink juices when it is pierced.

3 Meanwhile, mix the sauce ingredients in a container that is big enough to hold the pork.

4 When the meat is completely cooked, immediately put it in the sauce, and leave it to marinate for at least 2 hours, or overnight.

5 Cut the white part of the spring onions in half crossways, then in half lengthways. Remove the round cores, then lay the spring onion quarters flat on a chopping board. Slice them very thinly lengthways to make fine shreds.

6 Soak the shreds of spring onion in a bowl of ice-cold water. Repeat with the remaining parts of the spring onions. When the shreds curl up, drain and gather them into a loose ball.

7 Cut the drained wakame seaweed into 2.5cm/1in squares or narrow strips.

8 Slice the trimmed celery very thinly lengthways. Soak in cold water. When the shreds curl up, drain and gather them into a loose ball.

9 Remove the pork from the marinade and wipe it with kitchen paper to soak up any excess. Slice the pork into slices of medium thickness.

10 Strain the marinade into a gravy boat or jug (pitcher).

11 Arrange the sliced pork on a large serving plate and place the vegetables around it. Serve cold with the sauce.

Energy 198Kcal/830kJ; Protein 32.6g; Carbohydrate 0.9g, of which sugars 0.9g; Fat 6.2g, of which saturates 2.1g; Cholesterol 95mg; Calcium 24mg; Fibre 0.4g; Sodium 114mg.

CHAR-SIU PORK ★

LEAN PORK FILLET OR TENDERLOIN IS A DENSE MEAT, SO A LITTLE GOES A LONG WAY. IT TASTES WONDERFUL WHEN MARINATED, ROASTED AND GLAZED WITH HONEY, AND CAN BE SERVED HOT OR COLD.

SERVES 6

INGREDIENTS

    15ml/1 tbsp vegetable oil
    15ml/1 tbsp hoisin sauce
    15ml/1 tbsp yellow bean sauce
    1.5ml/¼ tsp five-spice powder
    2.5ml/½ tsp cornflour (cornstarch)
    15ml/1 tbsp caster
     (superfine) sugar
    1.5ml/¼ tsp salt
    1.5ml/¼ tsp ground white pepper
    450g/1lb pork fillet (tenderloin),
     trimmed of fat
    10ml/2 tsp clear honey
    shredded spring onion (scallion),
     to garnish
    rice, to serve

1 Mix the oil, sauces, five-spice powder, cornflour, sugar and seasoning in a shallow dish. Add the pork and coat it with the mixture. Cover and chill for 4 hours or overnight.

2 Preheat the oven to 190°C/375°F/ Gas 5. Drain the pork and place it on a wire rack over a deep roasting pan. Roast for 40 minutes, turning the pork over from time to time.

3 Check that the pork is cooked by inserting a skewer or fork into the meat; the juices should run clear. If they are still tinged with pink, roast the pork for 5–10 minutes more.

4 Remove the pork from the oven and brush it with the honey. Leave to cool for 10 minutes before cutting into thin slices. Garnish with spring onion and serve hot or cold with rice.

Energy 117Kcal/491kJ; Protein 16.1g; Carbohydrate 2.4g, of which sugars 2g; Fat 4.8g, of which saturates 1.3g; Cholesterol 47mg; Calcium 6mg; Fibre 0g; Sodium 94mg.

SINLESS SWEET AND SOUR PORK ★

SWEET AND SOUR PORK IS ONE OF THE MOST POPULAR CHINESE DISHES IN THE WEST, BUT THE CLASSIC RECIPE IS WOEFULLY HIGH IN FAT. THIS LOW-FAT VERSION IS JUST AS TASTY.

SERVES 4

INGREDIENTS
  15ml/1 tbsp Chinese rice wine or
    dry sherry
  350g/12oz lean pork steaks
  15ml/1 tbsp vegetable oil
  1 garlic clove, finely chopped
  ½ onion, diced
  1 small green (bell) pepper, seeded
    and cut into 2.5cm/1in squares
  1 small carrot, sliced
  75g/3oz/½ cup drained, canned
    pineapple chunks
  30ml/2 tbsp malt vinegar
  45ml/3 tbsp tomato ketchup
  150ml/¼ pint/⅔ cup pineapple juice
  10ml/2 tsp caster (superfine) sugar
  10ml/2 tsp cornflour (cornstarch)
  15ml/1 tbsp cold water
  salt and ground black pepper
  rice, to serve

1 Put the sherry in a bowl large enough to hold the pork steaks. Add 2.5ml/ ½ tsp salt and a large pinch of pepper. Add the pork, turn to coat, then cover and leave to marinate in a cool place for 15 minutes.

COOK'S TIP
This is a great way of giving leftover pork from the Sunday roast a new lease of life. Slice it into bitesize pieces and add it to the wok instead of the freshly cooked pork steaks. It is important that the pork is heated through completely before being served. This will probably take a few minutes longer than the time suggested in the recipe. When it is hot, thicken the sauce and serve.

2 Drain the pork steaks and place them on a rack over a grill (broiler) pan. Grill (broil) under high heat for 5 minutes on each side or until cooked, then remove and leave to cool. Cut the cooked pork into bitesize pieces.

3 Heat a non-stick frying pan or wok, then add the oil. When the oil is very hot, add the garlic and onion and stir-fry for a few seconds, then add the green pepper and carrot and stir-fry for 1 minute.

4 Stir in the pineapple chunks, vinegar, tomato ketchup, pineapple juice and caster sugar. Bring to the boil, lower the heat and simmer for 3 minutes, stirring the mixture once or twice.

5 Meanwhile, put the cornflour in a small bowl. Stir in the water to make a smooth paste.

6 Add the cooked pork to the vegetable mixture and toss over the heat for about 2 minutes.

7 Tip in the cornflour paste. Cook, stirring constantly with the chopsticks or a wooden spoon, until the sauce has thickened slightly. Serve with rice in heated bowls.

VARIATION
Skinless chicken, turkey or duck breast fillets could be used in place of the pork, and you could substitute canned apricots for the canned pineapple, if you like.

Energy 168Kcal/709kJ; Protein 19.7g; Carbohydrate 13.6g, of which sugars 13g; Fat 3.8g, of which saturates 1.3g; Cholesterol 55mg; Calcium 20mg; Fibre 1.1g; Sodium 251mg.

STICKY PORK RIBS ★★

MANY PEOPLE ASSUME PORK RIBS TO BE HIGH IN FAT, BUT THESE FALL WELL WITHIN ACCEPTABLE LIMITS. TAKE THE TIME TO MARINATE THE MEAT AS THIS ALLOWS ALL THE FLAVOURS TO PERMEATE.

SERVES 4

INGREDIENTS

- 30ml/2 tbsp caster (superfine) sugar
- 2.5ml/½ tsp five-spice powder
- 45ml/3 tbsp hoisin sauce
- 30ml/2 tbsp yellow bean sauce
- garlic cloves, finely chopped
- 15ml/1 tbsp cornflour (cornstarch)
- 2.5ml/½ tsp salt
- 16 meaty pork ribs
- chives and sliced spring onion (scallion), to garnish
- salad or rice, to serve

1 Combine the caster sugar, five-spice powder, hoisin sauce, yellow bean sauce, garlic, cornflour and salt in a bowl, then mix together well.

2 Place the pork ribs in an ovenproof dish and pour the marinade over. Mix thoroughly, cover and leave in a cool place for 1 hour.

3 Preheat the oven to 180°C/350°F/ Gas 4. Cover the dish tightly with foil and bake the pork ribs for 40 minutes. Baste the ribs from time to time with the cooking juices.

4 Remove the foil, baste the ribs and continue to cook for 20 minutes until glossy and brown.

5 Garnish the ribs with chives and sliced spring onion and serve with a salad or rice.

COOK'S TIP

- The ribs barbecue very well. Par-cook them in the oven for 40 minutes as described in the main recipe, then transfer them to the barbecue for 15 minutes to finish cooking. The sauce coating makes the ribs liable to burn, so watch them closely.
- Don't forget finger bowls when serving these. They are not called sticky ribs for nothing.

Energy 239Kcal/1006kJ; Protein 32.4g; Carbohydrate 14.5g, of which sugars 10.9g; Fat 6.1g, of which saturates 2.1g; Cholesterol 95mg; Calcium 17mg; Fibre 0.1g; Sodium 291mg.

STIR-FRIED PORK <u>WITH</u> LYCHEES ★★

PORK IS NOW LOWER IN FAT THAN EVER BEFORE, AND IS A GOOD CHOICE FOR A HEALTHY MEAL.
CHOOSE FILLET OR TENDERLOIN, WHICH COOK QUICKLY WHEN CUT INTO FINE STRIPS.

SERVES 4

INGREDIENTS

   450g/1lb lean pork
    fillet (tenderloin)
   30ml/2 tbsp hoisin sauce
   15ml/1 tbsp vegetable oil
   4 spring onions (scallions), sliced
   175g/6oz lychees, peeled, stoned
    (pitted) and cut into slivers
   salt and ground black pepper
   fresh lychees and fresh parsley
    sprigs, to garnish

1 Press the meat down on a chopping board, using the palm of your hand, and slice.it horizontally into strips. Cut the strips crossways into bitesize pieces and place them in a bowl.

2 Pour the hoisin sauce over the pork and marinate for 30 minutes.

3 Heat the wok until it is very hot, then add the pork and stir-fry for 5 minutes until it is cooked through and the outside is crisp and golden.

4 Add the spring onions and stir-fry for a further 2 minutes.

5 Sprinkle the lychee slivers over the pork, and season well with salt and pepper. Garnish with fresh lychees and fresh parsley, and serve.

Energy 198Kcal/833kJ; Protein 24.8g; Carbohydrate 8.7g, of which sugars 8.6g; Fat 7.4g, of which saturates 1.9g; Cholesterol 71mg; Calcium 16mg; Fibre 0.5g; Sodium 202mg.

STIR-FRIED PORK WITH MUSHROOMS ★★★

THE SWEET, ALMOST SCENTED FLAVOUR OF SUCCULENT LYCHEES MAKES THEM AN EXCELLENT ACCOMPANIMENT FOR ANY MEAT, BUT THEY ARE PARTICULARLY GOOD WITH PORK OR DUCK.

SERVES 4

INGREDIENTS
    30ml/2 tbsp vegetable oil
    450g/1lb pork fillet (tenderloin),
        cut into fine strips
    1 onion, halved and sliced
    1 fresh green chilli, seeded
        and chopped
    2 garlic cloves, sliced
    150g/5oz/1¾ cups oyster
        mushrooms, sliced
    200g/7oz green beans, sliced
    2 oranges, peeled and cut
        into segments
    15ml/1 tbsp clear honey
    30ml/2 tbsp sherry
    350g/12oz egg noodles, cooked
    30ml/2 tbsp sesame oil

1 Heat the oil in a wok or large frying pan until very hot. Stir-fry the pork for 5 minutes until it is tender and cooked through. Remove the pork with a slotted spoon and put it on a plate. Add the onion, chilli, garlic, mushrooms and green beans to the wok and stir-fry the vegetables for 3–5 minutes.

2 Return the pork to the wok. Add the orange segments, honey and sherry, and cook for a further 2 minutes, stirring frequently.

COOK'S TIP
When stir-frying, cut the ingredients into similar size strips so that they cook evenly and quickly, and prepare all the ingredients before you begin cooking.

3 Cook the egg noodles in a pan of boiling water, or according to the pack instructions, until tender. Drain thoroughly, then sprinkle with the sesame oil and toss to coat. Divide the noodles among individual warm serving bowls and spoon the pork stir-fry on top. Serve immediately.

Energy 243Kcal/1016kJ; Protein 26.6g; Carbohydrate 10g, of which sugars 9.1g; Fat 10.5g, of which saturates 2.3g; Cholesterol 71mg; Calcium 61mg; Fibre 2.8g; Sodium 85mg.

RIBS OF PORK WITH EGG-FRIED RICE ★★★

MEATY PORK RIBS WITH A GLORIOUS MARMALADE AND SOY SAUCE GLAZE ARE GREAT FOR INFORMAL DINNER PARTIES, AND LOOK IMPRESSIVE WHEN PRESENTED ON A MOUND OF EGG-FRIED RICE.

SERVES 4

INGREDIENTS
    2 shallots, chopped
    1 garlic clove, chopped
    30ml/2 tbsp tomato purée (paste)
    45ml/3 tbsp orange marmalade
    30ml/2 tbsp light soy sauce
    grated rind and juice of 1 orange
    grated rind and juice of 1 lemon
    1kg/2¼lb meaty pork ribs
    salt and ground black pepper
For the egg-fried rice
    30ml/2 tbsp vegetable oil
    6 spring onions (scallions), sliced
    1 red (bell) pepper, seeded
        and chopped
    175g/6oz/1½ cups peas
    2 eggs, lightly beaten
    350g/12oz/1⅔ cups long grain
        rice, cooked and cooled

1 Preheat the oven to 200°C/400°F/ Gas 6. Mix the shallots, garlic, tomato purée, marmalade, soy sauce, orange and lemon rind and juice in a pan. Bring to the boil, stirring all the time, then simmer until reduced to a syrupy glaze. Season with salt and pepper.

2 Arrange the ribs in a roasting pan and drizzle with glaze. Bake for 40 minutes, turning and basting occasionally.

3 Meanwhile prepare the egg-fried rice. Heat the oil in a large frying pan and when it is hot, cook the spring onions, pepper and peas until just tender.

4 Add the lightly beaten eggs. Cook until they are just beginning to set, then beat vigorously, so that the egg mixture breaks up. Add the cooked rice and cook, stirring often, until piping hot. Serve with the glazed ribs.

Energy 317kcal/1323kJ; Protein 36.3g; Carbohydrate 11.8g, of which sugars 7.4g; Fat 14.1g, of which saturates 3.4g; Cholesterol 164mg; Calcium 47mg; Fibre 3.4g; Sodium 147mg.

CELLOPHANE NOODLES <u>WITH</u> PORK ★

ADDING CHICKEN STOCK TO A STIR-FRY IN THE FINAL STAGES MIGHT SEEM A BIT STRANGE, BUT THE LIQUID IS ABSORBED BY THE NOODLES, WHICH BECOME BEAUTIFULLY TENDER AND FLAVOURSOME.

<u>SERVES 3–4</u>

INGREDIENTS

115g/4oz cellophane noodles
4 dried Chinese black mushrooms
225g/8oz lean pork fillet (tenderloin)
30ml/2 tbsp dark soy sauce
30ml/2 tbsp Chinese rice wine
2 garlic cloves, crushed
15ml/1 tbsp grated fresh root ginger
5ml/1 tsp chilli oil
30ml/2 tbsp vegetable oil
6 spring onions (scallions), chopped
5ml/1 tsp cornflour (cornstarch)
  blended with 175ml/6fl oz/³⁄₄ cup
  chicken stock
30ml/2 tbsp chopped fresh
  coriander (cilantro)
salt and ground black pepper
coriander sprigs, to garnish

1 Put the noodles and mushrooms in separate bowls and cover them with warm water. Leave them to soak for 20 minutes, until soft; drain well.

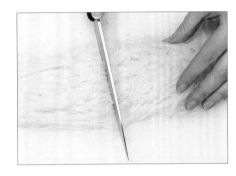

2 Cut the noodles into 13cm/5in lengths. Squeeze any water from the mushrooms, discard the stems and finely chop the caps.

3 Cut the pork into very small cubes. Put into a bowl with the soy sauce, rice wine, garlic, ginger and chilli oil, then leave for about 15 minutes. Drain, reserving the marinade.

4 Heat the oil in a wok and add the pork and mushrooms. Stir-fry for 3 minutes, then add the spring onions and stir-fry for 1 minute.

5 Add the cornflour and stock mixture with the marinade and seasoning.

6 Add the noodles and stir-fry for about 2 minutes, until the noodles absorb most of the liquid and the pork is cooked through. Stir in the coriander. Serve garnished with coriander sprigs.

Energy 198Kcal/834kJ; Protein 15.9g; Carbohydrate 24g, of which sugars 1.6g; Fat 4.9g, of which saturates 0.9g; Cholesterol 35mg; Calcium 18mg; Fibre 1.1g; Sodium 487mg.

PORK CHOW MEIN ★★★

PROVING THAT YOU DON'T NEED MASSIVE AMOUNTS OF MEAT TO MAKE A TASTY MEAL, THIS CLASSIC RECIPE TEAMS NOODLES WITH PORK, VEGETABLES AND FRESH HERBS IN A SAVOURY SAUCE.

SERVES 2–3

INGREDIENTS

175g/6oz medium egg noodles
275g/10oz pork fillet (tenderloin)
15ml/1 tbsp vegetable oil
2 garlic cloves, crushed
8 spring onions (scallions), sliced
1 red (bell) pepper, seeded and
  roughly chopped
1 green (bell) pepper, seeded and
  roughly chopped
30ml/2 tbsp dark soy sauce
45ml/3 tbsp dry sherry
5ml/1 tsp sesame oil
175g/6oz/3 cups beansprouts
45ml/3 tbsp chopped fresh flatleaf
  parsley or coriander (cilantro)
15ml/1 tbsp toasted sesame seeds

1 Soak the egg noodles in warm water according to the packet instructions. Drain well.

2 Thinly slice the pork fillet. Heat the sunflower oil in a wok or large frying pan. Add the pork to the wok or pan and cook over high heat, stirring constantly, until the meat is golden brown and cooked through.

3 Add the garlic, spring onions and peppers to the wok or pan. Cook the mixture over a high heat, stirring frequently, for 3–4 minutes, or until the vegetables just begin to soften. Reduce the heat slightly.

4 Add the noodles, with the soy sauce, sherry and sesame oil. Stir-fry for 2 minutes. Add the beansprouts and cook for a further 1–2 minutes. Stir in the parsley or coriander and serve in heated bowls. Sprinkle with the sesame seeds.

Energy 453Kcal/1906kJ; Protein 30.8g; Carbohydrate 53.7g, of which sugars 11.3g; Fat 14.2g, of which saturates 3.4g; Cholesterol 75mg; Calcium 86mg; Fibre 5.6g; Sodium 896mg.

MONGOLIAN FIREPOT ★★

IT IS WORTH INVESTING IN AN AUTHENTIC HOTPOT OR FIREPOT, JUST TO SEE THE DELIGHT ON YOUR GUESTS' FACES WHEN THEY SPY WHAT YOU HAVE IN STORE FOR THEM. THIS TASTES GREAT TOO.

SERVES 6–8

INGREDIENTS

750g/1²⁄₃lb boned leg of lamb,
   preferably bought thinly sliced
225g/8oz lamb's liver and/or kidneys
900ml/1½ pints/3¾ cups lamb stock
   (see Cook's Tip)
900ml/1½ pints/3¾ cups
   chicken stock
1cm/½in piece fresh root ginger,
   peeled and thinly sliced
45ml/3 tbsp rice wine or
   medium-dry sherry
½ head Chinese leaves
   (Chinese cabbage), rinsed
   and shredded
100g/3½oz young spinach leaves
250g/9oz fresh firm tofu, diced
115g/4oz cellophane noodles
salt and ground black pepper
For the dipping sauce
50ml/2fl oz/¼ cup red
   wine vinegar
7.5ml/½ tbsp dark soy sauce
1cm/½in piece fresh root ginger,
   peeled and finely shredded
1 spring onion (scallion),
   finely shredded
To serve
Steamed Flower Rolls
   bowls of tomato sauce, sweet chilli
   sauce, mustard oil and sesame oil
   dry-fried coriander seeds, crushed

COOK'S TIP
When buying the lamb, ask the butcher for the bones and make your own lamb stock. Rinse the bones and place them in a large pan with water to cover. Bring to the boil and skim the surface well. Add 1 peeled onion, 2 peeled carrots, 1cm/½in piece of peeled and bruised ginger, 5ml/1 tsp salt and ground black pepper to taste. Bring back to the boil, then simmer for about an hour until the stock is full of flavour. Strain, leave to cool, then skim and use.

1 Ask the butcher from whom you buy the lamb to slice it thinly on a slicing machine. If you have had to buy the lamb in one piece, however, trim off any fat, then put the leg in the freezer for about an hour, so that it is easier to slice thinly.

2 Trim the liver and remove the skin and core from the kidneys, if using. Place them in the freezer too. If you managed to buy sliced lamb, keep it in the refrigerator until needed.

3 Mix both types of stock in a large pan. Add the sliced ginger and rice wine or sherry, with salt and pepper to taste. Heat to simmering point; simmer for 15 minutes.

4 Slice all the meats thinly and arrange them on a large platter.

5 Place the shredded Chinese leaves, spinach leaves and the diced tofu on a separate platter.

6 Soak the noodles in a bowl of warm or hot water, following the instructions on the packet.

7 Make the dipping sauce by mixing all the ingredients together in a small bowl. The other sauces and the crushed coriander seeds should be spooned into separate small dishes and placed on a serving tray.

8 Have ready a basket of warm Steamed Flower Rolls.

9 Fill the moat of the hotpot with the simmering stock. Alternatively, fill a fondue pot and place it over a burner.

10 Each guest selects a portion of meat from the platter and cooks it in the hot stock, using chopsticks or a fondue fork. The meat is then dipped in one of the sauces and coated with the coriander seeds (if you like) before being eaten with a steamed flower roll.

11 When most of the meat has been eaten, top up the stock if necessary, then add the vegetables, tofu and drained noodles. Cook for a minute or two, until the noodles are tender and the vegetables retain a little crispness. Serve the soup in warmed bowls, with any remaining steamed flower rolls.

Energy 144Kcal/606kJ; Protein 12.3g; Carbohydrate 12g, of which sugars 1.2g; Fat 5.1g, of which saturates 1.1g; Cholesterol 128mg; Calcium 193mg; Fibre 0.9g; Sodium 49mg.

GLAZED LAMB ★★★

LEMON AND HONEY MAKE A CLASSICALLY GOOD COMBINATION IN SWEET DISHES, AND THIS LAMB RECIPE SHOWS HOW WELL THEY WORK TOGETHER IN SAVOURY DISHES, TOO.

SERVES 4

INGREDIENTS

350g/12oz lean boneless lamb
15ml/1 tbsp vegetable oil
175g/6oz mangetouts
  (snow peas), trimmed
3 spring onions (scallions), sliced
30ml/2 tbsp clear honey
juice of ½ lemon
30ml/2 tbsp fresh coriander
  (cilantro), chopped
10ml/2 tsp sesame seeds
salt and ground black pepper

1 Trim any visible fat from the lamb. Using a cleaver or sharp knife, cut the lamb into thin strips.

2 Heat the wok, then add the oil. When the oil is hot, stir-fry the lamb until browned all over. Remove from the wok and keep warm.

3 Add the mangetouts and spring onions to the hot wok and stir-fry for 30 seconds.

4 Return the lamb to the wok and add the honey, lemon juice, coriander and sesame seeds, and season well. Bring the sauce to the boil and bubble for 2–3 minutes until the lamb is cooked through and is well coated in the honey mixture.

Energy 223kcal/931kJ; Protein 19g; Carbohydrate 7.8g, of which sugars 7.4g; Fat 13.0g, of which saturates 4.9g; Cholesterol 67mg; Calcium 34mg; Fibre 1.2g; Sodium 78mg.

MINTED LAMB ★★★

No matter what cut you use, lamb is a fatty meat, so can't be eaten in huge quantities. Relish the flavour of this stir-fry and fill any gaps with couscous and a green salad.

SERVES 4

INGREDIENTS

300g/11oz boneless leg of lamb
30ml/2 tbsp chopped fresh mint
½ lemon
300ml/½ pint/1¼ cups natural
   (plain) low-fat yogurt
15ml/1 tbsp sunflower oil
salt and ground black pepper
lemon wedges and fresh mint sprigs,
   to garnish

1 Place the lamb on a board. Using a sharp knife or cleaver, cut the lamb into 6mm/¼in thick slices. Spread out the slices in a bowl or shallow dish.

2 Sprinkle half the chopped mint over the lamb, season well with salt and pepper and use your fingers to work the flavourings into the meat.

3 Cover the bowl with clear film (plastic wrap) and leave the lamb to marinate for 20 minutes.

4 Remove any visible seeds from the lemon and cut it into wedges, including the skin.

5 Place the lemon wedges in a food processor. Process until finely chopped.

6 Scrape the lemon into a bowl, then stir in the yogurt and the remaining chopped mint. Add salt and pepper to taste, if you like.

7 Heat a wok, then add the oil, trickling it around the inner rim so that it runs down to coat the surface. When the oil is hot, add the lamb and stir-fry for 4–5 minutes until cooked. Garnish with lemon wedges and fresh mint sprigs, and serve with the yogurt sauce.

Energy 268Kcal/1120kJ; Protein 25.9g; Carbohydrate 5.6g, of which sugars 5.6g; Fat 15.0g, of which saturates 6.6g; Cholesterol 86mg; Calcium 152mg; Fibre 0g; Sodium 159mg.

RICE AND NOODLES

This chapter introduces a range of recipes that should be in the repertoire of every low-fat cook. They are universally low in saturated fat, with several dishes registering below 1 gram. Stars in this regard include Five Ingredients Rice, Fusion Noodles, and Toasted Noodles with Vegetables. Sticky Rice Parcels and Noodles with Chicken, Prawns and Ham are designed to stand alone, but there are also some enticing accompaniments, including Noodles with Ginger and Coriander.

CHINESE FRIED RICE ★

ALTHOUGH THE RICE IN THIS RECIPE IS FRIED, WHICH MIGHT RING ALARM BELLS IN TERMS OF FAT, IT CONTAINS ONLY A LITTLE HAM AND COMES IN AT UNDER 4 GRAMS OF FAT.

SERVES 4

INGREDIENTS

50g/2oz cooked lean ham
50g/2oz cooked prawns
   (shrimp), peeled
2 eggs
pinch of salt
2 spring onions (scallions),
   finely chopped
30ml/2 tbsp vegetable oil
115g/4oz/1 cup green peas, thawed
   if frozen
15ml/1 tbsp light soy sauce
15ml/1 tbsp Chinese rice wine or
   dry sherry
450g/1lb/4 cups cooked white long
   grain rice

1 Dice the cooked ham finely. Pat the cooked prawns dry on kitchen paper.

VARIATIONS
This dish is ideal for using up leftovers. You can use cooked chicken instead of the ham and leave out the prawns, if you like.

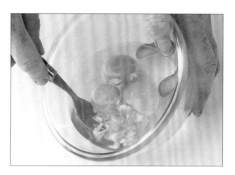

2 In a bowl, beat the eggs with a pinch of salt and a few spring onion pieces.

3 Heat a wok. When it is hot, add half the oil, trickling it around the inner rim of the wok so that it runs down to coat the surface. Stir-fry the peas, prawns and ham for 1 minute, then add the soy sauce and rice wine or sherry. Stir to combine, then transfer to a bowl and keep hot.

4 Heat the remaining oil in the wok and add the eggs. Stir over a low heat until lightly scrambled.

5 Add the prawn mixture, rice and the remaining spring onions. Stir to heat thoroughly. Serve hot or cold.

Energy 86Kcal/360kJ; Protein 9.8g; Carbohydrate 3.8g, of which sugars 1.2g; Fat 3.7g, of which saturates 1g; Cholesterol 127mg; Calcium 34mg; Fibre 1.4g; Sodium 477mg.

FRIED RICE WITH MUSHROOMS ★

A TASTY RICE AND MUSHROOM DISH THAT IS VERY LOW IN SATURATED FAT, YET SUFFICIENTLY FILLING TO BE ALMOST A MEAL IN ITSELF. SESAME OIL ADDS A HINT OF NUTTY FLAVOUR.

SERVES 4

INGREDIENTS
225g/8oz/1¼ cups long grain rice
15ml/1 tbsp vegetable oil
1 egg, lightly beaten
2 garlic cloves, crushed
175g/6oz/2¼ cups button (white) mushrooms or mixed wild and cultivated mushrooms, sliced
15ml/1 tbsp light soy sauce
1.5ml/¼ tsp salt
2.5ml/½ tsp sesame oil
cucumber matchsticks, to garnish

1 Rinse the rice until the water runs clear, then drain thoroughly. Place it in a pan. Measure the depth of the rice against your index finger, then bring the finger up to just above the surface of the rice and add cold water to the same depth as the rice.

2 Bring the water to the boil. Stir the rice, boil for a few minutes, then cover the pan. Lower the heat to a simmer and cook the rice gently for 5–8 minutes until all of the water has been absorbed.

3 Remove the pan from the heat and, without lifting the lid, leave for another 10 minutes before stirring or forking up the rice.

4 Heat 5ml/1 tsp of the vegetable oil in a non-stick frying pan or wok. Add the egg and cook, stirring with a chopstick or wooden spoon until scrambled. Immediately remove the pan from the heat and set aside.

5 Add the remaining vegetable oil in the pan or wok. When it is hot, stir-fry the garlic for a few seconds, then add the mushrooms and stir-fry for 2 minutes, adding a little water, if needed, to prevent burning.

6 Stir in the cooked rice and cook for about 4 minutes, or until the rice is hot, stirring from time to time.

7 Add the scrambled egg, soy sauce, salt and sesame oil. Mix together and cook for 1 minute to heat through. Serve the rice immediately, garnished with cucumber matchsticks.

COOK'S TIP
When you cook rice this way, you may find there is a crust at the bottom of the pan. Don't worry; simply soak the crust in water for a couple of minutes to break it up, then drain it and fry it with the rest of the rice.

Energy 275Kcal/1148kJ; Protein 7.1g; Carbohydrate 50.4g, of which sugars 0.4g; Fat 4.7g, of which saturates 0.8g; Cholesterol 48mg; Calcium 22mg; Fibre 0.5g; Sodium 287mg.

CHINESE JEWELLED RICE ★★

KEEP THE BASIC INGREDIENTS FOR THIS DISH IN YOUR KITCHEN AND YOU'LL ALWAYS HAVE THE MEANS TO MAKE A QUICK LOW-FAT MEAL. THE ONLY THING YOU'LL NEED TO BUY IS THE HAM.

SERVES 4

INGREDIENTS
  350g/12oz/1½ cups long grain rice
  30ml/2 tbsp vegetable oil
  1 onion, roughly chopped
  115g/4oz cooked lean ham, visible
    fat removed, diced
  175g/6oz/1¼ cups canned
    white crabmeat
  75g/3oz/½ cup canned water
    chestnuts, drained and cut
    into cubes
  4 dried black Chinese mushrooms,
    soaked, drained and diced
  115g/4oz/1 cup peas, thawed if frozen
  30ml/2 tbsp oyster sauce
  5ml/1 tsp sugar

2 Heat the wok, then add the oil, trickling it around the inner rim so that it runs down to coat the surface of the wok. When the oil is hot, add the chopped onion and cook until it has softened but not coloured.

3 Add the diced ham, white crab meat, cubed water chestnuts, diced Chinese mushrooms and peas. Mix lightly, then stir-fry for 2 minutes. Stir in the oyster sauce and sugar and mix well to thoroughly combine.

1 Rinse the raw rice under cold water, then cook for 10–12 minutes in 750–900ml/1¼–1½ pints water in a pan with a tight-fitting lid. When the rice is cooked, refresh it in a sieve (strainer) under cold running water. Set aside until required.

4 Add the rice to the wok. Toss all the ingredients together over high heat, until the rice is heated through.

5 Serve immediately in heated bowls.

Energy 474Kcal/1979kJ; Protein 22.5g; Carbohydrate 77.5g, of which sugars 4.3g; Fat 7.8g, of which saturates 1.1g; Cholesterol 48mg; Calcium 86mg; Fibre 1.9g; Sodium 710mg.

CHINESE LEAVES AND BLACK RICE STIR-FRY ★

*THE SLIGHTLY NUTTY, CHEWY BLACK GLUTINOUS RICE CONTRASTS BEAUTIFULLY WITH THE
CHINESE LEAVES IN THIS TASTY STIR-FRY, WHICH IS LOW IN SATURATED FAT.*

SERVES 4

INGREDIENTS

225g/8oz/1⅓ cups black glutinous
  rice or brown rice
900ml/1½ pints/3¾ cups
  vegetable stock
15ml/1 tbsp vegetable oil
225g/8oz Chinese leaves (Chinese
  cabbage), cut into 1cm/½in strips
4 spring onions (scallions),
  thinly sliced
salt and ground white pepper
2.5ml/½ tsp sesame oil

4 Drain the rice, stir it into the pan and cook for 4 minutes, using two spatulas or spoons to toss it with the Chinese leaves over the heat.

5 Add the spring onions, with salt and pepper to taste. Drizzle over the sesame oil. Cook for 1 minute more, stirring constantly. Serve immediately.

1 Rinse the rice until the water runs clear, then drain and tip into a pan. Add the stock and bring to the boil. Lower the heat, cover the pan and cook gently for 30 minutes.

2 Remove the pan from the heat and leave to stand for 15 minutes without lifting the lid.

3 Heat the vegetable oil in a non-stick frying pan or wok. Stir-fry the Chinese leaves over medium heat for 2 minutes, adding a little water to prevent them from burning.

Energy 243Kcal/1029kJ; Protein 4.8g; Carbohydrate 48.9g, of which sugars 3.8g; Fat 4.5g, of which saturates 0.7g; Cholesterol 0mg; Calcium 37mg; Fibre 2.4g; Sodium 6mg.

STICKY RICE PARCELS ★★

THIS IS A SUPERB DISH, PACKED WITH FLAVOUR. THE PARCELS LOOK PRETTY AND IT IS A PLEASURE TO CUT THEM OPEN AND DISCOVER THE DELICIOUS CHICKEN AND MUSHROOM FILLING INSIDE.

SERVES 4

INGREDIENTS
450g/1lb/2⅔ cups glutinous rice
20ml/4 tsp vegetable oil
15ml/1 tbsp dark soy sauce
1.5ml/¼ tsp five-spice powder
15ml/1 tbsp dry sherry
4 skinless, boneless chicken thighs,
  each cut into 4 pieces
8 dried Chinese mushrooms, soaked
  in hot water until soft
25g/1oz dried shrimps, soaked in
  hot water until soft
50g/2oz/½ cup canned bamboo
  shoots, drained and sliced
300ml/½ pint/1¼ cups
  chicken stock
10ml/2 tsp cornflour (cornstarch)
15ml/1 tbsp cold water
4 lotus leaves, soaked in warm
  water until soft
salt and ground white pepper

1 Rinse the glutinous rice in a sieve (strainer) until the water runs clear, then leave to soak in a bowl of water for 2 hours.

2 Drain the rice in a sieve and tip it into a bowl. Stir in 5ml/1 tsp of the oil and 2.5ml/½ tsp salt.

3 Line a large steamer with a piece of clean muslin or cheesecloth.

4 Scrape the soaked rice into the steamer, cover and steam over a large pan of boiling water for 45 minutes, stirring the rice from time to time and topping up the water if needed.

5 Mix the soy sauce, five-spice powder and sherry. Put the chicken pieces in a bowl, add the marinade, stir to coat, then cover and leave to marinate for 20 minutes.

6 Drain the Chinese mushrooms, remove and discard the stems, then chop the caps roughly. Drain the dried shrimps in a sieve.

7 Heat the remaining oil in a non-stick frying pan or wok. When the oil is hot, stir-fry the chicken for 2 minutes, then add the mushrooms, shrimps, bamboo shoots and stock. Mix well and simmer for 10 minutes.

8 Mix the cornflour to a paste with the cold water in a small bowl. Add to the pan and cook, stirring, until the sauce has thickened. Season to taste. Lift the cooked rice out of the steamer and let it cool slightly.

COOK'S TIP
The sticky rice parcels can be made several days in advance and simply re-steamed before serving. If you do this, allow an extra 20 minutes' cooking time to ensure that the filling is hot.

9 With lightly dampened hands, divide the rice into four equal portions. Put half of one portion in the centre of a lotus leaf. Spread it into a round and place a quarter of the chicken on top.

10 Cover with the remaining half portion of rice. Fold the leaf around the filling to make a neat rectangular parcel. Make three more parcels in the same way.

11 Put the rice parcels, seam side down, into the steamer, using two tiers if the parcels are too big to fit in one. Cover and steam over a high heat for about 30 minutes. Serve the parcels on individual heated plates, inviting each diner to unwrap their own.

Energy 565Kcal/2369kJ; Protein 37.3g; Carbohydrate 87.1g, of which sugars 0.3g; Fat 6.1g, of which saturates 0.7g; Cholesterol 102mg; Calcium 101mg; Fibre 0.2g; Sodium 336mg.

RED RICE WRAPPED IN OAK LEAVES ★★

THIS IS A SAVOURY VERSION OF A POPULAR JAPANESE SWEETMEAT. OAK TREES DON'T SHED THEIR OLD LEAVES UNTIL NEW ONES APPEAR, SO THEY REPRESENT THE CONTINUITY OF FAMILY LIFE.

SERVES 4

INGREDIENTS
  65g/2½oz/⅓ cup dried aduki beans
  5ml/1 tsp salt
  300g/11oz/1½ cups glutinous rice
  50g/2oz/¼ cup Japanese short
    grain rice
  12 *kashiwa* leaves (optional)
For the *goma-shio*
  45ml/3 tbsp sesame seeds (black
    sesame, if available)
  5ml/1 tsp ground sea salt

1 Put the aduki beans in a heavy pan and pour in 400ml/14fl oz/1⅔ cups plus 20ml/4 tsp water.

2 Bring to the boil, reduce the heat and simmer, covered, for 20–30 minutes, or until the beans look swollen but are still firm. Remove from the heat and drain. Reserve the liquid in a bowl and add the salt. Return the beans to the pan.

3 Wash all of the rice. Drain in a sieve (strainer) and leave for 30 minutes.

4 Bring another 400ml/14fl oz/1⅔ cups plus 20ml/4 tsp water to the boil. Add to the beans and boil, then simmer for 30 minutes. The beans' skins should start to crack. Drain and add the liquid to the bowl with the reserved liquid. Cover the beans and leave to cool.

5 Add the rice to the bean liquid. Leave to soak for 4–5 hours. Drain the rice and reserve the liquid. Mix the rice into the beans.

6 Bring a steamer of water to the boil. Turn off the heat. Place a tall glass in the centre of the steaming compartment. Pour the rice and beans into the steamer and gently pull the glass out. The hole in the middle will allow even distribution of the steam. Steam on high for 10 minutes.

7 Using your fingers, sprinkle the rice mixture with the reserved liquid from the bowl. Cover again and repeat the process twice more at 10 minute intervals, then leave to steam for 15 minutes more. Remove from the heat. Leave to stand for 10 minutes.

8 Make the *goma-shio*. Roast the sesame seeds and salt in a dry frying pan until the seeds start to pop. Leave to cool, then put in a small dish.

9 Wipe each *kashiwa* leaf with a wet dish towel. Scoop 120ml/4fl oz/½ cup of the rice mixture into a wet tea cup and press with wet fingers. Turn the cup upside down and shape the moulded rice with your hands into a flat ball. Insert into a leaf folded in two. Repeat this process until all the leaves are used. Alternatively, transfer the red rice to a large bowl wiped with a wet towel.

10 Serve the red rice with a sprinkle of *goma-shio*. The kashiwa leaves (except for fresh ones) are edible.

Energy 432Kcal/1807kJ; Protein 12.4g; Carbohydrate 78.7g, of which sugars 0.5g; Fat 7.2g, of which saturates 1g; Cholesterol 0mg; Calcium 105mg; Fibre 2.2g; Sodium 5mg.

FIVE INGREDIENTS RICE ✱

THE JAPANESE LOVE RICE SO MUCH THEY INVENTED MANY WAYS TO ENJOY IT. HERE, CHICKEN AND VEGETABLES ARE COOKED WITH SHORT GRAIN RICE MAKING A HEALTHY LIGHT LUNCH DISH.

SERVES 4

INGREDIENTS

275g/10oz/1¼ cups Japanese
   short grain rice
90g/3½oz carrot, peeled
2.5ml/½ tsp lemon juice
90g/3½oz gobo (burdock) or canned
   bamboo shoots
225g/8oz/3 cups oyster mushrooms
8 fresh mitsuba or parsley sprigs
350ml/12fl oz/1½ cups water
   and 7.5ml/1½ tsp instant
   dashi powder
150g/5oz skinless chicken breast
   fillet, cut into 2cm/¾in chunks
30ml/2 tbsp shoyu
30ml/2 tbsp sake
25ml/1½ tbsp mirin
pinch of salt

1 Put the rice in a large bowl and wash well with cold water. Keep changing the water until it remains clear, then tip the rice into a sieve (strainer) and drain for 30 minutes.

2 Using a sharp knife, cut the carrot into 5mm/¼in rounds, then cut the discs into flowers.

COOK'S TIP
Although gobo or burdock is recognized as a poisonous plant in the West, it has been eaten in Japan for centuries. To make it safe to eat, gobo must always be cooked, because it contains iron and other acidic elements that are harmful if they are eaten raw. By soaking it in alkaline water and then cooking it for a short time, gobo becomes edible.

3 Fill a small bowl with cold water and add the lemon juice. Peel the gobo and then slice it with a knife as if you were sharpening a pencil into the bowl.

4 Leave for 15 minutes, then drain. If using canned bamboo shoots, slice them into thin matchsticks.

5 Tear the oyster mushrooms into thin strips. Chop the mitsuba or parsley. Put it in a sieve and pour over hot water from the kettle to wilt the leaves. Allow to drain and then set aside.

6 Heat the dashi stock in a large pan and add the carrots and gobo or bamboo shoots. Bring to the boil and add the chicken. Remove any scum from the surface, and add the shoyu, sake, mirin and salt.

7 Add the rice and mushrooms and cover with a tight-fitting lid. Bring back to the boil, wait 5 minutes, then reduce the heat and simmer for 10 minutes. Remove from the heat without lifting the lid and leave to stand for 15 minutes. Add the wilted herbs and serve.

Energy 312Kcal/1308kJ; Protein 16.1g; Carbohydrate 58.4g, of which sugars 2.8g; Fat 1.2g, of which saturates 0.2g; Cholesterol 26mg; Calcium 30mg; Fibre 1.5g; Sodium 566mg.

CHICKEN AND EGG ON RICE ★★

THE AGE-OLD QUESTION OF WHICH CAME FIRST, THE CHICKEN OR THE EGG, IS ADDRESSED IN THIS JAPANESE DISH. IT IS TRADITIONALLY COOKED IN A LIDDED CERAMIC BOWL CALLED A DONI-BURI.

SERVES 4

INGREDIENTS
   250g/9oz skinless, boneless
      chicken thighs
   4 fresh mitsuba or parsley
      sprigs, trimmed
   300ml/½ pint/1¼ cups water
      and 25ml/1½ tbsp instant
      dashi powder
   30ml/2 tbsp caster (superfine) sugar
   60ml/4 tbsp mirin
   60ml/4 tbsp shoyu
   2 small onions, sliced
      thinly lengthways
   4 large (US extra large) eggs, beaten
   275g/10oz/scant 1½ cups Japanese
      short grain rice cooked with 375ml/
      13fl oz/scant 1⅔ cups water
   shichimi togarashi, to serve (optional)

1 Cut the chicken thighs into 2cm/¾in square bitesize chunks. Chop the roots of the fresh mitsuba or parsley into 2.5cm/1in lengths. Set aside.

2 Pour the dashi stock, sugar, mirin and shoyu into a clean frying pan with a lid and bring to the boil. Add the onion slices to the pan and lay the chicken pieces on top. Cook over a high heat for 5 minutes, shaking the pan frequently.

3 When the chicken is cooked, sprinkle with the mitsuba or parsley, and pour the beaten eggs over to cover the chicken. Cover and wait for 30 seconds. Do not stir.

4 Remove from the heat and leave to stand for 1 minute. The egg should be just cooked but still soft, rather than set. Do not leave it so that the egg becomes a firm omelette.

5 Scoop the warm rice on to individual plates, then pour the soft eggs and chicken on to the rice. Serve immediately with a little *shichimi-togarashi*, if you want spicy taste.

COOK'S TIP
Mitsuba, also known as Japanese wild parsley, tastes like angelica. Cut off the root before use.

Energy 417Kcal/1743kJ; Protein 25.2g; Carbohydrate 56.9g, of which sugars 1.9g; Fat 7.8g, of which saturates 2.1g; Cholesterol 256mg; Calcium 70mg; Fibre 0.2g; Sodium 935mg.

LUNCH-BOX RICE <u>WITH</u> THREE TOPPINGS ★★★

A GREAT DEAL MORE NUTRITIOUS THAN SOME OF THE PACKED LUNCHES TAKEN TO SCHOOL IN THE WEST, THIS JAPANESE SPECIALITY TOPS RICE WITH THREE DIFFERENT TOPPINGS.

MAKES 4 LUNCH BOXES

INGREDIENTS

275g/10oz/scant 1⅔ cups Japanese short grain rice cooked using 375ml/ 13fl oz/scant 1⅔ cups water, cooled
45ml/3 tbsp sesame seeds, toasted
salt
3 mangetouts (snow peas), to garnish
For the *iri-tamago* (yellow topping)
30ml/2 tbsp caster (superfine) sugar
5ml/1 tsp salt
3 eggs, beaten
For the *denbu* (pink topping)
115g/4oz cod fillet, skinned and boned
20ml/4 tsp caster (superfine) sugar
5ml/1 tsp salt
5ml/1 tsp sake
2 drops of red vegetable colouring, diluted with a few drops of water
For the *tori-soboro* (beige topping)
200g/7oz/scant 1 cup minced (ground) chicken
45ml/3 tbsp sake
15ml/1 tbsp caster (superfine) sugar
15ml/1 tbsp shoyu
15ml/1 tbsp water

1 To make the *iri-tamago*, mix the sugar and salt with the eggs in a pan. Cook over a medium heat, stirring with a whisk or fork as you would to scramble eggs. When the mixture is almost set, remove from the heat and stir until the egg becomes fine and slightly dry.

2 To make the *denbu*, cook the cod fillet for 2 minutes in a large pan of boiling water. Drain and dry well with kitchen paper. Skin and remove all the fish bones.

3 Put the cod and sugar into a pan, add the salt and sake, and cook over low heat for 1 minute, stirring with a fork to flake the cod. Reduce the heat to low and sprinkle on the colouring. Continue to stir for 15–20 minutes, or until the cod flakes become very fluffy and fibrous. Transfer the *denbu* to a plate.

4 To make the *tori-soboro*, put the minced chicken, sake, sugar, shoyu and water into a small pan. Cook over medium heat for about 3 minutes, then reduce the heat to medium-low and stir with a fork or whisk until the liquid has almost evaporated.

5 Blanch the mangetouts for about 3 minutes in lightly salted boiling water, drain and carefully slice into fine 3mm/⅛in sticks.

6 Mix the rice with the sesame seeds in a bowl. With a wet spoon, divide the rice among four 17 × 12cm/6½ × 4½in lunch boxes. Flatten the surface using the back of a wooden spoon.

7 Spoon a quarter of the egg into each box to cover a third of the rice. Cover the next third with a quarter of the *denbu*, and the last section with a quarter of the chicken topping. Use the lid to divide the boxes, if you like. Garnish with the mangetout sticks.

Energy 516Kcal/2162kJ; Protein 29.3g; Carbohydrate 72.2g, of which sugars 17.2g; Fat 11.8g, of which saturates 2.3g; Cholesterol 191mg; Calcium 124mg; Fibre 0.9g; Sodium 370mg.

SESAME NOODLE SALAD ★★★

TOASTED SESAME OIL ADDS A NUTTY FLAVOUR TO THIS ASIAN-STYLE SALAD. IT TASTES BEST WHEN IT IS SERVED WARM, AND IT IS SUBSTANTIAL ENOUGH TO SERVE AS A MAIN MEAL.

3 Meanwhile, make the dressing. Whisk together the soy sauce, sesame and sunflower oils, grated ginger and crushed garlic in a small bowl.

4 Cut the tomatoes in half and scoop out the seeds with a teaspoon, then chop roughly. Cut the spring onions into fine shreds.

SERVES 4

INGREDIENTS
 250g/9oz medium egg noodles
 200g/7oz/1¾ cup sugar snap peas
  or mangetouts (snow peas)
 2 tomatoes
 3 spring onions (scallions)
 2 carrots, cut into julienne
 30ml/2 tbsp chopped fresh coriander
  (cilantro)
 15ml/1 tbsp sesame seeds
 fresh coriander (cilantro), to garnish
For the dressing
 10ml/2 tsp light soy sauce
 15ml/1 tbsp toasted sesame seed oil
 15ml/1 tbsp vegetable oil
 4cm/1½in piece fresh root ginger,
  finely grated
 1 garlic clove, crushed

1 Bring a large pan of lightly salted water to the boil. Add the egg noodles, and bring back to the boil. Cook for 2 minutes.

2 Slice the sugar snap peas or mangetouts diagonally, add to the pan and cook for a further 2 minutes. Drain and rinse under cold running water.

5 Tip the noodles and the peas or mangetouts into a large bowl and add the carrots, tomatoes and coriander.

6 Pour the dressing over the top of the noodle mixture, and toss with your hands to combine. Sprinkle with the sesame seeds and top with the spring onions and coriander.

Energy 323Kcal/1364kJ; Protein 10.6g; Carbohydrate 50.1g, of which sugars 5.9g; Fat 10.3g, of which saturates 2.2g; Cholesterol 19mg; Calcium 76mg; Fibre 4.2g; Sodium 301mg.

CHILLED SOMEN NOODLES ★★

AT THE HEIGHT OF SUMMER, COLD SOMEN NOODLES SERVED IN ICE COLD WATER AND ACCOMPANIED BY A DIPPING SAUCE AND A SELECTION OF RELISHES MAKE A REFRESHING MEAL.

SERVES 4

INGREDIENTS
  300g/11oz dried somen noodles
For the dipping sauce
  105ml/7 tbsp mirin
  2.5ml/½ tsp sea salt
  105ml/7 tbsp shoyu
  400ml/14fl oz/1⅔ cups konbu and
    bonito stock or instant dashi
For the relishes
  2 spring onions (scallions), trimmed
    and finely chopped
  2.5cm/1in fresh root ginger, peeled
    and finely grated
  2 fresh shiso or basil leaves, finely
    chopped (optional)
  30ml/2 tbsp toasted sesame seeds
For the garnishes
  10cm/4in cucumber
  5ml/1 tsp sea salt
  ice cubes or a block of ice
  ice-cold water
  115g/4oz cooked, peeled small
    prawns (shrimp)
  orchid flowers or nasturtium flowers
    and leaves (optional)

1 To make the dipping sauce, put the mirin in a pan and bring to the boil to evaporate the alcohol. Add the salt and shoyu and shake the pan gently to mix. Add the konbu and bonito stock or instant dashi. Add the water and bring to the boil. Cook over a vigorous heat for 3 minutes without stirring. Remove from the heat and strain through muslin or cheesecloth. Cool, then chill for at least 1 hour.

2 Prepare the cucumber garnish. If the cucumber is bigger than 4cm/1½in in diameter, cut in half and scoop out the seeds, then slice thinly. For a smaller cucumber, cut into 5cm/2in lengths, then use a vegetable peeler to remove the seeds and make a hole in the centre. Slice thinly.

3 Sprinkle with the salt and leave in a sieve (strainer) for 20 minutes, then rinse in cold water and drain.

4 Bring at least 1.5 litres/2½ pints/ 6 cups water to the boil in a large pan. Have 75ml/2½fl oz/⅓ cup cold water to hand. Put the somen in the rapidly boiling water. When the water foams, pour the glass of cold water in. When the water boils again, the somen are ready. Drain into a colander.

5 Rinse under cold running water, and rub the somen with your hands to remove the starch. Drain well.

6 Put some ice cubes or a block of ice in the centre of a chilled, large glass bowl, and add the somen. Pour on enough ice-cold water to cover the somen, then arrange cucumber slices, prawns and flowers, if using, on top.

7 Prepare all the relishes separately and place them in small dishes or small sake cups.

8 Divide approximately one-third of the dipping sauce among four small cups. Put the remaining sauce in a jug (pitcher) or gravy boat.

9 Serve the noodles cold with the relishes. The guests are invited to put any combination of relishes into their dipping-sauce cup. The cup is then held over the somen bowl, and a mouthful of somen is picked up, dipped into the sauce and eaten. More dipping sauce is added from the jug and more relishes are spooned into the dipping-sauce cups as required.

Energy 368Kcal/1554kJ; Protein 15.9g; Carbohydrate 59g, of which sugars 3.5g; Fat 9.2g, of which saturates 0.7g; Cholesterol 56mg; Calcium 97mg; Fibre 2.9g; Sodium 1393mg.

FUSION NOODLES ★

WHAT HAPPENS WHEN ITALIANS SETTLE IN SHANGHAI? THEY EMBRACE THE COOKING STYLE OF THEIR ADOPTED COUNTRY BUT INTRODUCE THEIR FAVOURITE PASTA AND BALSAMIC VINEGAR.

SERVES 6

INGREDIENTS

    500g/1¼lb thin tagliarini
    1 red onion
    115g/4oz shiitake mushrooms
    15ml/1 tbsp vegetable oil
    45ml/3 tbsp dark soy sauce
    15ml/1 tbsp balsamic vinegar
    10ml/2 tsp caster (superfine) sugar
    5ml/1 tsp salt
    5ml/1 tsp sesame oil
    celery leaves, to garnish

1 Cook the tagliarini in a large pan of salted boiling water, following the instructions on the pack.

2 Thinly slice the red onion and the mushrooms, using a sharp knife.

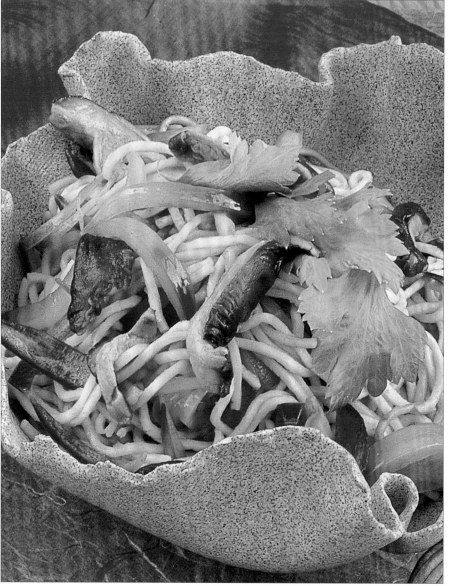

3 Heat a wok, then add the vegetable oil. When the oil is hot, stir-fry the onion and mushrooms for 2 minutes.

4 Drain the tagliarini, then add to the wok with the soy sauce, balsamic vinegar, sugar and salt.

5 Stir-fry for 1 minute, then add the sesame oil, mix well to combine thoroughly and serve garnished with celery leaves.

VARIATION
Use thin egg noodles instead of tagliarini, if you like.

Energy 72Kcal/306kJ; Protein 2.7g; Carbohydrate 14.1g, of which sugars 3.1g; Fat 1g, of which saturates 0.1g; Cholesterol 0mg; Calcium 10mg; Fibre 0.9g; Sodium 536mg.

NOODLES WITH GINGER AND CORIANDER ★★

*HERE IS A SIMPLE NOODLE DISH THAT IS LOW IN SATURATED FAT AND WOULD GO WELL WITH MOST
ORIENTAL DISHES. IT CAN ALSO BE SERVED AS A LIGHT MEAL FOR 2 OR 3 PEOPLE.*

SERVES 4

INGREDIENTS
handful of fresh coriander (cilantro)
225g/8oz dried egg noodles
10ml/2 tsp sesame oil
15ml/1 tbsp vegetable oil
5cm/2in piece fresh root ginger,
  cut into fine shreds
6–8 spring onions (scallions), cut
  into shreds
30ml/2 tbsp light soy sauce
salt and ground black pepper

1 Strip the leaves from the coriander
stalks. Pile them on to a chopping
board and coarsely chop them using
a cleaver or large, sharp knife.

2 Bring a large pan of lightly salted
water to the boil and cook the noodles
according to the packet instructions.

3 Rinse under cold water, drain well
and tip into a bowl. Add the sesame oil
and toss to coat.

VARIATION
If you don't like the flavour of coriander,
use flat leaf parsley.

4 Heat a wok until hot, add the
vegetable oil and swirl it around.
Add the ginger and stir-fry for a few
seconds, then add the noodles and
spring onions. Stir-fry for 3–4 minutes,
until the noodles are hot.

5 Drizzle over the soy sauce, then
sprinkle the chopped coriander on top
of the noodles.

6 Add salt and ground black pepper to
taste. Toss and serve in heated bowls.

Energy 253Kcal/1067kJ; Protein 7.4g; Carbohydrate 41.6g, of which sugars 2.2g; Fat 7.5g, of which saturates 1.6g; Cholesterol 17mg; Calcium 25mg; Fibre 1.9g; Sodium 637mg.

NOODLES WITH YELLOW BEAN SAUCE ★★★

SERVED SOLO, STEAMED LEEKS, COURGETTES AND PEAS MIGHT BE BLAND, BUT ADD A PUNCHY BEAN SAUCE AND THEY ACQUIRE ATTITUDE THAT EVEN THE ADDITION OF NOODLES CAN'T ASSUAGE.

3 Cover and stand over a wok of simmering water. Steam the vegetables for about 5 minutes, then remove and set aside. Drain and dry the wok.

4 Heat the vegetable oil in the wok and stir-fry the sliced garlic for 1–2 minutes.

5 In a separate bowl, mix together the yellow bean, sweet chilli and soy sauces, then pour into the wok. Stir to mix with the garlic, then add the steamed vegetables and the noodles and toss together to combine.

6 Cook the vegetables and noodles for 2–3 minutes, stirring frequently, until heated through.

7 Divide the vegetable noodles among four warmed serving bowls and sprinkle over the cashew nuts to garnish.

SERVES 4

INGREDIENTS
  150g/5oz thin egg noodles
  200g/7oz baby leeks, sliced
    lengthways
  200g/7oz baby courgettes (zucchini),
    halved lengthways
  200g/7oz sugarsnap peas, trimmed
  200g/7oz/1¾ cups fresh or
    frozen peas
  15ml/1 tbsp vegetable oil
  5 garlic cloves, sliced
  45ml/3 tbsp yellow bean sauce
  45ml/3 tbsp sweet chilli sauce
  30ml/2 tbsp sweet soy sauce
  50g/2oz/½ cup cashew nuts,
    to garnish

1 Cook the noodles according to the packet instructions, drain and set aside.

2 Line a large bamboo steamer with perforated baking parchment and add the leeks, courgettes, sugarsnaps and peas.

Energy 354Kcal/1487kJ; Protein 14.6g; Carbohydrate 46.4g, of which sugars 13g; Fat 13.5g, of which saturates 2.7g; Cholesterol 11mg; Calcium 76mg; Fibre 6.8g; Sodium 1008mg.

STIR-FRIED NOODLES WITH BEANSPROUTS ★★

*BEANSPROUTS ARE HIGHLY NUTRITIOUS AND MAKE A VALUABLE CONTRIBUTION TO THIS LOW-FAT DISH,
WHICH COMBINES EGG NOODLES WITH RED AND GREEN PEPPERS AND SOY SAUCE.*

SERVES 4

INGREDIENTS
   175g/6oz dried egg noodles
   15ml/1 tbsp vegetable oil
   1 garlic clove, finely chopped
   1 small onion, halved and sliced
   225g/8oz/4 cups beansprouts
   1 small red (bell) pepper, seeded
      and cut into strips
   1 small green (bell) pepper, seeded
      and cut into strips
   2.5ml/½ tsp salt
   1.5ml/¼ tsp ground white pepper
   30ml/2 tbsp light soy sauce

3 Stir in the cooked noodles and toss over the heat, using two spatulas or wooden spoons, for 2–3 minutes or until the ingredients are well mixed and have heated through.

4 Season to taste with salt and ground white pepper. Add the soy sauce and stir thoroughly before serving the noodle mixture in heated bowls.

1 Bring a pan of water to the boil. Cook the noodles for 4 minutes until just tender, or according to the instructions on the packet. Drain in a colander, refresh under cold water and drain again.

2 Heat the oil in a non-stick frying pan or wok. When the oil is very hot, add the garlic, stir briefly, then add the onion slices. Cook, stirring, for 1 minute, then add the beansprouts and peppers. Stir-fry for 2–3 minutes.

Energy 244Kcal/1030kJ; Protein 8g; Carbohydrate 39.9g, of which sugars 7.8g; Fat 7g, of which saturates 1.5g; Cholesterol 13mg; Calcium 34mg; Fibre 3.5g; Sodium 352mg.

NOODLES WITH ASPARAGUS ★★★

THIS DISH IS SIMPLICITY ITSELF WITH A WONDERFUL CONTRAST OF TEXTURES AND FLAVOURS. USE YOUNG ASPARAGUS WHICH IS BEAUTIFULLY TENDER AND COOKS IN MINUTES.

SERVES 2

INGREDIENTS

115g/4oz dried thin or medium
  egg noodles
15ml/1 tbsp oil
1 small onion, chopped
2.5cm/1in fresh root ginger, grated
2 garlic cloves, crushed
175g/6oz young asparagus, trimmed
115g/4oz/2 cups beansprouts
4 spring onions (scallions), sliced
45ml/3 tbsp light soy sauce
salt and ground black pepper

1 Bring a large pan of salted water to the boil. Add the noodles and cook until just tender. Drain, rinse under cold running water and set aside.

2 Heat a wok or frying pan, then add the oil. When the oil is very hot add the onion, ginger and garlic and stir-fry for 2–3 minutes.

3 Add the asparagus and stir-fry for a further 2–3 minutes.

4 Add the noodles and beansprouts and toss over fairly high heat for 2 minutes, to reheat the noodles.

5 Stir in the spring onions and soy sauce and mix well to combine. Season to taste, adding salt sparingly as the soy sauce will add quite a salty flavour.

6 Stir-fry the mixture for 1 minute, then serve immediately.

Energy 339kcal/1427kJ; Protein 12.6g; Carbohydrate 50.1g, of which sugars 7.9g; Fat 11.2g, of which saturates 2.2g; Cholesterol 17mg; Calcium 71mg; Fibre 4.8g; Sodium 1712mg.

FIVE-SPICE VEGETABLE NOODLES ★★

VARY THIS VEGETABLE STIR-FRY BY SUBSTITUTING MUSHROOMS, BAMBOO SHOOTS, BEANSPROUTS, MANGETOUTS OR WATER CHESTNUTS FOR SOME OR ALL OF THE VEGETABLES SUGGESTED BELOW.

SERVES 3–4

INGREDIENTS

225g/8oz dried egg noodles
10ml/2 tsp sesame oil
2 carrots
1 celery stick
1 small fennel bulb
15ml/1 tbsp vegetable oil
2 courgettes (zucchini), halved
 and sliced
1 fresh red chilli, seeded and chopped
2.5cm/1in fresh root ginger, grated
1 garlic clove, crushed
7.5ml/1½ tsp five-spice powder
2.5ml/½ tsp ground cinnamon
4 spring onions (scallions), sliced
thinly sliced fresh red chilli, to
 garnish (optional)

1 Bring a large pan of salted water to the boil. Add the noodles and cook for 2–3 minutes until just tender. Drain the noodles, return them to the pan and toss in the sesame oil. Set aside.

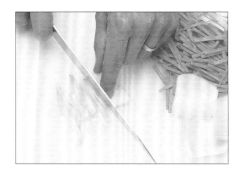

2 Cut the carrot and celery into julienne strips. Cut the fennel bulb in half and cut away the hard core. Cut into slices, then cut the slices into thin strips.

3 Heat the vegetable oil in a wok until very hot. Add all the vegetables, including the chopped chilli, and stir-fry for 7–8 minutes. Add the ginger and garlic and stir-fry for 2 minutes, then add the spices. Cook for 1 minute.

4 Add the spring onions, stir-fry for 1 minute and then stir in 60ml/4 tbsp warm water and cook for 1 minute. Stir in the noodles and toss well together. Serve in heated bowls, sprinkled with sliced red chilli, if you like.

Energy 286Kcal/1205kJ; Protein 8.8g; Carbohydrate 44.5g, of which sugars 5g; Fat 9.4g, of which saturates 2g; Cholesterol 17mg; Calcium 54mg; Fibre 3.8g; Sodium 116mg.

TOASTED NOODLES WITH VEGETABLES ★

SLIGHTLY CRISP NOODLE CAKES TOPPED WITH VEGETABLES MAKE A SUPERB DISH, AND THE VERY GOOD NEWS FOR THE HEALTH-CONSCIOUS IS THAT THE AMOUNT OF SATURATED FAT IS NEGLIGIBLE.

2 Heat 2.5ml/½ tsp oil in a non-stick frying pan or wok. When it starts to smoke, spread half the noodles over the base. Fry for 2–3 minutes until lightly toasted. Carefully turn the noodles over (they stick together like a cake), fry the other side, then slide on to a heated serving plate. Repeat with the remaining noodles to make two cakes. Keep hot.

3 Heat the remaining oil in the clean pan, then fry the garlic for a few seconds. Halve the corn cobs lengthways, add to the pan with the mushrooms, then stir-fry for 3 minutes, adding a little water, if needed, to prevent the mixture from burning. Add the celery, carrot, mangetouts and bamboo shoots. Stir-fry for 2 minutes or until the vegetables are crisp-tender.

SERVES 4

INGREDIENTS

175g/6oz dried egg vermicelli
15ml/1 tbsp vegetable oil
2 garlic cloves, finely chopped
115g/4oz/1 cup baby corn cobs
115g/4oz/1½ cups fresh shiitake
  mushrooms, halved
3 celery sticks, sliced
1 carrot, diagonally sliced
115g/4oz/1 cup mangetouts
  (snow peas)
75g/3oz/¾ cup sliced, drained,
  canned bamboo shoots
15ml/1 tbsp cornflour (cornstarch)
15ml/1 tbsp cold water
15ml/1 tbsp dark soy sauce
5ml/1 tsp caster sugar
300ml/½ pint/1¼ cups
  vegetable stock
salt and ground white pepper
spring onion curls, to garnish

1 Bring a pan of lightly salted water to the boil. Add the egg noodles and cook according to instructions on the packet until just tender. Drain the noodles in a sieve (strainer), refresh under cold water, drain again, then dry thoroughly on kitchen paper.

VARIATION
Sliced fennel tastes good in this stir-fry, either as an addition or instead of the sliced bamboo shoots.

4 Mix the cornflour to a paste with 15ml/1 tbsp cold water. Add to the pan with the soy sauce, sugar and stock. Cook, stirring, until the sauce thickens. Season to taste. Divide the vegetable mixture between the noodle cakes, garnish with the spring onion curls and serve immediately. Each noodle cake serves two people.

Energy 214Kcal/893kJ; Protein 7g; Carbohydrate 38.6g, of which sugars 3.5g; Fat 3.4g, of which saturates 0.4g; Cholesterol 0mg; Calcium 44mg; Fibre 2.4g; Sodium 353mg.

VEGETABLE NOODLES WITH PRAWNS ★★★

DRIED MUSHROOMS ADD AN INTENSE FLAVOUR TO THIS LIGHTLY CURRIED DISH, WHICH MATCHES A COLOURFUL MEDLEY OF VEGETABLES WITH FINE EGG NOODLES AND PRAWNS.

SERVES 4

INGREDIENTS

- 20g/¾oz/⅓ cup dried Chinese mushrooms
- 225g/8oz fine egg noodles
- 10ml/2 tsp sesame oil
- 30ml/2 tbsp vegetable oil
- 2 garlic cloves, crushed
- 1 small onion, chopped
- 1 fresh green chilli, seeded and thinly sliced
- 10ml/2 tsp curry powder
- 115g/4oz green beans, trimmed and halved
- 115g/4oz Chinese leaves (Chinese cabbage), thinly shredded
- 4 spring onions (scallions), sliced
- 30ml/2 tbsp soy sauce
- 115g/4oz cooked prawns (shrimp), peeled and deveined
- salt

3 Heat a wok and add the vegetable oil. When it is hot, stir-fry the garlic, onion and chilli for 3 minutes. Stir in the curry powder and cook for 1 minute. Add the mushrooms, green beans, Chinese leaves and spring onions. Stir-fry for 3–4 minutes until the vegetables are crisp-tender.

4 Add the noodles, soy sauce, reserved mushroom soaking water and prawns.

5 Using a pair of chopsticks or two spatulas, toss the mixture over the heat for 2–3 minutes until the noodles and prawns are heated through and thoroughly combined.

1 Place the mushrooms in a bowl. Cover with warm water and soak them for 30 minutes. Drain, reserving 30ml/2 tbsp of the soaking water, then slice.

2 Bring a pan of lightly salted water to the boil and cook the noodles according to the directions on the packet. Drain the noodles in a sieve (strainer), tip into a bowl and toss with the sesame oil.

VARIATION
Ring the changes with the vegetables used in this dish. Try mangetouts, broccoli, peppers or baby corn. The prawns can be omitted or substituted with ham or chicken.

Energy 329Kcal/1386kJ; Protein 13.4g; Carbohydrate 44.6g, of which sugars 4.5g; Fat 12.1g, of which saturates 2.2g; Cholesterol 73mg; Calcium 71mg; Fibre 3.3g; Sodium 337mg.

Noodles <u>with</u> Chicken, Prawns <u>and</u> Ham ★★

A mixture of meat and seafood works well in a stir-fry like this one. Raid the refrigerator for yesterday's leftovers or alter the ingredients to suit what you have.

SERVES 4–6

INGREDIENTS
275g/10oz dried egg noodles
15ml/1 tbsp vegetable oil
1 medium onion
1 garlic clove
2.5cm/1in fresh root ginger
50g/2oz/⅓ cup canned water
  chestnuts, drained and sliced
15ml/1 tbsp light soy sauce
30ml/2 tbsp Thai fish sauce
175g/6oz cooked chicken breast
  fillet, skinned and sliced
150g/5oz cooked lean ham, thickly
  sliced and cut into short fingers
225g/8oz cooked prawn (shrimp)
  tails, peeled
175g/6oz/3 cups beansprouts
200g/7oz baby corn cobs
2 limes, cut into wedges, and
  1 small bunch coriander (cilantro),
  shredded, to garnish

1 Cook the noodles according to the instructions on the packet. Drain well and set aside.

2 Chop the onion, crush the garlic and cut the ginger into fine slivers.

3 Heat a wok or large frying pan, add the oil and fry the onion, garlic and ginger for 3 minutes, until soft but not coloured. Add the chestnuts, soy sauce, fish sauce, chicken, ham and prawns.

4 Add the noodles, beansprouts and baby corn cobs and stir-fry for 6–8 minutes, until heated through. Transfer to a warmed serving dish, garnish with the lime and coriander and serve.

Energy 302Kcal/1277kJ; Protein 25.9g; Carbohydrate 35.5g, of which sugars 2.6g; Fat 7.3g, of which saturates 1.7g; Cholesterol 122mg; Calcium 56mg; Fibre 2.4g; Sodium 1031mg.

FIVE-FLAVOUR NOODLES ★★

CABBAGE IS ONE OF THE BEST VEGETABLES FOR STIR-FRYING, AND TASTES GOOD WITH GINGER AND GARLIC IN THIS SIMPLE DISH. DON'T LEAVE OUT THE SEAWEED; IT ADDS THE FINISHING TOUCH.

SERVES 4

INGREDIENTS

- 300g/11oz dried thin egg noodles
- 200g/7oz pork fillet (tenderloin), trimmed and thinly sliced
- 25ml/1½ tbsp oil
- 10g/¼oz fresh root ginger, grated
- 1 garlic clove, crushed
- 200g/7oz/1¾ cups green cabbage, roughly chopped
- 115g/4oz/2 cups beansprouts
- 1 green (bell) pepper, seeded and cut into fine strips
- 1 red (bell) pepper, seeded and cut into fine strips
- salt and ground black pepper
- 20ml/4 tsp *ao-nori* seaweed, to garnish (optional)

For the seasoning

- 60ml/4 tbsp Worcestershire sauce
- 15ml/1 tbsp light soy sauce
- 15ml/1 tbsp oyster sauce
- 15ml/1 tbsp sugar
- white pepper

1 Cook the egg noodles according to the packet instructions and drain.

2 Using a sharp chopping knife, carefully cut the pork fillet into 3–4cm/1¼–1½in strips and season with plenty of salt and pepper. Next, heat 7.5ml/1½ tsp of the oil in a large frying pan or wok and stir-fry the pork until just cooked, then transfer to a dish.

3 Wipe the pan with kitchen paper, and heat the remaining oil. When the oil is hot, add the ginger, garlic and cabbage and stir-fry for 1 minute.

4 Add the beansprouts and stir until softened, then add the green and red peppers and stir-fry for 1 minute, over medium heat. Return the strips of cooked pork fillet to the pan or wok and toss lightly to mix.

5 Add the drained cooked egg noodles. Stir in all the seasoning ingredients together with a little white pepper. Stir-fry for 2–3 minutes. Serve in heated bowls and sprinkle each portion with *ao-nori* seaweed, if you like.

Energy 425Kcal/1799kJ; Protein 28.2g; Carbohydrate 62.6g, of which sugars 9.4g; Fat 8.6g, of which saturates 2.6g; Cholesterol 67mg; Calcium 82mg; Fibre 4.4g; Sodium 844mg.

JAPANESE NOODLE CASSEROLES ★★★

NOT QUITE A SOUP NOR YET A STEW, THIS IS SERVED IN INDIVIDUAL CASSEROLES OR POTS. WHEN THE LIDS ARE LIFTED, EACH PORTION IS REVEALED TO HAVE A POACHED EGG NESTLING INSIDE.

SERVES 4

INGREDIENTS

115g/4oz skinless, boneless
  chicken thighs
2.5ml/½ tsp salt
2.5ml/½ tsp sake or dry white wine
2.5ml/½ tsp light soy sauce
1 leek
115g/4oz fresh spinach, trimmed
300g/11oz dried udon noodles or
  500g/1¼lb fresh udon noodles
4 shiitake mushrooms
4 eggs
shichimi-togarishi or seven-spice
  powder, to serve (optional)
For the soup
  1.5 litres/2½ pints/6 cups konbu
    and bonito stock or instant dashi
  25ml/1½ tbsp light soy sauce
  5ml/1 tsp salt
  15ml/1 tbsp mirin

1 Cut the chicken into small chunks and place in a shallow dish. Sprinkle with the salt, sake or wine and soy sauce.

2 Cut the leek diagonally into 4cm/1½in slices, and place in a bowl. Set aside until needed.

3 Cook the spinach in boiling water for 1–2 minutes, then drain and soak in cold water for 1 minute. Drain again, squeeze lightly, then cut it into 4cm/1½in lengths.

4 If you are using dried udon noodles, boil them according to the packet instructions, allowing 3 minutes less than the stated cooking time. If you are using fresh udon noodles, place them in boiling water, disentangle, then drain.

5 For the soup, bring the konbu and bonito stock or dashi stock, soy sauce, salt and mirin to the boil in a pan, then add the chunks of chicken and the sliced leek. Skim the broth, then simmer for 5 minutes.

6 Use a sharp knife to trim off the hard parts of the shiitake mushroom stems.

7 Divide the udon noodles among four individual flameproof casseroles. Pour the soup, chicken and leeks into the casseroles. Place over medium heat and add the shiitake mushrooms.

8 Gently break an egg into each casserole. Cover and simmer gently for 2 minutes.

9 Divide the spinach among the casseroles and simmer, covered, for a further 1 minute.

10 Serve immediately, standing the hot casseroles on plates or table mats.

11 Sprinkle with *shichimi-togarishi* or seven-spice powder if you like.

VARIATION
Assorted tempura, made from vegetables such as sweet potato, carrot and shiitake mushrooms, or fish such as squid and prawns, could be served in these noodle casseroles, instead of the chicken and the poached egg.

Energy 418Kcal/1765kJ; Protein 24.1g; Carbohydrate 59.4g, of which sugars 3.7g; Fat 11.1g, of which saturates 1.7g; Cholesterol 210mg; Calcium 109mg; Fibre 4g; Sodium 576mg.

VEGETABLES AND SALADS

All of the recipes in this chapter are low in fat, especially saturated fat, but they are also filling and full of flavour, so you won't feel any sense of sacrifice. You could combine a couple of dishes, such as New Potatoes Cooked in Dashi Stock and Pak Choi and Mushroom Stir-fry, and still stay well within sensible fat limits. If you are looking for a one-dish meal, try Stir-fried Greens, which includes pork and quail's eggs, or Steamed Aubergine with Sesame Sauce.

STIR-FRIED BEANSPROUTS ★

SPROUTED BEANS ARE HIGHLY NUTRITIOUS, ESPECIALLY IF YOU GROW THEM YOURSELF AND USE THEM WHEN THEY ARE REALLY FRESH. THEY MAKE FOR A CRISP AND CRUNCHY STIR-FRY.

SERVES 4

INGREDIENTS

15ml/1 tbsp vegetable oil
1 garlic clove, finely chopped
5ml/1 tsp grated fresh root ginger
1 small carrot, cut into
   fine matchsticks
50g/2oz/½ cup drained,
   canned bamboo shoots, cut
   into fine matchsticks
450g/1lb/8 cups beansprouts
2.5ml/½ tsp salt
large pinch of ground white pepper
15ml/1 tbsp dry sherry
15ml/1 tbsp light soy sauce
2.5ml/½ tsp sesame oil

1 Heat a non-stick frying pan or wok. Add the vegetable oil, just below the rim so that it trickles down to coat the surface. When the oil is hot, add the chopped garlic and grated ginger and stir-fry for 2 minutes.

2 Toss the carrot and bamboo shoot matchsticks into the pan or wok and stir-fry for 2–3 minutes.

3 Add the beansprouts to the pan or wok with the salt and pepper. Drizzle over the dry sherry and toss the beansprouts over the heat for 3 minutes until they have heated through.

4 Sprinkle over the light soy sauce and sesame oil, toss to mix thoroughly, then serve immediately.

COOK'S TIP
Beansprouts keep best when stored in the refrigerator or other cool place in a bowl of cold water, but you must remember to change the water daily.

Energy 76Kcal/318kJ; Protein 3.9g; Carbohydrate 6.9g, of which sugars 4.5g; Fat 3.4g, of which saturates 0.5g; Cholesterol 0mg; Calcium 31mg; Fibre 2.3g; Sodium 278mg.

STIR-FRIED CHINESE LEAVES ★

THIS SIMPLE WAY OF COOKING CHINESE LEAVES PRESERVES THEIR DELICATE FLAVOUR. THE RIBS REMAIN BEAUTIFULLY CRUNCHY AND PROVIDE A CONTRAST TO THE SOFTER PARTS OF THE LEAVES.

SERVES 4

INGREDIENTS

675g/1½lb Chinese leaves
   (Chinese cabbage)
15ml/1 tbsp vegetable oil
2 garlic cloves, finely chopped
2.5cm/1in piece fresh root ginger,
   finely chopped
2.5ml/½ tsp salt
15ml/1 tbsp oyster sauce
4 spring onions (scallions), cut
   into 2.5cm/1in lengths

1 Stack the Chinese leaves together and cut them into 2.5cm/1in slices using a sharp knife.

2 Heat a wok or large sauté pan. When the wok or pan is hot, add the oil just below the rim so that it trickles down to coat the surface. When the oil is hot, add the garlic and ginger and stir-fry for 1 minute.

VARIATION

If you are catering for vegetarians, substitute 15ml/1 tbsp light soy sauce and 5ml/1 tsp caster sugar for the oyster sauce.

3 Add the Chinese leaves to the wok or pan and stir-fry for 2 minutes. Sprinkle the salt over and drizzle with the oyster sauce. Toss the leaves over the heat for 2 minutes more.

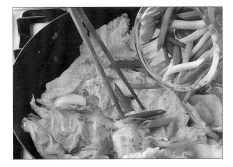

4 Tip the spring onions into the wok or pan and stir-fry for 1 minute more. Toss the mixture well, transfer it to a heated serving plate or bowl and serve.

Energy 77Kcal/321kJ; Protein 2.6g; Carbohydrate 9.8g, of which sugars 9.6g; Fat 3.2g, of which saturates 0.3g; Cholesterol 0mg; Calcium 87mg; Fibre 3.7g; Sodium 74mg.

CHOI SUM AND MUSHROOM STIR-FRY ★

USE THE MUSHROOMS RECOMMENDED FOR THIS DISH – WILD OYSTER AND SHIITAKE MUSHROOMS HAVE PARTICULARLY DISTINCTIVE, DELICATE FLAVOURS THAT WORK WELL WHEN STIR-FRIED.

SERVES 4

INGREDIENTS

    4 dried black Chinese mushrooms
    150ml/¼ pint/⅔ cup hot water
    450g/1lb choi sum
    50g/2oz/¾ cup oyster mushrooms,
      preferably wild
    50g/2oz/¾ cup shiitake mushrooms
    15ml/1 tbsp vegetable oil
    1 garlic clove, crushed
    30ml/2 tbsp oyster sauce

1 Soak the dried Chinese mushrooms in the hot water for 15 minutes to soften.

2 Tear the choi sum into bitesize pieces with your fingers. Place in a bowl and set aside.

3 Halve any large oyster and shiitake mushrooms, using a sharp knife.

4 Strain the Chinese mushrooms and cut off the stems. Heat a wok, then add the oil. When the oil is hot, stir-fry the garlic until it has softened but not coloured.

5 Add the choi sum to the wok and stir-fry for 1 minute. Toss in the oyster and shiitake mushrooms with the Chinese mushroom caps, and stir-fry for 1 minute.

6 Add the oyster sauce, toss well and serve immediately.

COOK'S TIP
Pak choi, also called bok choy, pok choi and spoon cabbage, is an attractive member of the cabbage family, with long, smooth white stems and dark green leaves. It has a pleasant flavour which does not, in any way, resemble that of ordinary green cabbage.

Energy 57Kcal/237kJ; Protein 3.7g; Carbohydrate 2.1g, of which sugars 1.8g; Fat 3.8g, of which saturates 0.5g; Cholesterol 0mg; Calcium 193mg; Fibre 2.7g; Sodium 159mg.

DAIKON, BEETROOT AND CARROT STIR-FRY ★★

THIS IS A DAZZLINGLY COLOURFUL DISH WITH A CRUNCHY TEXTURE AND FRAGRANT TASTE. IT IS LOW IN SATURATED FAT AND CHOLESTEROL-FREE AND WOULD BE IDEAL FOR A SUMMER LUNCH.

SERVES 4

INGREDIENTS
    25g/1oz/¼ cup pine nuts
    115g/4oz daikon (mooli), peeled
    115g/4oz raw beetroot (beet), peeled
    115g/4oz carrots, peeled
    15ml/1 tbsp vegetable oil
    1 orange
    30ml/2 tbsp chopped fresh
        coriander (cilantro)
    salt and ground black pepper

1 Heat a non-stick wok or frying pan. Add the pine nuts and toss over medium heat until golden brown. Remove and set aside.

2 Using a sharp knife, cut the daikon, beetroot and carrots into long, thin strips. Keep them separate on a chopping board.

3 Reheat the wok or frying pan, then add the oil. When the oil is hot, add the daikon, raw beetroot and carrots and stir-fry for 2–3 minutes.

4 Remove the vegetables from the wok and set aside.

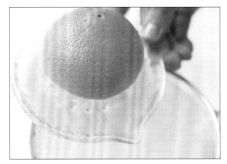

5 Cut the orange in half. Squeeze the juice, using a citrus juicer or a reamer, and pour the juice into a bowl.

6 Arrange the vegetables attractively on a warmed platter, sprinkle over the coriander and season to taste with salt and ground black pepper.

7 Reheat the wok or frying pan, then pour in the orange juice and simmer for 2 minutes.

8 Drizzle the reduced orange juice over the top of the stir-fried vegetables, sprinkle the top with the pine nuts, and serve immediately.

Energy 103Kcal/427kJ; Protein 2.1g; Carbohydrate 7.8g, of which sugars 7.5g; Fat 7.2g, of which saturates 0.7g; Cholesterol 0mg; Calcium 33mg; Fibre 2.1g; Sodium 31mg.

BROCCOLI WITH SOY SAUCE ★

A WONDERFULLY SIMPLE DISH THAT YOU WILL WANT TO MAKE AGAIN AND AGAIN. THE BROCCOLI COOKS IN NEXT TO NO TIME, SO DON'T START COOKING UNTIL YOU ARE ALMOST READY TO EAT.

SERVES 4

INGREDIENTS
    450g/1lb broccoli
    15ml/1 tbsp vegetable oil
    2 garlic cloves, sliced
    30 ml/2 tbsp light soy sauce
    salt

COOK'S TIP
Broccoli is a rich source of vitamin C and folic acid and is also believed to have antioxidant properties.

1 Trim the thick stems of the broccoli and cut the head into large florets.

2 Bring a pan of lightly salted water to the boil. Add the broccoli and cook for 3–4 minutes until crisp-tender.

3 Drain the broccoli thoroughly and transfer it to a heated serving dish.

4 Heat the oil in a small pan. Fry the sliced garlic for 2 minutes to release the flavour, then remove it with a slotted spoon. Pour the oil carefully over the broccoli, taking care as it will splatter.

5 Drizzle the soy sauce over the broccoli, sprinkle over the fried garlic and serve.

VARIATIONS
Cos lettuce or Chinese leaves (Chinese cabbage) taste delicious prepared this way.

Energy 65Kcal/271kJ; Protein 5.2g; Carbohydrate 2.7g, of which sugars 2.2g; Fat 3.8g, of which saturates 0.6g; Cholesterol 0mg; Calcium 64mg; Fibre 2.9g; Sodium 543mg.

BROCCOLI WITH SESAME SEEDS ★★★

THIS SIMPLE TREATMENT IS IDEAL FOR BROCCOLI AND OTHER BRASSICAS, INCLUDING BRUSSELS SPROUTS. ADDING A SPRINKLING OF TOASTED SESAME SEEDS IS AN INSPIRED TOUCH.

SERVES 2

INGREDIENTS

225g/8oz purple sprouting broccoli
15ml/1 tbsp vegetable oil
15ml/1 tbsp soy sauce
15ml/1 tbsp toasted sesame seeds
salt and ground black pepper

VARIATIONS

- Sprouting broccoli has been used for this recipe, but when it is not available an ordinary variety of broccoli, such as calabrese, will also work very well.
- An even better choice would be Chinese broccoli, which is often available in Asian markets under the name *gailan*.

1 Using a sharp knife, cut off and discard any thick stems from the broccoli and cut the broccoli into long, thin florets. Stems that are young and tender can be sliced into rounds.

2 Remove any bruised or discoloured portions of the stem along with any florets that are no longer firm and tightly curled.

3 Heat the vegetable oil in a wok or large frying pan and add the broccoli. Stir-fry for 3–4 minutes, or until tender, adding a splash of water if the pan becomes too dry.

4 Mix the soy sauce with the sesame seeds, then season with salt and ground black pepper. Add to the broccoli, toss to combine and serve immediately.

Energy 135Kcal/558kJ; Protein 6.6g; Carbohydrate 2.7g, of which sugars 2.3g; Fat 10.9g, of which saturates 1.5g; Cholesterol 0mg; Calcium 115mg; Fibre 3.5g; Sodium 545mg.

SPRING VEGETABLE STIR-FRY ★

FAST, FRESH AND PACKED WITH HEALTHY VEGETABLES, THIS STIR-FRY IS DELICIOUS SERVED WITH MARINATED TOFU AND RICE OR NOODLES. THIS RECIPE CONTAINS VERY LITTLE SATURATED FAT.

3 Heat a frying pan or wok over high heat. Add the vegetable oil and the sesame oil, and reduce the heat. Add the garlic and sauté for 2 minutes.

4 Add the chopped ginger, carrots, broccoli and asparagus tips to the pan and stir-fry for 4 minutes.

5 Add the spring onions and spring greens or collard greens and stir-fry for a further 2 minutes.

6 Add the soy sauce and apple juice and cook for 1–2 minutes until the vegetables are tender; add a little water if they appear dry. Sprinkle the sesame seeds on top and serve.

SERVES 4

INGREDIENTS
  2 spring onions (scallions)
  175g/6oz spring greens or
    collard greens
  15ml/1 tbsp vegetable oil
  5ml/1 tsp toasted sesame oil
  1 garlic clove, chopped
  2.5cm/1in piece fresh root ginger,
    finely chopped
  225g/8oz baby carrots
  350g/12oz broccoli florets
  175g/6oz asparagus tips
  30ml/2 tbsp light soy sauce
  15ml/1 tbsp apple juice
  15ml/1 tbsp sesame seeds, toasted

1 Trim the spring onions and cut them diagonally into thin slices.

2 Wash the spring greens or collard greens and drain in a colander, then shred finely.

Energy 105Kcal/434kJ; Protein 7.1g; Carbohydrate 9.4g, of which sugars 8.6g; Fat 4.4g, of which saturates 0.7g; Cholesterol 0mg; Calcium 170mg; Fibre 5.9g; Sodium 565mg.

ORIENTAL GREEN BEANS ★

THIS IS A SIMPLE AND DELICIOUS WAY OF ENLIVENING GREEN BEANS. THE DISH CAN BE SERVED HOT OR COLD AND, ACCOMPANIED BY AN OMELETTE, MAKES A PERFECT LIGHT LUNCH OR SUPPER.

SERVES 4

INGREDIENTS

450g/1lb/3 cups green beans
15ml/1 tbsp vegetable oil
5ml/1 tsp sesame oil
2 garlic cloves, crushed
2.5cm/1in piece fresh root ginger
30ml/2 tbsp dark soy sauce

2 Meanwhile, peel the ginger, using a sharp knife, slice it into matchstick strips, then chop the strips finely.

3 Heat the vegetable and sesame oils in a heavy pan, add the garlic and sauté for 2 minutes.

4 Stir in the ginger and soy sauce and cook, stirring constantly, for a further 2–3 minutes until the liquid has reduced, then pour this mixture over the warm beans. Leave for a few minutes to allow all the flavours to mingle before serving.

1 Steam the beans over a pan of boiling lightly salted water for 4 minutes or until just tender.

VARIATIONS

- Substitute other green beans, if you wish. Runner beans and other flat varieties should be cut diagonally into thick slices before steaming. This recipe also works well with mangetouts (snow peas) or sugar snap peas.
- Broccoli goes well with ginger and garlic, but don't steam calabrese broccoli or its vibrant colour will become dull. Blanch the broccoli in boiling water instead.

Energy 62Kcal/254kJ; Protein 2.4g; Carbohydrate 4.2g, of which sugars 3.1g; Fat 4.1g, of which saturates 0.6g; Cholesterol 0mg; Calcium 42mg; Fibre 2.5g; Sodium 534mg.

BRAISED AUBERGINE AND COURGETTES ★

AUBERGINE, COURGETTES AND SOME FRESH RED CHILLIES ARE COMBINED WITH BLACK BEAN SAUCE IN THIS DISH TO CREATE A SIMPLE, SPICY AND QUITE SENSATIONAL ACCOMPANIMENT TO ANY MEAL.

SERVES 4

INGREDIENTS

  1 aubergine (eggplant), about
    350g/12oz
  2 small courgettes (zucchini)
  2 fresh red chillies
  2 garlic cloves
  15ml/1 tbsp vegetable oil
  1 small onion, diced
  15ml/1 tbsp black bean sauce
  15ml/1 tbsp dark soy sauce
  45ml/3 tbsp cold water
  salt
  chilli flowers (optional), to garnish
    (see Cook's Tip)

COOK'S TIP
Chilli flowers make a pretty garnish.

1 Using a sharp knife, slit a fresh red chilli from the tip to within 1cm/½in of the stem end. Repeat this at regular intervals around the chilli so that you have slender "petals" attached at the stem.

2 Rinse the chilli to remove the seeds, then place it in a bowl of iced water for at least 4 hours until the "petals" curl. Rinse well.

1 Trim the aubergine and slice it in half lengthways, then across into 1cm/½in thick slices.

2 Layer all the slices of aubergine in a colander, sprinkling each layer with salt. Leave the aubergine in the sink to stand for about 20 minutes.

3 Roll cut each courgette in turn by slicing off one end diagonally, then rolling the courgette through 180 degrees and cutting off another diagonal slice, so that you create a triangular wedge.

4 Make more wedges of courgette in the same way.

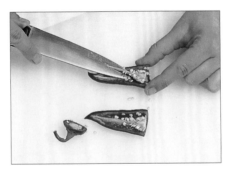

5 Remove the stalks from the chillies, cut them in half lengthways and scrape out and discard the pith and seeds. Chop the chillies finely.

VARIATION
You can vary the intensity of the chilli in this dish. For a fiery result, retain the chilli seeds and add to the mixture; for a milder result, reduce the amount of chilli or even omit it altogether.

6 Cut the garlic cloves in half. Place them cut side down and chop them finely by slicing first in one direction and then in the other.

7 Rinse the aubergine slices well, drain and dry thoroughly on kitchen paper.

8 Heat the oil in a wok or non-stick frying pan. Stir-fry the garlic, chillies and onion with the black bean sauce for a few seconds.

9 Add the aubergine and stir-fry for 2 minutes, sprinkling over a little water to prevent them from burning. Stir in the courgettes, soy sauce and water. Cook, stirring often, for 5 minutes. Serve hot. Add a garnish of chilli flowers.

Energy 66Kcal/276kJ; Protein 3g; Carbohydrate 6.1g, of which sugars 4.2g; Fat 3.5g, of which saturates 0.5g; Cholesterol 0mg; Calcium 34mg; Fibre 2.9g; Sodium 270mg.

STIR-FRIED GREENS ★

WHEN YOU'VE GOT A SINGLE CHICKEN BREAST FILLET OR SMALL PIECE OF PORK FILLET IN THE REFRIGERATOR, THIS IS THE IDEAL RECIPE TO USE. IT TASTES GREAT AND IS LOW IN FAT.

3 When the meat is cooked, add the sliced stems first and cook them quickly; then add the torn leaves, quail's eggs and chilli. Spoon in the oyster sauce and a little boiling water, if necessary. Cover and cook for 1–2 minutes only.

SERVES 4

INGREDIENTS

2 bunches spinach or 1 head Chinese leaves (Chinese cabbage) or 450g/1lb curly kale
3 garlic cloves, crushed
5cm/2in piece fresh root ginger, peeled and cut in matchsticks
15ml/1 tbsp vegetable oil
115g/4oz skinless chicken breast fillet or pork fillet (tenderloin), very finely sliced
8 quail's eggs, hard-boiled and shelled (optional)
1 fresh red chilli, seeded and shredded
30–45ml/2–3 tbsp oyster sauce
15ml/1 tbsp brown sugar
10ml/2 tsp cornflour (cornstarch), mixed with 60ml/4 tbsp cold water
salt

1 Wash the chosen leaves well and shake them dry. Strip the tender leaves from the stems and tear them into pieces. Discard the lower, tougher part of the stems and slice the remainder evenly, with a sharp knife.

2 Fry the garlic and ginger in the hot oil, without browning, for 1 minute. Add the chicken or pork and keep stirring it in the wok until the meat changes colour.

4 Remove the cover, stir the mixture and add sugar and salt to taste. Stir in the cornflour and water mixture and toss thoroughly. Cook until the mixture is well coated in a glossy sauce.

5 Serve immediately, while still very hot and the colours are bright and positively jewel-like.

COOK'S TIP
As with all stir-fries, don't start cooking until you have prepared all of the ingredients. Cut everything into small, even-size pieces so that the food can be cooked very quickly and all the colours and flavours are preserved.

VARIATION
The quail's eggs look very attractive, but if you don't have any, you can substitute some baby corn, halved at an angle.

Energy 111Kcal/465kJ; Protein 10.3g; Carbohydrate 8.9g, of which sugars 8.7g; Fat 4g, of which saturates 0.5g; Cholesterol 20mg; Calcium 196mg; Fibre 2.5g; Sodium 358mg.

COURGETTES WITH NOODLES ★

ANY COURGETTE OR MEMBER OF THE SQUASH FAMILY CAN BE USED IN THIS SIMPLE DISH, WHICH IS LOW IN FAT, YET FILLING ENOUGH TO MAKE A GOOD LIGHT LUNCH FOR FOUR.

SERVES 4

INGREDIENTS

    450g/1lb courgettes (zucchini)
    1 onion, finely sliced
    1 garlic clove, finely chopped
    15ml/1 tbsp vegetable oil
    2.5ml/½ tsp ground turmeric
    2 tomatoes, chopped
    45ml/3 tbsp water
    115g/4oz cooked, peeled
       prawns (shrimp) (optional)
    25g/1oz cellophane noodles
    salt

1 Use a potato peeler to cut thin strips from the outside of each courgette so that they have a stripy appearance. Use a sharp knife to cut the courgettes into neat slices.

2 Heat the oil in a wok. Add the onions and garlic and stir-fry for 2 minutes. Add the turmeric, courgette slices, chopped tomatoes and water. If using the prawns, add them to the wok.

3 Put the noodles in a pan and pour over boiling water to cover. Leave for 1 minute and then drain. Cut the noodles in 5cm/2in lengths and add to the vegetables.

4 Cover with a lid and cook in their own steam for 2–3 minutes. Toss everything well together. Season with salt to taste and serve while still hot.

Energy 54Kcal/225kJ; Protein 2.1g; Carbohydrate 6.1g, of which sugars 2.7g; Fat 2.5g, of which saturates 0.3g; Cholesterol 0mg; Calcium 24mg; Fibre 1.2g; Sodium 3mg.

STEAMED AUBERGINE WITH SESAME SAUCE ★

SERVE THIS TASTY VEGETABLE MEDLEY ON ITS OWN, OR AS AN ACCOMPANIMENT TO GRILLED STEAK. IT CONTAINS VERY LITTLE FAT, SO CAN EASILY BE ACCOMMODATED IN A HEALTHY DIET.

SERVES 4

INGREDIENTS
2 large aubergines (eggplants)
400ml/14fl oz/1²/₃ cups water
  with 5ml/1 tsp instant
  dashi powder
25ml/1½ tbsp caster
  (superfine) sugar
15ml/1 tbsp shoyu
15ml/1 tbsp sesame seeds, finely
  ground in a mortar and pestle
15ml/1 tbsp sake or dry sherry
15ml/1 tbsp cornflour (cornstarch)
salt
For the accompanying vegetables
130g/4½oz shimeji mushrooms
115g/4oz/¾ cup fine green beans
100ml/3fl oz/scant ½ cup water
  with 5ml/1 tsp instant
  dashi powder
25ml/1½ tbsp caster
  (superfine) sugar
15ml/1 tbsp sake or dry sherry
1.5ml/¼ tsp salt
dash of shoyu

1 Peel the aubergines and cut them in quarters lengthways. Prick them all over with a skewer, then plunge them into a bowl of salted water. Leave them to stand for 30 minutes.

2 Drain the aubergines and lay them side by side in a steamer, or in a wok half filled with simmering water and with a bamboo basket supported on a tripod inside, for 20 minutes, or until the aubergines are soft. If the quarters are too long to fit in the steamer, cut them in half.

3 Mix the dashi stock, sugar, shoyu and 1.5ml/¼ tsp salt together in a large pan. Gently transfer the aubergines to this pan, then cover and cook over a low heat for a further 15 minutes. Take a few tablespoonfuls of stock from the pan and mix with the ground sesame seeds. Add this mixture to the pan.

4 Thoroughly mix the sake with the cornflour in small bowl, then add to the pan with the aubergines and stock and shake the pan gently, but quickly. When the sauce becomes quite thick, remove the pan from the heat.

5 While the aubergines are cooking, prepare and cook the accompanying vegetables. Wash the mushrooms and cut off the hard base part. Separate the large block into smaller chunks with your fingers. Trim the green beans and cut in half.

6 Mix the stock with the sugar, sake, salt and shoyu in a shallow pan. Add the green beans and mushrooms and cook for 7 minutes until just tender. Serve the aubergines and their sauce in individual bowls with the accompanying vegetables over the top.

Energy 93Kcal/390kJ; Protein 2.9g; Carbohydrate 13.6g, of which sugars 9.6g; Fat 2.9g, of which saturates 0.5g; Cholesterol 0mg; Calcium 52mg; Fibre 3.3g; Sodium 274mg.

NEW POTATOES COOKED IN DASHI STOCK ★

AS THE STOCK EVAPORATES IN THIS DELICIOUS DISH, THE ONION BECOMES MELTINGLY SOFT AND CARAMELIZED, MAKING A WONDERFUL SAUCE THAT COATS THE POTATOES.

SERVES 4

INGREDIENTS

15ml/1 tbsp toasted sesame oil
1 small onion, thinly sliced
1kg/2¼lb baby new
  potatoes, unpeeled
200ml/7fl oz/scant 1 cup water with
  5ml/1 tsp instant dashi powder
45ml/3 tbsp shoyu

COOK'S TIP
Japanese chefs use toasted sesame oil for its distinctive strong aroma. If the smell is too strong, use a mixture of half sesame and half vegetable oil.

1 Heat the sesame oil in a wok or large pan. Add the onion slices and stir-fry for 30 seconds, then add the potatoes. Stir constantly, until all the potatoes are well coated in sesame oil, and have begun to sizzle.

2 Pour on the dashi stock and shoyu and reduce the heat to the lowest setting. Cover and cook for 15 minutes, turning the potatoes every 5 minutes so that they cook evenly.

3 Uncover the wok or pan for a further 5 minutes to reduce the liquid. If there is already very little liquid remaining, remove the wok or pan from the heat, cover and leave to stand for 5 minutes. Check that the potatoes are cooked, then remove from the heat.

4 Transfer the potatoes and onions to a deep serving bowl. Pour the sauce over the top and serve immediately.

Energy 210Kcal/890kJ; Protein 4.8g; Carbohydrate 42.4g, of which sugars 4.9g; Fat 3.5g, of which saturates 0.7g; Cholesterol 0mg; Calcium 21mg; Fibre 2.7g; Sodium 829mg.

TURNIPS WITH PRAWNS AND MANGETOUTS ★

THIS IS SOMETHING OF A CINDERELLA DISH, TRANSFORMING TURNIPS, THOSE SOMEWHAT NEGLECTED VEGETABLES, INTO SOMETHING THAT IS AS SOPHISTICATED AS IT IS SURPRISING.

SERVES 4

INGREDIENTS

   8 small turnips, peeled
   600ml/1 pint/2½ cups water and
     7.5ml/1½ tsp instant dashi powder
   10ml/2 tsp shoyu (use the Japanese
     pale *awakuchi* soy sauce
     if available)
   60ml/4 tbsp mirin
   30ml/2 tbsp sake
   16 medium raw tiger prawns (jumbo
     shrimp), heads and shells removed
     but with tails left intact
   dash of rice vinegar
   90g/3½oz mangetouts (snow peas)
   5ml/1 tsp cornflour (cornstarch)
   salt

1 Par-boil the turnips in boiling water for 3 minutes. Drain, then place them side by side in a deep pan. Add the dashi stock and cover with a saucer to submerge the turnips. Bring to the boil, then add the shoyu, 5ml/1 tsp salt, the mirin and sake. Reduce the heat to very low, cover and simmer for 30 minutes.

2 Insert a cocktail stick (toothpick) into the back of each prawn, and gently scoop up the thin black vein running down its length. Very carefully pull the vein out, then discard.

3 Blanch the prawns in boiling water with the vinegar until the colour just changes. Drain. Cook the mangetouts in lightly salted water for 3 minutes. Drain well, then set aside.

4 Remove the saucer from the turnips and add the cooked prawns to the stock for about 4 minutes to warm through. Scoop out the turnips, drain and place in individual bowls. Transfer the prawns to a small plate.

5 Mix the cornflour with 15ml/1 tbsp water and add to the pan that held the turnips. Increase the heat a little bit and shake the pan gently until the liquid thickens slightly.

6 Place the mangetouts on the turnips and arrange the prawns on top, then pour about 30ml/2 tbsp of the hot liquid from the pan into each bowl. Serve immediately.

Energy 80Kcal/339kJ; Protein 10.4g; Carbohydrate 6.1g, of which sugars 4.6g; Fat 0.6g, of which saturates 0.1g; Cholesterol 98mg; Calcium 87mg; Fibre 2.3g; Sodium 375mg.

SLOW-COOKED SHIITAKE WITH SHOYU ★★

Shiitake mushrooms cooked slowly are so rich and filling, that some people call them "vegetarian steak". This is a useful and flavoursome addition to other dishes.

SERVES 4

INGREDIENTS
    20 dried shiitake mushrooms
    30ml/2 tbsp vegetable oil
    30ml/2 tbsp shoyu
    5ml/1 tsp toasted sesame oil

1 Start soaking the dried shiitake the day before. Put them in a large bowl almost full of water. Cover the shiitake with a plate or lid to stop them floating to the surface of the water. Leave to soak overnight.

VARIATION
Cut the slow-cooked shiitake into thin strips. Mix with 600g/1⅓lb/5¼ cups cooked brown rice and 15ml/1 tbsp finely chopped chives. Sprinkle with toasted sesame seeds.

2 Remove the shiitake from the soaking water and gently squeeze out the water with your fingers.

3 Measure 120ml/4fl oz/½ cup of the liquid in the bowl, and set aside.

4 Heat the oil in a wok or a large frying pan. Stir-fry the shiitake over a high heat for 5 minutes, stirring continuously.

5 Reduce the heat to the lowest setting, then add the liquid and the shoyu.

6 Cook the mushrooms until there is almost no moisture left, stirring frequently. Sprinkle with the toasted sesame oil and remove from the heat.

7 Leave to cool, then slice and arrange the shiitake on a large plate.

Energy 66Kcal/272kJ; Protein 1.1g; Carbohydrate 0.8g, of which sugars 0.7g; Fat 6.5g, of which saturates 0.8g; Cholesterol 0mg; Calcium 4mg; Fibre 0.6g; Sodium 537mg.

SAUTÉED GREEN BEANS ★

THE SMOKY FLAVOUR OF THE DRIED SHRIMPS ADDS AN EXTRA DIMENSION TO THESE GREEN BEANS, AND BECAUSE THIS DISH IS SO LOW IN SATURATED FAT, YOU CAN EAT IT TO YOUR HEART'S CONTENT.

3 Bring a large pan of lightly salted water to the boil and cook the beans for 3–4 minutes until crisp-tender. Drain, refresh under cold water and drain again. Pat the beans dry with kitchen paper.

4 Drain the dried shrimps, reserving the soaking water for adding to fish soup, if you like.

SERVES 4

INGREDIENTS
  450g/1lb green beans
  25g/1oz dried shrimps
  15ml/1 tbsp vegetable oil
  3 garlic cloves, finely chopped
  5 spring onions (scallions), cut
    into 2.5cm/1in lengths
  15ml/1 tbsp light soy sauce
  salt

COOK'S TIP
Don't be tempted to use too many dried shrimps. As well as being high in salt, dried shrimps have a very strong flavour that could overwhelm the more delicate taste of the beans.

1 Put the dried shrimps in a bowl and pour over the warm water to cover. Stir, cover the bowl with clear film (plastic wrap) and leave to soak for 1 hour.

2 Using a sharp knife, trim the green beans neatly, then bunch them together on a board and slice them in half.

5 Heat the oil in a non-stick frying pan or wok until very hot. Stir-fry the garlic and spring onions for 30 seconds, then add the shrimps. Mix lightly.

6 Add the green beans and soy sauce. Toss the mixture over the heat until the beans are hot. Serve immediately.

Energy 64Kcal/264kJ; Protein 4.5g; Carbohydrate 4g, of which sugars 2.9g; Fat 3.5g, of which saturates 0.5g; Cholesterol 19mg; Calcium 90mg; Fibre 2.7g; Sodium 163mg.

BAMBOO SHOOT SALAD ★

THIS HOT, SHARP-FLAVOURED SALAD IS POPULAR THROUGHOUT FAR EAST ASIA. USE CANNED WHOLE BAMBOO SHOOTS, IF YOU CAN FIND THEM — THEY HAVE MORE FLAVOUR THAN SLICED ONES.

SERVES 4

INGREDIENTS
400g/14oz canned bamboo shoots, in large pieces
25g/1oz/about 3 tbsp glutinous rice
30ml/2 tbsp chopped shallots
15ml/1 tbsp chopped garlic
45ml/3 tbsp chopped spring onions (scallions)
30ml/2 tbsp Thai fish sauce
30ml/2 tbsp fresh lime juice
5ml/1 tsp sugar
2.5ml/½ tsp dried chilli flakes
20–25 small fresh mint leaves
15ml/1 tbsp toasted sesame seeds

COOK'S TIP
Glutinous rice does not, in fact, contain any gluten – it's just sticky.

1 Rinse the bamboo shoots under cold running water, then drain them and pat them thoroughly dry with kitchen paper and set them aside.

2 Dry-roast the rice in a frying pan until it is golden brown. Leave to cool slightly, then tip into a mortar and grind to fine crumbs with a pestle.

3 Transfer the rice to a bowl and add the shallots, garlic, spring onions, fish sauce, lime juice, sugar, chillies and half the mint leaves. Mix well.

4 Add the bamboo shoots to the bowl and toss to mix. Serve sprinkled with the toasted sesame seeds and the remaining mint leaves.

Energy 88Kcal/368kJ; Protein 4.4g; Carbohydrate 11.5g, of which sugars 4.6g; Fat 2.8g, of which saturates 0.4g; Cholesterol 0mg; Calcium 51mg; Fibre 2g; Sodium 274mg.

JAPANESE SALAD ★★

HIJIKI IS A MILD-TASTING SEAWEED AND, COMBINED WITH RADISHES, CUCUMBER AND BEANSPROUTS, IT MAKES A REFRESHING SALAD THAT IS THE PERFECT ACCOMPANIMENT TO A RICH MAIN DISH.

SERVES 4

INGREDIENTS
15g/½oz/½ cup hijiki seaweed
250g/9oz/1¼ cups radishes, sliced
    into very thin rounds
1 small cucumber, cut into
    thin sticks
75g/3oz/1½ cups beansprouts
For the dressing
15ml/1 tbsp sunflower oil
15ml/1 tbsp toasted sesame oil
5ml/1 tsp light soy sauce
30ml/2 tbsp rice vinegar or 15ml/
    1 tbsp wine vinegar
15ml/1 tbsp mirin

1 Soak the hijiki in a bowl of cold water for 10–15 minutes until it is rehydrated, then drain, rinse under cold running water and drain again. It should almost triple in volume.

2 Place the hijiki in a pan of water. Bring the water to the boil, then reduce the heat and simmer the hijiki for about 30 minutes or until tender.

COOK'S TIP
Hijiki is a type of seaweed that is popular in Japan. It resembles wakame and is generally sold dried and finely shredded. It is available in many supermarkets and Asian stores.

3 Meanwhile, make the dressing. Whisk the oils with the vinegar and mirin in a bowl until combined, and then whisk in the soy sauce.

4 Drain the cooked hijiki in a sieve (strainer) and arrange it in a shallow bowl or platter with the prepared radishes, cucumber and beansprouts. Pour over the dressing and toss lightly to combine.

Energy 68Kcal/280kJ; Protein 1.4g; Carbohydrate 2.8g, of which sugars 2.4g; Fat 5.8g, of which saturates 0.8g; Cholesterol 0mg; Calcium 23mg; Fibre 1.1g; Sodium 276mg.

ASSORTED SEAWEED SALAD ★

SEAWEED IS A NUTRITIOUS, ALKALINE FOOD WHICH IS RICH IN FIBRE. ITS UNUSUAL FLAVOURS ARE A GREAT COMPLEMENT TO FISH AND TOFU DISHES. THIS SALAD IS EXTREMELY LOW IN FAT.

SERVES 4

INGREDIENTS
   5g/⅛oz each dried wakame, dried
      arame and dried hijiki seaweeds
   about 130g/4½oz fresh
      enokitake mushrooms
   15ml/1 tbsp rice vinegar
   6.5ml/1¼ tsp salt
   2 spring onions (scallions)
   a few ice cubes
   ½ cucumber, cut lengthways
   250g/9oz mixed salad leaves
For the dressing
   60ml/4 tbsp rice vinegar
   7.5ml/1½ tsp toasted sesame oil
   15ml/1 tbsp shoyu
   15ml/1 tbsp water with a pinch
      of instant dashi powder
   2.5cm/1in piece fresh root ginger,
      finely grated

1 Soak the dried wakame seaweed for 10 minutes in one bowl of water and, in a separate bowl of water, soak the dried arame and hijiki seaweeds together for 30 minutes.

2 Trim the hard end of the enokitake mushroom stalks, then cut the bunch in half and separate the stems.

3 Cook the wakame and enokitake in boiling water for 2 minutes, then add the arame and hijiki for a few seconds. Immediately remove from the heat.

4 Drain in a sieve (strainer) and sprinkle over the vinegar and salt while still warm. Chill until needed.

5 Slice the spring onions into thin, 4cm/1½in long strips, then soak the strips in a bowl of cold water with a few ice cubes added to make them curl up. Drain. Slice the cucumber into thin, half-moon shapes.

6 Mix the dressing ingredients in a bowl. Arrange the mixed salad leaves in a large bowl with the cucumber on top, then add the seaweed and enokitake mixture. Decorate the salad with spring onion curls and serve with the dressing.

Energy 26Kcal/107kJ; Protein 1.5g; Carbohydrate 2.2g, of which sugars 2g; Fat 1.3g, of which saturates 0.2g; Cholesterol 0mg; Calcium 28mg; Fibre 1.2g; Sodium 272mg.

DESSERTS

Desserts have never been central to culinary tradition in China
and Far East Asia. At the conclusion of a meal you are more
likely to be offered fresh fruit than a fancy sweet dish. Iced
Fruit Mountain, for instance, consists simply of a wide variety
of fresh fruits tumbling over a sculpted sierra of crushed ice.
Flavoured ices are said to have originated in China, and dishes
such as Lychee and Elderflower Sorbet, Ginger Granita and
Iced Oranges are excellent for cleansing the palate.

LYCHEE AND ELDERFLOWER SORBET ★

THE FLAVOUR OF ELDERFLOWERS IS FAMOUS FOR BRINGING OUT THE ESSENCE OF GOOSEBERRIES, BUT WHAT IS LESS WELL KNOWN IS HOW WONDERFULLY IT COMPLEMENTS LYCHEES.

SERVES 4

INGREDIENTS
175g/6oz/¾ cup caster
   (superfine) sugar
400ml/14fl oz/1⅔ cups water
500g/1¼lb fresh lychees, peeled
   and stoned (pitted)
15ml/1 tbsp elderflower cordial
   or lime syrup
dessert biscuits (cookies),
   to serve (optional)

COOK'S TIP
For the best result, switch the freezer to the coldest setting before making the sorbet – the faster the mixture freezes, the smaller the ice crystals that form, and the better the final texture of the sorbet will be.

1 Place the sugar and water in a pan and heat gently until the sugar has dissolved, stirring several times. Increase the heat and boil for 5 minutes.

2 Add the lychees. Lower the heat and simmer for 7 minutes. Remove from the heat and pour into a jug (pitcher) or bowl. Set aside until cool.

3 Purée the fruit and syrup in a blender or food processor. Place a sieve (strainer) over a bowl and pour the purée into it. Press through as much of the purée as possible with a spoon.

4 Stir the elderflower cordial or lime syrup into the strained purée, then pour the mixture into a freezerproof container. Freeze for 2 hours, until ice crystals start to form around the edges.

5 Remove the sorbet from the freezer and process briefly in a food processor or blender to break up the crystals. Repeat this twice more, then freeze until firm. Transfer to the refrigerator for 10 minutes to soften slightly before serving in scoops, with dessert biscuits, if you like.

Energy 249Kcal/1064kJ; Protein 1.4g; Carbohydrate 64.7g, of which sugars 64.7g; Fat 0.1g, of which saturates 0g; Cholesterol 0mg; Calcium 31mg; Fibre 0.9g; Sodium 4mg.

LEMON SORBET ★

REFRESHINGLY TANGY AND YET DELICIOUSLY SMOOTH, THIS FAT-FREE SORBET QUITE LITERALLY MELTS IN THE MOUTH, AND IS THE PERFECT DESSERT FOR SERVING AFTER A SPICY STIR-FRY.

SERVES 6

INGREDIENTS
    200g/7oz/1 cup caster
      (superfine) sugar
    300ml/½ pint/1¼ cups water
    4 lemons, well scrubbed
    1 egg white
    sugared lemon rind, to decorate

1 Put the sugar and water into a medium pan and bring to the boil, stirring occasionally until the sugar has just dissolved.

2 Using a swivel vegetable peeler pare the rind thinly from two of the lemons so that it falls straight into the pan.

3 Simmer for 2 minutes without stirring, then take the pan off the heat. Leave to cool, then chill.

4 Squeeze the juice from all the lemons and add it to the syrup. Strain the syrup into a shallow freezerproof container, reserving the rind. Freeze the mixture for 4 hours until it is mushy and ice crystals have begun to form around the edges of the mixture.

5 Scoop the sorbet into a food processor and beat until smooth. Lightly whisk the egg white until just frothy. Spoon the sorbet back into the tub, beat in the egg white and return to the freezer for 4 hours. Before serving, transfer the sorbet to the refrigerator for 10 minutes to soften slightly.

6 Scoop into bowls or glasses and decorate with sugared lemon rind.

COOK'S TIP
Cut one third off the top of a lemon and retain as a lid. Squeeze the juice out of the larger portion. Remove any membrane and use the shell as a container. Scoop or pipe sorbet into the shell, top with the lid and add lemon leaves or bay leaves.

VARIATION
Sorbet can be made from any citrus fruit. As a guide you will need 300ml/ ½ pint/1¼ cups fresh fruit juice and the pared rind of half the squeezed fruits. Use 4 oranges, or 2 oranges and 2 lemons, or, for a grapefruit sorbet, use the rind of one ruby grapefruit and the juice of two. For lime sorbet, combine the pared rind of three limes with the juice of six.

If you have an ice cream maker, simply strain the syrup and lemon juice and churn the mixture until thick. Add the egg white to the mixture and continue to churn for 10–15 minutes until the sorbet is firm enough to scoop. Either eat the sorbet straight away or store in the freezer.

Energy 134Kcal/571kJ; Protein 0.7g; Carbohydrate 35g, of which sugars 35g; Fat 0g, of which saturates 0g; Cholesterol 0mg; Calcium 19mg; Fibre 0g; Sodium 12mg.

GINGER GRANITA ★

THIS FULL-BODIED GRANITA IS A MUST FOR GINGER LOVERS. SERVED SOLO, IT IS A SIMPLE AND INEXPENSIVE DESSERT, YET IS SMART ENOUGH TO SERVE TO THE MOST SOPHISTICATED GUESTS.

SERVES 6

INGREDIENTS
150g/5oz/¾ cup caster
(superfine) sugar
1 litre/1¾ pints/4 cups water
75g/3oz fresh root ginger
a little ground cinnamon, to decorate

1 Bring the sugar and water to the boil in a pan, stirring until all the sugar has dissolved. Take the pan off the heat.

VARIATION
For a stronger ginger flavour, use lemon and ginger tea. Make up 1 litre/1¾ pints/4 cups of the tea and boil it with the sugar before adding the chopped ginger. Cool completely before chilling.

2 Peel the ginger, chop it finely, then stir it into the hot sugar syrup. Leave for at least 1 hour to infuse (steep) and cool, then pour into a bowl and chill.

3 Strain the chilled syrup into a large, shallow plastic container, making sure the depth is no more than 2.5cm/1in.

4 Cover and freeze for 2 hours or until the mixture around the sides of the container has become mushy.

5 Using a fork, break up the ice crystals and mash finely. Return the granita to the freezer for 2 hours more, beating every 30 minutes until the ice becomes soft and very fine with even size ice crystals.

6 After the final beating, return the now slushy granita to the freezer. Serve in tall glasses decorated with ground cinnamon.

COOK'S TIP
Make sure you buy very fresh, young root ginger for this dessert. Look for firm pieces with smooth skin.

Energy 99Kcal/420kJ; Protein 0.1g; Carbohydrate 26.1g, of which sugars 26.1g; Fat 0g, of which saturates 0g; Cholesterol 0mg; Calcium 13mg; Fibre 0g; Sodium 2mg.

RUBY GRAPEFRUIT GRANITA ★

THIS IS SHARPER THAN SOME OTHER GRANITAS, BUT IS VERY REFRESHING. IT LOOKS STUNNING IF YOU SERVE IT IN THE EMPTY GRAPEFRUIT SHELLS, WITH A FEW GRAPEFRUIT SEGMENTS ON THE SIDE.

SERVES 6

INGREDIENTS
200g/7oz/1 cup caster
(superfine) sugar
300ml/½ pint/1¼ cups water
4 ruby grapefruit
tiny mint leaves, to decorate

1 Put the sugar and water into a pan. Bring the water to the boil, stirring until the sugar has dissolved. Pour the syrup into a bowl. Leave to cool, then chill.

2 Cut the grapefruit in half. Squeeze the juice, taking care not to damage the grapefruit shells. Set these aside.

3 Strain the juice into a large plastic container. Stir in the chilled syrup, making sure that the depth of the mixture does not exceed 2.5cm/1in.

4 Cover and freeze for 2 hours or until the mixture around the sides of the container is mushy.

5 Using a fork, break up the ice crystals and mash the granita finely.

6 Freeze for 2 hours more, mashing the mixture every 30 minutes until the grapefruit granita consists of fine, even crystals.

7 Select the six best grapefruit shells for use as the serving dishes. Using a sharp knife, remove the grapefruit pulp, leaving the shells as clean as possible on the inside.

8 Scoop the sorbet into the grapefruit shells, decorate with the tiny mint leaves and serve immediately.

COOK'S TIP
Grapefruit shells make very good, eye-catching serving dishes. For a more modern treatment, consider the effect you would like to achieve when halving the grapefruit. They look great when tilted at an angle, or with a zig-zag pattern around the edge. Having squeezed the juice and removed the membrane, trim a little off the base of each shell so that it will remain stable when filled with granita.

Energy 163Kcal/695kJ; Protein 1g; Carbohydrate 42.1g, of which sugars 42.1g; Fat 0.1g, of which saturates 0g; Cholesterol 0mg; Calcium 42mg; Fibre 1.4g; Sodium 5mg.

ICED FRUIT MOUNTAIN ★

WITH ONLY THE MEREST TRACE OF FAT, THIS IS ONE MOUNTAIN YOU CAN CONQUER WITHOUT WORRYING ABOUT THE CONSEQUENCES. IT MAKES A STUNNING CENTREPIECE FOR A SPECIAL MEAL.

SERVES 6–8

INGREDIENTS

  1 star fruit (carambola)
  4 kumquats
  6 physalis
  225g/8oz seedless black grapes
  1 apple and/or 1 Asian pear
  2 large oranges, peeled
  8 fresh lychees, peeled (optional)
  1 Charentais melon and/or
    ½ watermelon
  225g/8oz large strawberries
  caster (superfine) sugar, for dipping
  wedges of lime, to decorate

COOK'S TIP
This list of fruits is just a suggestion. Use any colourful seasonal fruits you like.

1 Slice the star fruit and halve the kumquats. Do not remove the hulls from the strawberries. Cut the apple and/or Asian pear into wedges, and the oranges into segments. Use a melon baller for the melon or, alternatively, cut the melon into neat wedges. Chill all the fruit.

2 Prepare the ice cube "mountain". Choose a wide, shallow bowl that, when turned upside down, will fit neatly on a serving platter. Fill the bowl with crushed ice cubes. Put it in the freezer, with the serving platter. Leave in the freezer for at least 1 hour.

3 Remove the serving platter, ice cubes and bowl from the freezer. Invert the serving platter on top of the bowl of ice, then turn platter and bowl over. Lift off the bowl and arrange the pieces of fruit on the mountain.

4 Decorate the mountain with the lime wedges, and serve the fruit immediately, handing round a bowl of sugar separately for guests with a sweet tooth.

Energy 56Kcal/239kJ; Protein 1.1g; Carbohydrate 13.4g, of which sugars 13.4g; Fat 0.2g, of which saturates 0g; Cholesterol 0mg; Calcium 35mg; Fibre 1.7g; Sodium 17mg.

ICED ORANGES ★

THE ULTIMATE LOW-FAT TREAT — THESE DELECTABLE ORANGE SORBETS SERVED IN FRUIT SHELLS ARE
FUN TO SERVE AND EASY TO EAT. KEEP SOME IN THE FREEZER FOR IMPROMPTU DESSERTS.

SERVES 8

INGREDIENTS
  150g/5oz/⅔ cup sugar
  juice of 1 lemon
  14 medium oranges
  8 fresh bay leaves, to decorate

1 Put the sugar in a heavy pan. Add half the lemon juice, then add 120ml/ 4fl oz/½ cup water. Heat until the sugar has dissolved, stirring occasionally. Bring to the boil and boil for 2–3 minutes until the syrup is clear.

2 Slice the tops off eight of the oranges to make lids. Scoop out the flesh of the oranges and reserve.

3 Freeze the empty shells and lids until needed. Grate the rind of the remaining oranges and add to the syrup.

4 Squeeze the juice from the oranges, and from the reserved flesh. There should be 750ml/1¼ pints/3 cups.

5 Squeeze another orange or add bought orange juice, if necessary, to make up the volume.

6 Stir the orange juice and remaining lemon juice into the syrup, then add 90ml/6 tbsp cold water.

7 Taste, and add more lemon juice or sugar if you think the mixture needs it, bearing in mind that freezing will dull the taste a little.

8 Pour the mixture into a shallow freezer container and freeze for 3 hours.

9 Turn the orange sorbet mixture into a bowl and whisk thoroughly to break up the ice crystals. Freeze for 4 hours more, until firm, but not solid.

10 Pack the mixture into the hollowed- out orange shells, mounding it up, and set the lids on top. Freeze until ready to serve. Just before serving, push a skewer into the tops of the lids and push in a bay leaf, to decorate.

Energy 152Kcal/647kJ; Protein 2.4g; Carbohydrate 37.5g, of which sugars 37.5g; Fat 0.2g, of which saturates 0g; Cholesterol 0mg; Calcium 109mg; Fibre 3.6g; Sodium 12mg.

MANDARINS IN SYRUP ★

MANDARINS, TANGERINES, CLEMENTINES, MINEOLAS; ANY OF THESE LOVELY CITRUS FRUITS ARE SUITABLE FOR THIS RECIPE, WHICH IS BOTH FAT FREE AND VERY LOW IN ADDED SUGAR.

2 Peel the remaining fruit, removing as much of the white pith as possible. Arrange the peeled fruit whole in a wide dish or bowl.

3 Mix the mandarin juice, sugar and orange flower water and pour it over the fruit. Cover the dish and chill in the refrigerator for at least 1 hour.

SERVES 4

INGREDIENTS
  10 mandarin oranges
  15ml/1 tbsp icing
   (confectioners') sugar
  10ml/2 tsp orange flower water
  15ml/1 tbsp chopped pistachio nuts

1 Thinly pare a little of the rind from one mandarin and use a small, sharp knife to cut it into fine shreds for decoration. Squeeze the juice from two mandarins and set aside.

COOK'S TIP
Mandarin oranges look very attractive if you leave them whole, but you may prefer to separate the segments.

4 Bring a small pan of water to the boil. Add the shreds of mandarin rind and blanch them for 30 seconds. Drain and set aside.

5 When the shreds of rind are cold, sprinkle them over the mandarins, with the pistachio nuts. Serve in chilled dessert bowls.

Energy 121Kcal/512kJ; Protein 3.2g; Carbohydrate 23.4g, of which sugars 23.3g; Fat 2.3g, of which saturates 0.3g; Cholesterol 0mg; Calcium 112mg; Fibre 4.1g; Sodium 31mg.

CLEMENTINES IN SPICED SYRUP ★

STAR ANISE IS A VERY USEFUL SPICE. NOT ONLY DOES IT ADD A DELICATE FLAVOUR, BUT IT ALSO MAKES AN ATTRACTIVE DECORATION, ESPECIALLY WITH CITRUS FRUITS.

SERVES 6

INGREDIENTS
350ml/12fl oz/1½ cups sweet
   dessert wine
75g/3oz/6 tbsp caster
   (superfine) sugar
6 star anise
1 cinnamon stick
1 vanilla pod (bean)
30ml/2 tbsp Cointreau or another
   orange liqueur, such as Grand
   Marnier or Van der Hum
1 strip of thinly pared lime rind
12 clementines

1 Put the wine, sugar, star anise and cinnamon in a large pan. Split the vanilla pod and add it to the pan with the lime rind.

2 Bring to the boil, lower the heat and simmer for 10 minutes.

3 Pour the spiced vanilla syrup into a bowl and set aside to cool. When it is completely cold, stir in the Cointreau.

VARIATION
Tangerines or oranges can be used instead of clementines, if you prefer.

4 Peel the clementines. Leave some clementines whole and cut the rest in half. Arrange them in a glass dish. Pour over the spicy syrup and chill overnight.

Energy 143Kcal/605kJ; Protein 0.9g; Carbohydrate 23.5g, of which sugars 23.5g; Fat 0.1g, of which saturates 0g; Cholesterol 0mg; Calcium 40mg; Fibre 1g; Sodium 12mg.

MELON, GINGER AND GRAPEFRUIT ★

THIS IS A REAL PALATE-CLEANSER. THE WATERMELON ABSORBS THE FLAVOUR OF THE GINGER SYRUP WHILE CHILLING, AND CONTRASTS BEAUTIFULLY WITH THE SEGMENTS OF RUBY OR PINK GRAPEFRUIT.

SERVES 4

INGREDIENTS
   500g/1¼lb diced watermelon flesh
   2 ruby or pink grapefruit
   2 pieces preserved stem ginger
     in syrup, plus 30ml/2 tbsp syrup
     from the jar

COOK'S TIP
Take care to toss the fruits gently –
grapefruit segments break up easily and
if that happens, the appearance of the
dish will be spoiled.

1 Remove any seeds from the
watermelon and discard. Cut into bitesize
chunks and put in a serving bowl.

2 Using a small sharp knife, cut away
all the peel and white pith from the
grapefruits, then carefully slice out
the segments, catching any juice in a
bowl placed below. Add the segments
and the juice to the watermelon chunks
in the serving bowl.

3 Finely chop the stem ginger and put
it in the serving bowl containing the
melon cubes and grapefruit segments.

4 Spoon over the ginger syrup and toss
the fruits lightly to mix evenly. Chill
before serving.

VARIATION
Use an orange-fleshed melon such as
cantaloupe, if watermelon is out of season.

Energy 85Kcal/362kJ; Protein 1.3g; Carbohydrate 20.3g, of which sugars 20.3g; Fat 0.5g, of which saturates 0.1g; Cholesterol 0mg; Calcium 28mg; Fibre 1.2g; Sodium 25mg.

APPLES AND RASPBERRIES IN ROSE POUCHONG ★

THIS DELIGHTFULLY FRAGRANT AND QUICK-TO-PREPARE ASIAN DESSERT COUPLES THE SUBTLE FLAVOURS OF APPLES AND RASPBERRIES WITH AN INFUSION OF ROSE-SCENTED TEA.

SERVES 4

INGREDIENTS
    5ml/1 tsp rose pouchong tea
    5ml/1 tsp rose water (optional)
    50g/2oz/¼ cup sugar
    5ml/1 tsp lemon juice
    5 dessert apples
    175g/6oz/1½ cups
        fresh raspberries

1 Warm a large teapot. Add the rose pouchong tea and 900ml/1½ pints/3¾ cups of boiling water together with the rose water, if using. Allow to stand and infuse for 4 minutes.

2 Measure the sugar and the lemon juice into a stainless-steel pan. Pour the tea through a small sieve (strainer) into the pan, and stir to dissolve the sugar.

VARIATION
A fruit tea such as rosehip and hibiscus could be used instead of the rose pouchong, or try cranberry and raspberry to highlight the flavour of the berries.

3 Peel the apples, then cut into quarters and core.

4 Add the apples to the pan of syrup. Return the pan to the heat and bring the syrup to simmering point. Cook the apples for about 5 minutes, until just tender.

5 Transfer the apples and syrup to a large metal tray and leave to cool to room temperature.

6 Pour the cooled apples and syrup into a bowl, add the raspberries and mix to combine. Spoon into individual dishes or bowls and serve immediately.

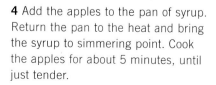

Energy 90Kcal/384kJ; Protein 0.9g; Carbohydrate 22.5g, of which sugars 22.5g; Fat 0.2g, of which saturates 0.1g; Cholesterol 0mg; Calcium 21mg; Fibre 2.4g; Sodium 4mg.

TOFFEE APPLES ★★

THIS HEALTHIER VERSION OF THE CLASSIC CHINESE DESSERT RETAINS ALL THE FLAVOUR AND TEXTURE WITHOUT THE FUSS AND FAT OF DEEP-FRYING.

SERVES 6

INGREDIENTS
  25g/1oz/2 tbsp butter
  75ml/6 tbsp cold water
  40g/1½oz/6 tbsp plain
    (all-purpose) flour
  1 egg
  1 dessert apple
  5ml/1 tsp vegetable oil
  175g/6oz/¾ cup caster
    (superfine) sugar
  5ml/1 tsp sesame seeds

1 Preheat the oven to 200°C/400°F/ Gas 6. Put the butter and water into a small pan and bring to the boil over a high heat.

2 Remove the pan from the heat and add the flour all at once.

3 Stir vigorously with a wooden spoon until the mixture forms a smooth paste which leaves the sides of the pan clean.

4 Leave the choux paste to cool for 5 minutes, then beat in the egg, mixing thoroughly until the mixture is smooth and glossy.

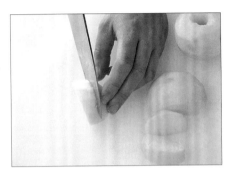

5 Peel and core the apple, then cut it into 1cm/½in chunks.

6 Stir the chopped apple into the cooled choux paste and place teaspoonfuls of the mixture on a dampened non-stick baking sheet.

7 Bake the choux pastry in the oven for 20–25 minutes until it is brown and crisp on the outside, but still soft on the inside.

8 Remove the baking sheet from the oven and leave the pastry to cool.

9 While the pastries are cooling, gently heat the oil in a clean small pan over a low heat and add the caster sugar.

10 Cook, without stirring, until the sugar has melted and turned golden brown, then sprinkle in the sesame seeds. Remove the pan from the heat.

11 Have ready a bowl of iced water. Add the pastries, a few at a time, to the caramel and toss to coat them all over.

12 Remove with a slotted spoon and quickly dip in the iced water to set the caramel; drain well.

13 Serve immediately. If the caramel becomes too thick before all the choux have been coated, re-heat it gently until it liquefies before continuing.

VARIATIONS
A slightly unripe banana can be used instead of an apple, to ring the changes. Alternatively, use chunks of pear or Asian pear, or even peaches or nectarines.

Energy 192Kcal/811kJ; Protein 2.1g; Carbohydrate 36.7g, of which sugars 31.6g; Fat 5.1g, of which saturates 2.6g; Cholesterol 47mg; Calcium 32mg; Fibre 0.4g; Sodium 42mg.

PEARS WITH GINGER AND STAR ANISE ★

PEARS POACHED IN SPICED WINE SYRUP BECOME TRANSLUCENT AND BEAUTIFULLY TENDER. THEY LOOK LOVELY SLICED ON A DESSERT PLATE AND COATED WITH THE REDUCED SYRUP.

SERVES 4

INGREDIENTS

   1 lemon
   75g/3oz/6 tbsp caster (superfine) sugar
   300ml/½ pint/1¼ cups white
     dessert wine
   5 star anise
   10 cloves
   600ml/1 pint/2½ cups cold water
   7.5cm/3in fresh root ginger
   6 slightly unripe pears
   25g/1oz/3 tbsp drained, preserved
     ginger in syrup, sliced
   whipped cream, to serve

1 Pare the lemon thinly and squeeze the juice. Place in a pan just large enough to hold the pears snugly in an upright position. Add the sugar, wine, star anise, cloves and water. Bruise the ginger and add it. Bring to the boil.

2 Meanwhile, peel the pears, leaving the stems intact. Immerse them in the wine mixture.

3 Return the wine mixture to the boil, lower the heat, cover and simmer for 15–20 minutes or until the pears are tender. Lift out the pears with a slotted spoon and place them in a heatproof dish. Boil the wine syrup rapidly until it is reduced by about half, then pour over the pears. Leave to cool, then chill.

4 Cut the pears into thick slices and arrange these on four serving plates. Remove the ginger and whole spices from the wine sauce, stir in the preserved ginger and spoon the sauce over the pears. Serve with cream.

Energy 235Kcal/991kJ; Protein 0.9g; Carbohydrate 46.5g, of which sugars 46.5g; Fat 0.2g, of which saturates 0g; Cholesterol 0mg; Calcium 45mg; Fibre 5g; Sodium 18mg.

MANGO AND GINGER CLOUDS ★

THE SWEET, PERFUMED FLAVOUR OF RIPE MANGO COMBINES BEAUTIFULLY WITH GINGER, AND THIS LOW-FAT DESSERT MAKES THE VERY MOST OF THEM BOTH.

SERVES 6

INGREDIENTS

   3 ripe mangoes
   3 pieces preserved stem ginger plus
     45ml/3 tbsp syrup from the jar
  75g/3oz/½ cup silken tofu
   3 egg whites
   6 pistachio nuts, chopped

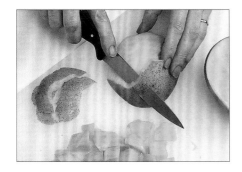

1 Cut the mangoes in half, remove and discard the stones (pits) and peel the fruit, using a sharp knife. Roughly chop the mango flesh.

2 Cut the tofu into rough cubes to make it easier to process.

3 Put the chopped mango in a food processor and add the ginger, the syrup from the jar and the chopped tofu.

4 Process the mixture until it is smooth, then scrape into a mixing bowl.

COOK'S TIP
This dessert can be served lightly frozen. If you prefer not to use ginger, omit the ginger pieces and syrup and use 45ml/ 3 tbsp clear honey instead.

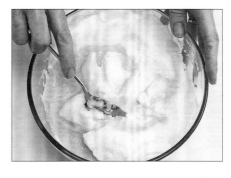

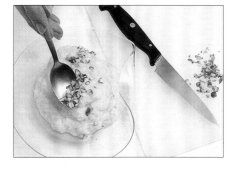

5 Put the egg whites in a bowl and whisk them either by hand or with an electric whisk, until they form soft peaks. Fold them into the mango mixture.

6 Spoon the mixture into wide dishes or tall sundae glasses and cover with clear film (plastic wrap). Chill before serving, sprinkled with the chopped pistachios.

Energy 110Kcal/466kJ; Protein 3.9g; Carbohydrate 17g, of which sugars 16.6g; Fat 3.5g, of which saturates 0.5g; Cholesterol 0mg; Calcium 80mg; Fibre 2.3g; Sodium 79mg.

CHINESE FRUIT SALAD ★

FOR AN UNUSUAL FRUIT SALAD WITH AN ORIENTAL FLAVOUR, TRY THIS MIXTURE OF FRUITS IN A TANGY LIME AND LYCHEE SYRUP, TOPPED WITH A LIGHT SPRINKLING OF TOASTED SESAME SEEDS.

SERVES 4

INGREDIENTS

   115g/4oz/½ cup caster
     (superfine) sugar
   300ml/½ pint/1¼ cups water
   thinly pared rind and juice of 1 lime
   1 eating apple
   400g/14oz can lychees in syrup
   1 ripe mango, peeled, stoned
     (pitted) and sliced
   1 star fruit (carambola),
     sliced (optional)
   2 bananas
   5ml/1 tsp sesame seeds, toasted

COOK'S TIP
Don't prepare the apples and bananas in advance or they will discolour.

1 Place the sugar in a pan with the water and the lime rind. Heat gently until the sugar dissolves, stirring several times, then increase the heat and bring the mixture to the boil. Boil gently for 7–8 minutes. Remove from the heat and pour the syrup into a jug (pitcher). Set aside to cool.

2 Core the apple, and slice it. Drain the lychees and reserve the juice. Pour the juice into the cooled lime syrup with the lime juice. Place all the prepared fruit in a bowl and pour over the syrup. Chill for about 1 hour. Just before serving, slice the banans into the bowl and sprinkle with toasted sesame seeds.

Energy 259Kcal/1102kJ; Protein 2.5g; Carbohydrate 60.4g, of which sugars 59.4g; Fat 2.5g, of which saturates 0.4g; Cholesterol 0mg; Calcium 54mg; Fibre 2.7g; Sodium 5mg.

COOL GREEN FRUIT SALAD ★

A MONOCHROMATIC FRUIT SALAD LOOKS MORE SOPHISTICATED THAN A MEDLEY OF MIXED COLOURS. USE THE FRUITS SUGGESTED OR MAKE UP COMBINATIONS OF YOUR OWN.

SERVES 6

INGREDIENTS

3 Ogen or Galia melons
115g/4oz green seedless grapes
2 kiwi fruit
1 star fruit (carambola)
1 green-skinned eating apple
1 lime
175ml/6fl oz/¾ cup sparkling
    grape juice

1 Cut the melons in half and scoop out the seeds. Keeping the shells intact, scoop out the fruit with a melon baller, or spoon it out and cut into bitesize cubes. Set the melon shells aside.

2 Remove any stems from the grapes, and, if they are large, cut them in half. Peel and chop the kiwi fruit. Thinly slice the star fruit. Core and thinly slice the apple and place the slices in a bowl, with the melon, grapes, kiwi fruit and star fruit.

COOK'S TIP
If you're serving this dessert on a hot summer day, serve the filled melon shells nestling on a platter of crushed ice to keep them beautifully cool.

3 Thinly pare the lime, cut the rind in fine strips and blanch the strips in boiling water for 30 seconds. Drain, dip in cold water, and drain again. Squeeze the juice from the lime and gently mix it with the fruit.

4 Spoon the prepared fruit into the melon shells and chill in the refrigerator until required. Just before serving, spoon the sparkling grape juice over the fruit and sprinkle it with the blanched lime rind.

Energy 102Kcal/436kJ; Protein 1.7g; Carbohydrate 24.4g, of which sugars 24.4g; Fat 0.4g, of which saturates 0g; Cholesterol 0mg; Calcium 46mg; Fibre 1.9g; Sodium 81mg.

HEAVENLY JELLIES WITH FRUIT ★

DELICATE, VANILLA-FLAVOURED JELLY, SET WITH RIBBONS OF EGG WHITE WITHIN IT, MAKES A DELIGHTFUL DESSERT THAT TASTES GREAT WHEN SERVED WITH FRESH FRUIT.

SERVES 6

INGREDIENTS
  10g/¼oz *agar-agar*
  900ml/1½ pints/3¾ cups
    boiling water
  115g/4oz/½ cup caster
    (superfine) sugar
  5ml/1 tsp vanilla extract
  1 egg white, lightly beaten
  225g/8oz/1½ cups strawberries
  450g/1lb fresh lychees, or 425g/15oz
    can lychees, drained

1 Put the *agar-agar* into a pan. Stir in the boiling water, return to the boil and then lower the heat. Simmer the mixture for 10–15 minutes, stirring occasionally, until the *agar-agar* has dissolved completely.

2 Stir in the sugar. As soon as it has dissolved, strain the syrup through a fine sieve (strainer) placed over a bowl. Return the mixture to the pan.

VARIATION
The jelly can be made with equal amounts of reduced-fat coconut milk and water instead of just water.

3 Immediately stir in the vanilla extract, then gently pour in the egg white in a steady stream; the heat will cook the egg white. Gently stir the mixture just once to distribute the threads of cooked egg white.

4 Pour the mixture into a shallow 28 x 18cm/11 x 7in baking tray and allow to cool. The jelly will set at room temperature, but it will set faster and taste better if it is transferred to the refrigerator to set as soon as it has cooled completely.

5 Hull most of the strawberries, keeping the green part on a few for decoration. If the strawberries are large, cut them into smaller bitesize pieces.

6 If using fresh lychees, peel them and remove the stones (pits). If using canned lychees, drain them in a sieve. Divide them among six small serving dishes or cups, then add some strawberries to each portion.

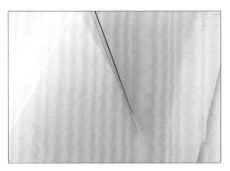

7 Turn the jelly out of the tray and cut it into diamond shapes to serve with the strawberries and lychees.

Energy 131Kcal/559kJ; Protein 1.6g; Carbohydrate 33g, of which sugars 33g; Fat 0.1g, of which saturates 0g; Cholesterol 0mg; Calcium 21mg; Fibre 0.9g; Sodium 14mg.

TAPIOCA AND TARO PUDDING ★

USUALLY SERVED WARM, THIS IS A LIGHT AND REFRESHING "SOUP", POPULAR THROUGHOUT CHINA AND FAR EAST ASIA WITH CHILDREN AND ADULTS ALIKE.

3 Peel the *taro* and cut it into diamond-shaped slices, about 1cm/½in thick. Pour the remaining water into a pan and bring it to the boil. Add the *taro* and cook for 10–15 minutes or until it is just tender.

4 Using a slotted spoon, lift out half of the *taro* slices and set them aside. Continue to cook the remaining taro until it is very soft.

5 Tip the *taro* and cooking liquid into a food processor and process until smooth.

6 Return the *taro* "soup" to the clean pans; stir in the sugar and simmer, stirring occasionally, until the sugar has dissolved, and the mixture is hot.

7 Stir in the tapioca, reserved taro and coconut milk. Cook for a few minutes. Serve immediately in heated bowls or cool and chill before serving.

SERVES 4–6

INGREDIENTS
 115g/4oz/⅔ cup tapioca
 1.5 litres/2½ pints/6 cups cold water
 225g/8oz *taro*
 150g/5oz/⅔ cup rock sugar
 300ml/½ pint/1¼ cups reduced-fat
  coconut milk

1 Rinse the tapioca, drain well, then put into a bowl with enough water to cover. Leave to soak for 30 minutes.

COOK'S TIP
Taro is a starchy tuber that tastes rather like a floury potato. If it is difficult to locate, use sweet potato instead.

2 Drain the tapioca and put it in a pan with 900ml/1½ pints/3¾ cups water. Bring to the boil, lower the heat and simmer for about 6 minutes or until the tapioca is transparent. Tip into a sieve (strainer), drain well, refresh under cold water, and drain again.

VARIATION
If children's comments about frogspawn put you off tapioca for life, add fine cooked noodles, such as vermicelli, to the taro soup instead.

Energy 211Kcal/901kJ; Protein 0.8g; Carbohydrate 54.8g, of which sugars 30.7g; Fat 0.3g, of which saturates 0.1g; Cholesterol 0mg; Calcium 38mg; Fibre 1g; Sodium 72mg.

GOLDEN STEAMED SPONGE CAKE ★★

CAKES ARE NOT TRADITIONALLY SERVED FOR DESSERT IN CHINA, BUT THIS LIGHT SPONGE IS VERY POPULAR AND IS OFTEN SERVED ON THE DIM SUM TROLLEY AT LUNCHTIME.

SERVES 8

INGREDIENTS

175g/6oz/1½ cups plain
  (all-purpose) flour
5ml/1 tsp baking powder
1.5ml/¼ tsp bicarbonate of soda
  (baking soda)
3 large (US extra large) eggs
115g/4oz/⅔ cup soft light
  brown sugar
45ml/3 tbsp walnut oil
30ml/2 tbsp golden
  (light corn) syrup
5ml/1 tsp vanilla extract

1 Sift the flour, baking powder and bicarbonate of soda into a bowl. Line an 18cm/7in diameter bamboo steamer or cake tin (pan) with baking parchment.

2 In a mixing bowl, whisk the eggs with the sugar until thick and frothy. Beat in the walnut oil and syrup, then set the mixture aside for about 30 minutes.

VARIATION
Maple syrup can be substituted for golden syrup, but make sure you use the real thing.

3 Add the sifted flour, baking powder and bicarbonate of soda to the egg mixture with the vanilla extract, and beat rapidly by hand or with an electric whisk to form a thick batter that is free from lumps.

4 Pour the batter into the paper-lined steamer or tin. Cover and steam over boiling water for 30 minutes or until the sponge springs back when gently pressed with a finger. Leave to cool for a few minutes before serving.

Energy 150Kcal/632kJ; Protein 4.4g; Carbohydrate 20g, of which sugars 3.3g; Fat 6.5g, of which saturates 1g; Cholesterol 71mg; Calcium 42mg; Fibre 0.7g; Sodium 37mg.

PANCAKES <u>WITH</u> RED BEAN PASTE ★

IN CHINA, SWEETENED RED BEANS ARE OFTEN USED IN DESSERTS AND SWEETMEATS BECAUSE THE RICH COLOUR IS TRADITIONALLY ASSOCIATED WITH GOOD LUCK.

SERVES 4

INGREDIENTS
  600ml/1 pint/2½ cups cold water
  175g/6oz/1 scant cup aduki beans,
    soaked overnight in cold water
  115g/4oz/1 cup plain
    (all-purpose) flour
  1 large (US extra large) egg,
    lightly beaten
  300ml/½ pint/1¼ cups semi-
    skimmed (low-fat) milk
  5ml/1 tsp vegetable oil
  75g/3oz/6 tbsp caster
    (superfine) sugar
  2.5ml/½ tsp vanilla extract
  fromage frais or natural (plain)
    yogurt, to serve (optional)

3 Meanwhile, make the pancakes. Sift the flour into a bowl and make a well in the centre. Pour in the egg and half the milk. Beat, gradually drawing in the flour until it has all been incorporated. Beat in the remaining milk to make a smooth batter. Cover; set aside for 30 minutes.

1 Bring the water to the boil in a pan. Drain the beans in a sieve (strainer), add them to the pan and boil rapidly for 10 minutes.

2 Skim off any scum from the surface of the liquid, then lower the heat, cover the pan and simmer, stirring occasionally, for 40 minutes or until the beans are soft.

VARIATION
Instead of serving these sweet pancakes with fromage frais, which would increase the fat content of the dessert, try using whipped tofu instead. Cut 450g/1lb firm tofu into squares and put it in a blender with 60ml/4 tbsp golden (light corn) syrup and 10ml/2 tsp vanilla extract. Add 15ml/1 tbsp water. Blitz until it becomes smooth. If the mixture is too thick, add a little more water and blitz again to combine.

4 Heat a 20cm/8in non-stick omelette pan and brush lightly with the vegetable oil. Pour in a little of the batter, swirling the pan to cover the base thinly.

5 Cook the pancake for 2 minutes until the bottom has browned lightly. Flip the pancake over, either with chopsticks or by flipping in the air, and cook the second side for about 1 minute. Slide the pancake on to a plate.

6 Make seven more pancakes in the same way. Cover the pancakes with foil and keep hot.

7 When the beans are soft and all the water has been absorbed, tip them into a food processor and process until almost smooth. Add the sugar and vanilla extract and process briefly until the sugar has dissolved.

8 Preheat the grill (broiler). Spread a little of the bean paste on the centre of each pancake and fold them into parcels, pressing them down with your fingers to flatten.

9 Place on a baking sheet and cook under the grill for a few minutes until crisp and lightly toasted on each side.

10 Serve the hot pancakes immediately, either on their own or with a little fromage frais or low-fat yogurt.

COOK'S TIP
Both the pancakes and the bean paste can be made well in advance and kept frozen, ready for thawing, reheating and assembling when needed.

Energy 368Kcal/1562kJ; Protein 17.2g; Carbohydrate 69.1g, of which sugars 24.8g; Fat 4.5g, of which saturates 1.6g; Cholesterol 52mg; Calcium 183mg; Fibre 4.5g; Sodium 59mg.

KABOCHA SQUASH CAKE ★

THIS IS A VERY SWEET JAPANESE DESSERT OFTEN MADE WITH ADUKI BEANS, TO BE EATEN AT TEA TIME WITH GREEN TEA. THE BITTERNESS OF THE TEA BALANCES THE SWEETNESS OF THE CAKE.

SERVES 4

INGREDIENTS
    1 × 350g/12oz kabocha squash
    30ml/2 tbsp plain
      (all-purpose) flour
    15ml/1 tbsp cornflour (cornstarch)
    10ml/2 tsp caster (superfine) sugar
    1.5ml/¼ tsp salt
    1.5ml/¼ tsp ground cinnamon
    25ml/1½ tbsp water
    2 egg yolks, beaten
To serve (optional)
    ½ Asian pear
    ½ persimmon

1 Cut off the hard part from the top and bottom of the kabocha, then cut it into three to four wedges. Scoop out the seeds with a spoon. Cut into chunks.

2 Steam the kabocha squash in a covered steamer for about 15 minutes over a medium heat. It will be ready when a chopstick or skewer can be pushed into the centre easily. Remove and leave, covered, for 5 minutes.

3 Remove the skin from the kabocha. Mash the flesh and push it through a sieve (strainer) using a wooden spoon, or purée it in a blender or food processor. Scrape the purée into a mixing bowl. Add the flour, cornflour, caster sugar, cinnamon, water and beaten egg yolks. Mix well.

4 Roll out a *makisu* sushi mat as you would if making a sushi roll. Wet some muslin or cheesecloth slightly with water and lay it on the mat. Spread the kabocha cake mixture evenly on the wet cloth. Hold the nearest end and tightly roll up the *makisu* to the other end. Close both outer ends by rolling up or folding the cloth over.

5 Put the *makisu* containing the rolled kabocha cake back into the steamer for 5 minutes. Remove from the heat and leave to set for 5 minutes.

6 If serving with fruit, peel, trim and slice the Asian pear and persimmon very thinly lengthways.

7 Open the *makisu* when the roll has cooled down. Cut the cake into 2.5cm/1in thick slices and serve cold on four small plates with the thinly sliced fruit, if using.

Energy 97Kcal/409kJ; Protein 4.5g; Carbohydrate 13.8g, of which sugars 4.2g; Fat 3.1g, of which saturates 0.9g; Cholesterol 95mg; Calcium 52mg; Fibre 1.1g; Sodium 37mg.

EXOTIC FRUIT SUSHI ★

THIS IDEA CAN BE ADAPTED TO INCORPORATE A WIDE VARIETY OF FRUITS, BUT TO KEEP TO THE EXOTIC THEME TAKE YOUR INSPIRATION FROM THE TROPICS. THE SUSHI NEEDS TO CHILL OVERNIGHT.

SERVES 4

INGREDIENTS
150g/5oz/⅔ cup short grain
   pudding rice
350ml/12fl oz/1½ cups water
400ml/14fl oz/1⅔ cups reduced-fat
   coconut milk
75g/3oz/⅓ cup caster
   (superfine) sugar
a selection of exotic fruit, such as
   1 mango, 1 kiwi fruit, 2 figs and
   1 star fruit (carambola),
   thinly sliced
30ml/2 tbsp apricot jam, sieved
For the raspberry sauce
225g/8oz/2 cups raspberries
25g/1oz/¼ cup icing
   (confectioners') sugar

1 Rinse the rice well under cold running water, drain and place in a pan with 300ml/½ pint/1¼ cups of the water. Pour in 175ml/6fl oz/¾ cup of the coconut milk. Cook over very low heat for 25 minutes, stirring often and gradually adding the remaining coconut milk, until the rice has absorbed all the liquid and is tender.

2 Grease a shallow 18cm/7in square tin (pan) and line it with clear film (plastic wrap). Stir 30ml/2 tbsp of the caster sugar into the rice mixture and pour it into the prepared tin. Cool, then chill overnight.

COOK'S TIP
To cut the rice mixture into bars, turn out of the tin, cut in half lengthways, then make 7 crossways cuts for 16 bars. Shape into ovals with damp hands.

3 Cut the rice mixture into 16 small bars, shape into ovals and flatten the tops. Place on a baking sheet lined with baking parchment. Arrange the sliced fruit on top, using one type of fruit only for each sushi.

4 Place the remaining sugar in a small pan with the remaining 60ml/4 tbsp water. Bring to the boil, then lower the heat and simmer until the liquid becomes thick and syrupy. Stir in the jam and cool slightly.

5 To make the raspberry sauce, put the raspberries in a food processor or blender, and add the icing sugar. Process in short bursts, using the pulse button if your machine has one, until the raspberries are a purée. Press through a sieve, then divide among four small bowls.

6 Arrange a few different fruit sushi on each plate and spoon over a little of the cool apricot syrup. Serve with the raspberry sauce.

Energy 323Kcal/1372kJ; Protein 4.5g; Carbohydrate 77.1g, of which sugars 47g; Fat 0.8g, of which saturates 0.3g; Cholesterol 0mg; Calcium 73mg; Fibre 2.9g; Sodium 118mg.

SWEET ADUKI BEAN PASTE JELLY ★

BASED ON AGAR-AGAR, A SETTING AGENT MADE FROM SEAWEED, THESE JELLIES LOOK LIKE BLOCKS OF MOUNTAIN ICE IN WHICH SEMI-PRECIOUS STONES HAVE BEEN TRAPPED FOR CENTURIES.

SERVES 12

INGREDIENTS
    200g/7oz can aduki beans
    40g/1½oz/3 tbsp caster
        (superfine) sugar
For the *agar-agar* jelly
    2 × 5g/⅛oz sachets powdered
        agar-agar
    100g/3¾oz/½ cup caster sugar
    rind of ¼ orange in one piece

1 Drain the beans, then tip into a pan over a medium heat. When steam begins to rise, reduce the heat to low.

2 Add the sugar one-third at a time, stirring constantly until the sugar has dissolved and the moisture evaporated. Remove from the heat.

3 Pour 450ml/¾ pint/scant 2 cups water into a pan, and mix with one *agar-agar* sachet. Stir until dissolved, then add 40g/1½oz of the sugar and the orange rind. Bring to the boil and cook for about 2 minutes, stirring constantly until the sugar has all dissolved.

4 Remove from the heat and discard the orange rind.

5 Transfer 250ml/8fl oz/1 cup of the hot liquid into a 15 × 10cm/6 × 4in container so that it fills only 1cm/½in. Leave at room temperature to set.

6 Add the bean paste to the *agar-agar* liquid in the pan, and mix well. Move the pan on to a wet dish towel and keep stirring for 8 minutes.

7 Pour the bean and *agar-agar* liquid into an 18 × 7.5 × 2cm/7 × 3 × ¾in container and leave to set for 1 hour at room temperature, then 1 hour in the refrigerator. Turn upside down on to a chopping board covered with kitchen paper. Leave for 1 minute, then cut into 12 rectangular pieces.

8 Line 12 ramekins with clear film (plastic wrap). With a fork, cut the set kanten block into 12 squares. Put one square in each ramekin, then place a bean and kanten cube on top of each.

9 Pour 450ml/¾ pint/scant 2 cups water into a pan and mix with the remaining kanten sachet. Bring to the boil, add the remaining sugar, then stir constantly until dissolved. Boil for a further 2 minutes, and remove from the heat. Place the pan on a wet dish towel to cool quickly and stir for 5 minutes, or until the liquid starts to thicken.

10 Ladle the liquid into the ramekins to cover the cubes. Twist the clear film at the top. Leave to set in the refrigerator for at least 1 hour. Carefully remove the ramekins and clear film and serve cold on serving plates.

Energy 63Kcal/267kJ; Protein 1.2g; Carbohydrate 15.2g, of which sugars 12.8g; Fat 0.1g, of which saturates 0g; Cholesterol 0mg; Calcium 18mg; Fibre 1g; Sodium 66mg.

STICKY RICE IN BEAN PASTE ★

*THIS TEA-TIME SNACK IS AN ABSOLUTE FAVOURITE AMONG ALL AGES IN JAPAN. IT IS ALSO MADE ON
OCCASIONS SUCH AS BIRTHDAYS AND FESTIVALS, WHEN IT IS DECORATED WITH CAMELLIA LEAVES.*

MAKES 12

INGREDIENTS
    150g/5oz/scant 1 cup glutinous rice
    50g/2oz/⅓ cup Japanese short
        grain rice
    410g/14¼oz can aduki beans
        (canned in water, with sugar and salt)
    90g/3½oz/6½ tbsp caster
        (superfine) sugar
    pinch of salt

1 Mix both kinds of rice in a sieve
(strainer), wash well under running
water, then drain. Leave for at least
1 hour to dry.

2 Tip the rice into a heavy cast-iron pan
or flameproof casserole with a lid, and
add 200ml/7fl oz/scant 1 cup water.

3 Cover and bring to the boil, then
reduce the heat to low and simmer for
15 minutes, or until a slight crackling
noise is heard from the pan.

4 Remove from the heat and leave to
stand for 5 minutes. Remove the lid,
cover and leave to cool.

5 Pour the contents of the aduki bean
can into a pan and cook over a medium
heat. Add the sugar a third at a time,
mixing well after each addition.

6 Reduce the heat to low and mash
the beans using a potato masher.
Add the salt and remove from the
heat. The consistency should be like
that of mashed potatoes. Heat gently to
remove any excess liquid. Leave to cool.

7 Wet your hands. Shape the sticky rice
into 12 balls, each about the size of a
golf ball.

8 Dampen some muslin or cheesecloth
and place on the work surface.

9 Scoop up 30ml/2 tbsp of the aduki
bean paste and spread it in the centre
of the cloth to a thickness of about
5mm/¼in.

COOK'S TIP
Make sure the muslin or cheesecloth is
really damp, or the rice mixture will stick
to it and prove difficult to remove.

10 Put a rice ball in the middle, then
wrap it up in the paste using the
muslin. Open the cloth and remove the
ball. Repeat until all the rice balls are
used up. Serve at room temperature.

Energy 123Kcal/518kJ; Protein 3.6g; Carbohydrate 27.1g, of which sugars 9g; Fat 0.3g, of which saturates 0g; Cholesterol 0mg; Calcium 31mg; Fibre 2.1g; Sodium 130mg.

GLOSSARY

Abura-age Fried thin rectangular blocks of tofu. Available frozen and fresh.

Aduki beans Small, brownish red beans that are often used in sweet recipes.

Agar-agar A gelling agent made from seaweed.

Aka miso A medium-strength flavoured dark red soybean paste.

Ao nori Green seaweed flakes.

Arame A brown variety of seaweed.

Atsu-age Thick, deep-fried tofu. These are usually bought in pieces: 1 atsu-age = 1 piece.

Awakuchi shoyu Pale soy sauce.

Choi sum A mild-tasting brassica.

Chow chow A Chinese relish made from pickled vegetables.

Daikon A long, white vegetable of the radish family.

Dashi-konbu Dried kelp seaweed.

Dashi-no-moto Freeze-dried stock granules for making a quick dashi stock with water.

Dashi stock A stock for soups and hotpots using kezuri-bushi and konbu. It is possible to make your own dashi stock but stock granules (dashi-no-moto) are also available.

Denbu Pink topping for rice, made from cod fillet, salt, sake and food colouring.

Enokitake Small delicately flavoured mushrooms with slender stalks.

Gari Thinly sliced and pickled ginger.

Left: Lotus root and seeds

Gobo (burdock root) A long, stick-like root vegetable.

Golden needles Dried tiger lily buds.

Goma shio Sesame salt.

Hakusai (Chinese cabbage) A vegetable with white stem and green leaves.

Hatcho miso Dark brown soybean paste.

Hijiki Twiggy, black marine algae (seaweed) available dried.

Iri-tamago Yellow topping for rice, made from egg, salt and sugar

Kabocha A squash with dark green skin and yellow flesh, and a nutty flavour.

Kashiwa Salted Japanese oak leaves.

Katsuo-bushi Whole cooked and dried block of katsuo (skipjack tuna), ready for shaving.

Kezuri-bushi Ready shaved, dried katsuo (skipjack tuna) flakes for use in dashi fish stock.

Kiku nori Dried chrysanthemum petals in a sheet.

Konbu Giant kelp seaweed, usually sold dried as dashi-konbu.

Konnyaku A dense, gelatinous cake made from the konnyaku, a yam-like plant.

Lotus root A white-fleshed root from the lotus plant.

Left: Dried tiger lily buds, which are also known as "Golden needles".

Makisu Sushi rolling mat.

Mirin Sweet rice wine, used for cooking rather than drinking.

Miso Mixture of fermented soybeans and grains that matures into a paste of different strengths.

Mitsuba Aromatic herb used mostly for soups. Member of the parsley family.

Mizuna Japanese greens.

Nori Dried, paper-thin seaweed product.

Pak choi (bok choy) Loose-leafed brassica with white stems.

Ramen Thin egg noodles.

Saikyo miso Pale yellow soybean paste, lightly flavoured.

Sake A traditional rice wine for drinking and cooking.

Sansho Ground Japanese pepper with a minty aroma.

Sashimi Raw fish and shellfish sliced thinly and arranged decoratively.

Satoimo Oval-shaped potato, covered in a hairy skin.

Sencha Green tea made from the young leaves.

Shichimi togarashi (seven-spice powder) Containing chilli, sesame, poppy, hemp, shiso, sansho and nori.

Right: A bamboo makisu

Above: Shimeji mushrooms

Shiitaki A variety of fungus with a brown cap and white stem.

Shimeji Meaty-textured mushroom, similar to oyster mushrooms.

Shiro miso Pale yellow soybean paste, lightly flavoured.

Shiso Basil-flavoured leaves used as a herb garnish.

Shoyu Ordinary Japanese soy sauce.

Shungiku Edible leaves from the vegetable chrysanthemum (not the garden plant).

Soba Dried buckwheat noodles.

Somen Very fine wheat noodles.

Sora mame Broad (fava) beans.

Sukiyaki Wafer-thin meat and vegetables cooked in a sauce.

Su-meshi Vinegared rice, the essential basis for all sushi.

Sushi Small rolls of *su-meshi* and flavourings topped with thin slices of raw fish.

Takanotsume Fresh red chilli.

Takenoko Fresh, young bamboo shoots.

Takuan Pickled and dyed daikon.

Tamari shoyu Naturally fermented dark soy sauce.

Taro A starchy tuber that tastes rather like a potato.

Tempura A lumpy batter made with ice-cold water for deep-frying fish and sliced vegetables.

Tofu A nutritious, coagulated soya bean protein.

Tori-soboro Beige topping for rice, made from chicken, sake, sugar, shoyu and water.

Tsuma Daikon cut very thinly into strands, for decorative purposes.

Udon Thick wheat noodles.

Usukuchi shoyu Reduced salt soy sauce.

Usu zukuri Very thin slices of fish.

Wakame A curly seaweed, available in a dried form.

Wasabi A Japanese pungent root similar to horseradish, available as a paste or in powder form.

Yakitori Skewered grilled chicken.

Below: Bamboo steamers

ACKNOWLEDGEMENTS

Left: Somen noodles

Recipes

Catherine Atkinson, Alex Barker, Ghillie Basan, Judy Bastyra, Carla Capalbo, Kit Chan, Roz Denny, Joanna Farrow, Rafi Fernandez, Christine France, Silvano Franco, Linda Fraser, Yasuko Fukuoka, Elaine Gardner, Sarah Gates, Shirley Gill, Brian Glover, Nicola Graimes, Deh-Ta Hsiung, Shehzad Husain, Christine Ingram, Becky Johnson, Emi Kazuko, Soheila Kimberley, Lucy Knox, Masaki Ko, Elizabeth Lambert Ortiz, Ruby Le Bois, Patricia Lousada, Norma MacMillan, Lesley Mackley, Sue Maggs, Sarah Maxwell, Maggie Mayhew, Jane Milton, Sallie Morris, Janice Murfitt, Annie Nichols, Angela Nilsen, Maggie Pannell, Keith Richmond, Anne Sheasby, Marlena Spieler, Liz Trigg, Hilaire Walden, Laura Washburn, Steven Wheeler, Jenny White, Kate Whiteman, Elizabeth Wolf-Cohen

Home Economists

Julie Beresford, Carla Capalbo, Kit Chan, Joanne Craig, Joanna Farrow, Annabel Ford, Nicola Fowler, Christine France, Carole Handslip, Jane Hartshorn, Tonia Hedley, Shehzad Husain, Kate Jay, Becky Johnson, Wendy Lee, Sara Lewis, Lucy McKelvie, Annie Nichols, Bridget Sargeson, Jennie Shapter, Jane Stevenson, Sunil Vijayakar, Steven Wheeler, Elizabeth Wolf-Cohen.

Photographers

Edward Allwright, Peter Anderson, David Armstrong, Steve Baxter, Martin Brigdale, Nicki Dowey, James Duncan, Gus Filgate, Michelle Garrett, Amanda Heywood, Janine Hosegood, Tim Hill, David Jordan, Dave King, Don Last, William Lingwood, Patrick McLeavey, Michael Michaels, Thomas Odulate, Peter Reilly, Craig Robertson, Simon Smith

INDEX